UNMASKING

SAMANTHA COOKES

Alan Bradley is an award-winning Irish documentary director, actor and writer. In 2024 he won the Young Director Award for Documentary in Cannes and has directed multiple critically acclaimed documentaries for RTÉ, BBC and VMTV, including *Patrick: A Young Traveller Lost*, which won the Radharc Award. This is his debut book.

UNMASKING SAMANTHA COOKES

THE MANY LIVES OF A SERIAL FRAUDSTER

ALAN BRADLEY

First published in 2026 by
Merrion Press
10 George's Street
Newbridge
Co. Kildare
Ireland
www.merrionpress.ie

978 1 78537 593 4 (Paper)
978 1 78537 597 2 (eBook)

A CIP catalogue record for this book is available from the British Library.

Typeset in Calluna 12/18 pt

Cover design by Fiachra McCarthy

Front cover image courtesy of Ronan Kelly, RTÉ

Merrion Press is a member of Publishing Ireland.

CONTENTS

AUTHOR'S NOTE

Some stories are so extraordinary, involving an intricate mesh of deceit that entangles so many people, that the telling of them requires more than just a recording of the facts – it demands empathy and respect for those whose lives are forever changed. This is one of those stories.

For over a decade, Samantha Cookes moved under the radar, slipping through identities and lives across the UK and Ireland. Posing as a therapist, a nanny and even a terminally ill award-winning author, she wove a tapestry of lies so intricate that many who crossed her path were left shattered and searching for answers. Yet, by her various acts of deception, she unknowingly forged a community of remarkable women, mothers, caregivers and survivors, each carrying their own burdens and some caring for children with profound needs, bound together by their shared pain and a growing resolve to stop Cookes from wreaking any further damage.

This book draws on extensive interviews with Samantha's many victims and those who knew her best, as well as court records, multiple news sources, Samantha's own discarded writings, documents and social media content, and the documentary *Bad Nanny*, produced by the author with Alleycats Films and commissioned by RTÉ and BBC Northern Ireland, which illuminated Samantha's decade-long trail of deceit. Through the voices of those she targeted, we uncover not only her manipulations, but also the fierce strength and solidarity of the women she thought she could break.

Due to the sensitive nature of the experiences shared here, some names and locations have been changed to protect the identities of individuals involved. The events remain undeniably vivid, and the impact of Samantha's actions echoes far beyond these pages. For legal reasons the identities and genders of Samantha's living children have been concealed.

As you read, you will enter a world where trust is weaponised and shattered, but also where resilience and courage rise, defying even the most skilful of predators.

PROLOGUE

Carrie Jade was dazzling. That was the image she had built and burnished, brick by brick. She was terminally ill. A disability activist. A fierce advocate for Huntington's disease awareness. A guest voice on Newstalk radio, a featured profile in the *Irish Independent*. An award-winning author with a leading London literary agent and even a *Financial Times* essay award to her name. A groundbreaking entrepreneur with backing and funding from legitimate institutions like the Alzheimer's Society UK. She spoke eloquently about life with Huntington's disease, telling audiences that she was on borrowed time. She filmed TikTok videos about resilience, wrote online blogs about lifting others up, positioned herself as the heroic underdog elevated by intellect and courage.

Who could argue with this story? She was courageous, tragic, inspiring. The kind of figure people rallied behind without question. To thousands online, Carrie Jade Williams was a phoenix emerging proudly through the flames.

Then, one ordinary evening, she opened her TikTok app and the phoenix stumbled.

The screen was alive. The notification icon along the bottom bar was pulsing red with new activity. Hashtags blossomed like a rash.

At first, it was outrage, the story she'd told having done its work. She had claimed that guests staying at her home as part of an Airbnb let were suing her because her disability aids had 'triggered' them. TikTok fumed on Carrie Jade's behalf, comments piling in, allies rallying to defend her:

> @Mazxxxxxxxxx 'What the hell? I am so shocked and sickened. How can this woman who is TERMINALLY ILL be treated so badly?!?! Shame on Air BnB!! 😠😠😠'

> @PrimalEmpress 'What the hell is wrong with the world? This woman has Huntington's disease!! Can we all go and support her please?!'

Anger and outrage were Carrie Jade's shield, her currency. Her hashtag, #thisworldcanbeaccessible, was trending across TikTok for all to see. For a heartbeat, she felt the familiar sweet burn of success. But then she saw them. The other comments.

'Oh, it's Lucy ...'

'Sophia?'

'OMG that's her, she's back!'

'Don't you remember us Rebecca?'

'She's a scammer. BEWARE!'

The words sprawled across her carefully curated identity like graffiti on a shrine. She scrolled, numb, breath held.

These messengers weren't supposed to know. They weren't supposed to find her here. Carrie hit delete, delete, delete, delete, in frantic repetition, her screen a battlefield she could no longer control. When more appeared, she shut off the comments altogether. Silence.

But silence wasn't enough. You can't kill the past by flicking a switch. It had found her.

Cold panic rolled up her spine, that familiar shiver that always came when the mask began to slip. She knew this feeling all too well. The sensation of walls closing in. Of stories unravelling.

It was happening again.

She wasn't really Carrie Jade. Just as she hadn't really been Rebecca, or Lucy, or Claudia, or Sophia before that. She was Samantha. Samantha Jade Cookes. Behind the awards and interviews and carefully lit TikTok videos, she remained the same restless figure she had always been, a fraud constructed from borrowed names and stolen narratives.

And so, Samantha once more pulled the move that she had perfected over a decade of reinvention. She packed only the essentials into a holdall and closed the front door on her latest life. Under the cover of darkness, she disappeared. Somewhere out there was the next place, the next identity, the next set of victims waiting for the latest version of herself she hadn't yet created. But this time the Garda Síochána was hot on her heels.

1

THE MAKING OF A LIAR

In a discarded journal, Samantha Cookes left behind a revealing statement: 'Lies? Yes, everyone lies. I've lied ever since I could remember. It's the only thing I do well, and I think we should all play to our strengths, don't you?'

Despite becoming a prolific scam artist, Cookes was not born a master manipulator. She grew into it, layer by deceitful layer, honing her craft slowly, until the lies she wrapped around herself were like a second skin. By the time people knew her as Carrie Jade Williams, she could spin a story so convincingly that even the wary would lean in to listen. In the very beginning, however, her lies were too obvious, too loud, betraying their maker.

Samantha Jade Cookes was born on 7 November 1988, in Gloucester Maternity Hospital, to Janice and Leslie Cookes. Three years later, her younger brother, Adam, was born. A picture-perfect family, the Cookes children grew up in the lower-middle-class suburb of Watson Grove in Abbeymead, Gloucester. Samantha's childhood was set against a backdrop of modest semi-detached houses and a close-knit community, where families lived stable, orderly lives. The streets were lined with tidy gardens and, in the quiet, tree-lined avenues of Watson Grove, there was a steady, unhurried rhythm to daily life. While Abbeymead was not overly affluent, it was a place where children could roam the streets safely and neighbours knew each other by name. Yet, behind the façade of calm suburban streets and tidy gardens, where childhood innocence and routine prevailed, something complex was taking root within young Samantha.

Samantha's mother described her as a quiet child, one who found refuge in the pages of books, a world where stories unfolded with comforting order and certainty. But as Samantha grew, those stories began to take on a different shape. She didn't just read about other lives and adventures; she created them, weaving intricate fantasies. What had started as harmless daydreaming now carried a malignant undertone, a whisper of the darker craft to come, where truth became as malleable as the tales she told. The young Samantha – Sam to friends – quickly earned a reputation not for brilliance or scandal, but for the sheer audacity of her stories. They were outlandish, sprawling things, impossible to prove yet told with such conviction that they left listeners momentarily spellbound.

Though she later claimed to have attended a bohemian Steiner school, the truth was far more polished. Samantha was educated at the prestigious Denmark Road High School for Girls in Gloucester. Denmark Road, a high-achieving grammar school, became to her a sanctuary, stage and audience rolled into one. She thrived there, initially at least. Classmates recall how charming she could be, how easily she disarmed you with a glance or a laugh. She had the kind of presence that made you listen when she spoke, hungry for whatever came next.

One girl, plagued by relentless bullying, still remembers

Samantha with a kind of awe and gratitude. Samantha was among the few pupils who showed her kindness, a glimmer of warmth amidst the cruelty of school corridors. That, too, was Samantha – a friend you thought you needed.

But alongside this warmth came fabrication, and the stories spilled into lesson breaks and lunch hours like small performances. She once declared she had a sewing machine she intended to bring into school, only later to spin a ludicrous tale of falling down the stairs, the contraption miraculously flying out of her hands and through the window on impact. At first, girls gasped, wide-eyed at the slapstick horror of it. Then, after a string of such melodramas, the gasps turned into glances, the glances into smirks.

For weeks, Samantha wore gloves inside the classroom, murmuring about a terrible skin condition that left her hands raw and unsightly. No one saw so much as a blemish. Then, just as suddenly, the gloves vanished, never to return, as though the condition had healed overnight. Her tall tales always came with expiry dates, never polished enough to last, never planned beyond the moment. It wasn't long before her schoolmates began to see through them, recognising how quickly the seams came undone. The wary girls learned to take what Samantha Cookes said with a pinch of salt.

There was no real need for the theatrics. These girls lived surrounded by comfort, by friends, by stability, yet Samantha seemed compelled to continue. She began carrying around small notebooks into which she scribbled constantly, as though she needed a written ledger of her inventions, a record to stop one lie colliding too dangerously with another, something she would continue fastidiously in later years as her cons developed. It was during these school years that the patterns were laid for

Samantha's instinct to embroider the truth, to cut and stitch reality into what she wished it to be. Lies became less a tactic for seeking attention and more a habit, as natural and necessary as breathing. If one collapsed under scrutiny, another was ready to replace it, more elaborate, more alluring. She had learned, even then, that drama drew people close, that sympathy and intrigue were currencies as valuable as charm or pedigree.

Her first boyfriend, Mark (not his real name), remembers a girl whose lying ran so deep it felt like compulsion. So entrenched was her deceit that, on the day they finally broke up, he set up a Google alert for the name 'Samantha Cookes'. Mark was certain, utterly certain, that one day his first love would resurface, not in his life, but in the headlines.

The two met in 2005, when Samantha was seventeen. To the shy, bookish teenager that Mark was, she seemed to be everything a girl should be: blonde hair falling effortlessly about her shoulders, striking blue eyes, wit as sharp as it was playful, funny, confident and dazzlingly quick. Mark was hooked instantly. Their relationship unfurled with the intoxicating recklessness of first love. To him, it was perfection.

Samantha painted herself as a girl with a heart for others, working a part-time job at the high-end Laura Ashley store in town and volunteering on weekends at a local school for blind children. Between her beauty, her charm and her apparent selflessness, she seemed too good to be true. And she was.

The cracks first appeared in small, awkward slips, details that didn't quite add up, inconsistencies that at first Mark told himself were misunderstandings. But one lie crumbled after another, and soon her entire backstory dissolved. She wasn't employed by Laura Ashley. Instead, she clocked in for shifts behind the counter at

Marks & Spencer in central Gloucester. *Why lie about such a thing?* Mark wondered. The volunteering with blind children? Nothing more than another fabrication. Mark's head was spinning. This was his first serious romance and he was in love, so in love that he tried to explain it away. When he did confront her, Samantha crumbled, collapsing into floods of tears. He comforted her, convincing himself it was insecurity, a misguided way of trying to impress him, and swallowed his doubts.

Mark recalls how Samantha would daydream about the future constantly, doodling in notebooks, picking out names for their future children, picking out fantasy careers for them to follow as young parents-to-be. She would often ask him to 'put a baby in her', a request he found odd and off-putting at his age, when dreams of fatherhood were far from his mind.

Then came a meeting with her mother, Janice. Mark still remembers the line she delivered with frightening bluntness: 'You can't believe a word she [Samantha] says. Be careful.' He laughed nervously, unsettled by the idea of a mother warning a boyfriend against her own daughter. In the weeks that followed, the stories Samantha concocted took on a less benign tone. One night she claimed that Janice had cancer, an aggressive form. She spoke of her mother's hair falling out in clumps, of hospital visits and whispered prognoses. Mark believed her because what sort of person would invent such a thing? Weeks later, arriving at the Cookes' family home, he found Janice entirely healthy, hair thick and intact. The lie was so grotesque, so brazen, that it left him disturbed and confused. He confronted Samantha only to be met with tears and hysterics, making him wary of broaching his suspicions going forward.

No honest acknowledgement of any wrongdoing came from

Samantha. To explain away the lies, she invented further fabrications with which to distract, muddy the waters and garner sympathy. Then, one day, Mark received a handwritten letter from her:

> Dear Mark,
>
> I'm trying to decide what to say. I thought about just handing you my medical records and the photographs of me when I was sick and waiting for your response, but I wanted you to know what happened in my own words. I don't expect you to understand my anorexia, I suffered from it and I don't really understand! Instead I just want you to be aware of it. We both come with a history and I just hope you realise that I'm <u>not</u> that person any more. I was young, impressionable, confused and hurting; that's not an excuse, just a fact. I'm telling you this because I didn't want there to be any secrets. I can't open up to people, not even you, the way you've been able to, but after you've read this I am prepared to discuss it.
>
> There's no particular point when my eating disorder began; it would be easier if there was! If I could pinpoint the exact moment that it started, I'd be able to have a reason to show people why, but instead I woke up and found myself in the middle of it. I'm probably making no sense! I hope you don't mind me writing this and I hope I'm not being too dull. I'm very ashamed, VERY ASHAMED of it and part of me really doesn't want you to know, but the other part of me knows that if I don't tell you, it could become an issue.

> The first time I was hospitalised was a few weeks after my 12th birthday and was awful. I was fragile and hurting so much that nothing mattered. God, I was such a mess. You can't make someone eat, nor can you make someone happy when they're in such a state. I didn't want to die, but I couldn't eat, so when I got extremely ill I was hooked up to a feeding tube. Being force fed via a feeding tube is one of the most traumatic and undignified things I have ever been through, I hated it, but at the time it probably saved my life.
>
> You probably think I'm a terribly selfish person. I probably was but I've worked really hard to try and prove to everyone that I'm not and that it was the anorexia.

Sure this was another fabrication, and fearful of how deep the deceit went, Mark broke things off. However, Samantha had one more twist reserved for him. Tearfully, she told him she was pregnant. For two weeks he reeled, caught between terror and guilt, until he discovered that the pregnancy too was a lie. As he permanently severed ties with her, he didn't feel heartbroken so much as haunted. Who had he really been with during those months? What, if anything, had been real?

Mark suspects now that Samantha was honing her craft on him, that their relationship was less a romance and more a rehearsal. Years later, the doubt still lingers – the sense that he never truly knew his girlfriend at all, or what she was capable of becoming.

* * *

Leaving Mark reeling in her wake, Samantha wasted no time in moving on. By the summer after her A-levels, she had drawn another boy into her orbit, an eighteen-year-old named Peter (not his real name). Vulnerable, shy and already weathering a turbulent time, Peter was drifting, at odds with both home and school, uncertain of where he belonged when Samantha appeared.

She was everything he believed he wasn't – beautiful, effervescent and effortlessly confident, the kind of girl who seemed to stride through the world while others stumbled. That she should notice him at all felt miraculous. 'I just couldn't believe a beautiful, confident girl like that would be interested in me,' he later confessed. For Peter, life had suddenly swung in his favour. He was instantly smitten, convinced he had somehow stumbled into a dream he didn't deserve. 'Things moved pretty quickly; before I knew it, we were boyfriend and girlfriend. I was on cloud nine!'

Then a mutual friend pulled him aside during a night out, issuing the stark warning: 'You can't trust her, everything she says is a lie.' Peter felt a knot tighten in his stomach, but he ignored it. The thought of losing Samantha, of severing this unlikely connection, was unbearable. He drowned out the doubt, rushing headlong into the relationship.

Once again, it didn't take long for the cracks to show. There were inconsistencies, small at first, but strange enough to unsettle Peter. On one occasion, Samantha invited him to a barbecue for her vegan friends. In Gloucester, in the early 2000s, veganism was hardly a fashion, not really believable at all. It seemed odd, but Peter accepted it, wanting to please her. Then, without explanation, the barbecue was abruptly cancelled, vanishing as though it had never been planned. He never met her vegan friends – they too vanished. Other nights, she claimed to be out partying with friends, painting vivid pictures of laughter and chaos, only for Peter to discover, when he turned up to the very same venues, that there was no trace of her. Her stories collapsed on inspection, leaving behind only a hollow feeling of absence.

According to Peter, Samantha told her stories with the kind of casual ease that suggested a habit of spinning tales. Sometimes, she seemed to talk as if caught between reality and fantasy, embellishing details so effortlessly it was hard to tell where truth ended and invention began. Yet she never appeared to relish deception in the usual sense; rather, her stories seemed like a world she inhabited as much as created. Samantha's brilliance was always in the moment, so when she was with him, Peter forgot his doubts. He remembered only that she made him feel seen, wanted, transformed. 'She made me feel special, no one had ever made me feel like that before.' It was intoxicating, the way she lit up his difficult life. And that intoxication was stronger, for a time, than truth itself.

Peter recalls that Samantha often spoke, as though idly daydreaming, of a future filled with a quaint, perfect family life. She painted pictures of a house of her own, a devoted husband and a child she could cherish. It was the kind of idyll she returned to again and again, spoken about with such wistful sincerity that it caught Peter off guard. For all her wild stories and dizzying lies, there was something believable in that longing. It seemed to be what she wanted most – a family of her own. A place to belong, where she might anchor herself against the restlessness that hummed beneath her skin. For Peter, hearing her speak that way softened everything. It made the inconsistencies easier to overlook, the doubts easier to silence. What harm could there be, after all, in a girl who dreamed out loud about love and stability?

By the time school drew to its inevitable close, Samantha's

web of lies had left her increasingly isolated, ostracised by many of the friends she once had. So, rather than hanging out with Samantha's friends, Peter found himself spending a lot of time with the Cookes family. They welcomed him with easy warmth. Janice was sociable and engaging, a stark contrast to Leslie, who guarded himself behind a quiet reserve. The family dynamics felt ordinary, even reassuring, to Peter. Little did he know just how quickly the ground beneath him would shift.

As summer faded, Samantha left for York University to study politics and law, carrying with her the bright promise of a future they both imagined. The couple attempted to hold together the fragile threads of their young relationship across the miles. Peter recalls visiting Samantha for the weekend at her university halls in October 2007. She was excited to see him, but he remembers that, strangely, she kept him separate from the new friends she had spoken about so often in the previous weeks. The couple spent the entire weekend squirrelled away in Samantha's room, avoiding all others. Samantha assured Peter she was using contraception – the coil – so there was no need to use condoms as they always had done in the past. 'It's completely safe, don't be such a worrier,' she giggled. It was a moment Peter would later look back on with deep regret.

On the Sunday evening, as the October air cut thin and sharp, Peter caught the train from York to Birmingham and then onwards to Gloucester. With distance growing by the second between himself and his girlfriend, he knew in his heart that something wasn't right about their relationship. Why had she hidden him away from her new friends? Did these people even exist? Did he want to be in a relationship with a girl who made him question such basic things? Peter made the decision there and then to end things. By text. At the same time, he changed his Facebook status from 'in a relationship' to 'single' for the whole world to see. It is a moment he now recalls with shame.

What followed was relentless. There was a barrage of messages from Samantha, a storm of emotion and tactics, sometimes furious, shouting into the void, other times fragile, pleading for his return. Weeks passed and Peter attempted to move on with his life. Then, one night, out of the blue, his Nokia 3210 mobile phone buzzed in the quiet stillness of his small, cluttered room. It was a message from Samantha. He stared at the screen, hesitant, a pit growing in his stomach. Slowly, he unlocked it.

The words hit him like a blow.

'I'm pregnant.'

For a heartbeat, nothing registered but the cold flush seeping through his veins.

Pregnant.

The word felt foreign, dangerous, too heavy for a boy still unsteady on the edge of adulthood. His mind recoiled, scrambling for reasons, for excuses. It had to be another story, a trick spun to trap him in her web. He thought back to that moment in Samantha's bedroom in York University Halls. 'I'm on birth control, I have the coil, there's nothing to worry about.' Was she lying to him? She had dreamt aloud so often of having a baby with him, could she have tricked him into it? Peter didn't know what to think.

His fingers trembled as he reread the message, hoping somehow the weight of those two words would dissipate with time. What he didn't know then, what he couldn't know, was that Samantha was, this time, telling the truth. She was, in fact, pregnant. As Peter lay there, in that quiet hour, he felt the ground shift beneath him as his life began unravelling before him.

Over the coming weeks, as the news sank in, Peter told no one of the pregnancy – it was a secret he kept to himself. Sticking his head in the sand, he ignored further messages from Samantha, declining her phone calls. Young and terrified of the prospect of fatherhood with a woman he couldn't trust, he fled. He booked a one-way ticket to New Zealand and cut off all contact from Samantha. He still sincerely doubted she was telling the truth about this baby, but he wasn't going to hang around to find out for sure. This is a moment in his life that he looks back on with little pride. He left Samantha in the lurch, he knows that now. In quiet moments he often thinks how different things might have been for both of them if he had made a different decision. But that was not to be.

For Samantha, the pregnancy marked a fissure in her carefully built illusions, a turning point from which there was no retreat. It heralded a spiral into a world of fabricated identities, betrayals and deceptions that would fracture hundreds of lives across both the UK and Ireland for over a decade.

2

BABY MARTHA

Only a handful of people knew the truth Samantha hadn't dared speak aloud, a secret as fragile as the life growing within her, alone in her room, at halls in York University.

At university Samantha could be whoever she wanted to be. Having run out of road with her friends at Denmark Road High School for Girls, York University presented a second chance for her. Studying politics and law, this was an opportunity to redefine herself as an altogether new person, a habit she would grow increasingly accustomed to in the coming years. A more 'Received Pronunciation' accent appeared, in contrast to the broader Gloucester accent of her family and friends.

However, a surprise pregnancy was not the start to the new life she had envisioned. Adding to Samantha's turmoil, her parents had recently separated. Samantha's world had truly been turned on its axis.

She sided with Janice in the divorce, but her brother Adam sided with their father, which led to another loss in young Samantha's life. Samantha never told her father about the baby and barely spoke of the pregnancy to anyone beyond her mother.

Peter, her ex-boyfriend, having completely cut her off, left a gap no one else could fill.

Isolated and lonely, as the weeks crept forward and this new life grew inside her, the world around Samantha was falling apart. Single, her family separated, the future she once daydreamed about – of a husband, a child and a home together – seemed to unravel in the cold light of reality. At thirty weeks of pregnancy, Samantha made a quiet, resolute choice that settled over her like a shadow. This baby would not be hers to keep. She could not see herself as a mother, not in the way she had once imagined. She reached out to Gloucester Council, asking it to arrange for her unborn child to be adopted. It was a choice she knew would change everything.

Without sharing the news with her college friends, Samantha left university and moved into Magnolia House, supportive housing for women and young babies. On 9 July 2008, at the tender age of nineteen, she gave birth to her first child, Martha Isobel Cookes. The moment Martha took her first tiny breath in the world, a light seemed to shine through the shadows that had gathered around Samantha's life. She was perfect, so small, so fragile.

The following four months were a complicated start to baby Martha's life. The adoption process was already underway, so Martha was taken into foster care immediately after birth. Two weeks passed and the baby then spent four days with Samantha at her request, followed by another stint in foster care. Following this, again upon Samantha's request, Martha was returned to her care while awaiting adoption.

Exactly nineteen weeks after her birth, on 18 November 2008, Martha was due to be given up for adoption. The significance of that day hung in the air. Unbeknownst to all, it was to be the day that would change everything, altering the course of Samantha and Martha's futures irrevocably.

* * *

1st April 2009. Coroner's Court. Shire Hall, Gloucestershire.

Coroner's Court Transcript

Female Police Officer:

Sam Cookes woke up between 6.30 and 7.00 hours on the 18th of November, 2008, and gave Martha her first feed of the day. Sam was aware the adoption worker was arriving that morning, and was looking forward to signing the adoption paperwork.

___________ the adoption worker from ___________, arrived at Magnolia House at approximately 09.30 hours and remained for approximately one hour.

The adoption paperwork was signed by Sam and ___________ played with Martha and observed Sam caring for Martha. ___________ left the room at approximately 10.30 and was waved off from the building by Sam and Martha. Sam had planned to take Martha to the Lane Children Centre later that afternoon, however between 12.00 hours and 14.00 hours Martha would normally have a sleep.

Sam placed Martha on her back and placed her into a v-shaped pillow.

Martha was placed at the bottom of the bed with her head towards the cot. She was placed on top of the quilt, not under any sheets or quilts.

Martha fell asleep and Sam went downstairs to clean out the baby bottles and baby bath. She was fastidious with the bottles and baby baths. Within a short period of time, Sam returned upstairs and saw that Martha was still asleep on the bed. Sam lay on the bed next to Martha. Her intention was never to fall asleep. She wanted to lie next to Martha and watch her.

She placed a rectangular shaped pillow above the v-shaped pillow so that she could rest her left shoulder area on it. This would be similar to when you lie in bed reading a book and you prop yourself up. Sam was lying on the left-hand side with Martha between herself and the wall.

Sam had stated to police that she had previously lain next to Martha but never slept in a bed with her. In fact, other witnesses have stated Sam was very concerned about overlaying and would lecture the other mothers about the dangers of overlaying.

Sam has stated that she would place the pillows at the bottom of the bed so that her head was closer to the cot. Sam would never sleep with Martha, she did not want to build a dependence bond between mother and child. The reason being that she was aware that Martha was to be adopted. Therefore, each morning Sam would then return the pillows to the headboard side so it did not look peculiar and the room looked tidy.

Sam has told police when she fell asleep, sorry that she then fell asleep, she had no intention of falling asleep and

> did not know why she woke up. Sam believes that she fell asleep approximately at 1 p.m. and awoke at about 2.30 p.m.
>
> When Sam woke up, she saw that the rectangular pillow was over Martha's face and the v-shaped pillow was slightly wrapped around the neck of Martha.

The police officer became overwhelmed with emotion, so a court official read the following extract from her statement:

> Sam pulled Martha from underneath the pillows. She was lifeless, and according to Martha [*sic*; should read Samantha] she was a funny colour. Sam then picked Martha up and went to run out of the bedroom. She went to open the door and found that it was locked from the inside.
>
> Sam then had to put Martha down and open the door. She opened the door and picked Martha up again. Sam started screaming and the residents and workers of Magnolia House were alerted. ___________ the Magnolia House worker, then started cardiopulmonary resuscitation on Martha and the ambulance were [*sic*] called.

The evidence read aloud by police in the court was devastating. It reported how Emergency Services responded rapidly to the scene. Martha was rushed to A&E in Cheltenham and later moved to City General Hospital Stoke-on-Trent, but despite the medical staff's best efforts, they were unable to save her and Martha died at the age of just four months old.

While at Cheltenham Hospital Samantha told her mother, 'We went to sleep. I woke up and she was blue.' Witnesses recalled that Samantha was completely traumatised and remained inconsolable at Martha's bedside. In a discarded note years later, Samantha wrote: 'Losing a child, no matter what age, makes your heart break in places that you never knew existed.'

As the Coroner's Court was coming to the conclusion of the inquest in 2009, the following exchange took place between the coroner, Alan Crickmore, and Samantha:

> **Crickmore**: On this particular morning, you'd had a meeting with the adoption people and you'd effectively signed paperwork. Did you know that you could change your mind about the adoption at any time, right up to the last minute?
>
> **Samantha**: Yes.
>
> **Crickmore**: Although you signed this paperwork, you knew that you could change your mind?
>
> **Samantha**: Yeah, from my perspective that was just the step forward. It was to get the Social Services to, you know, move things along.
>
> **Crickmore**: Okay, then the next question is a harder question, but it's a question that should be put for fairness to you. Did you do anything on that day to deliberately harm your daughter?
>
> **Samantha**: No.

Upon hearing all the evidence presented to him, the coroner ruled that Martha Cookes died an accidental death with no suspicion of foul play from her mother, Samantha. 'I'm satisfied that she is blameless in this particular matter,' he stated. Martha's cause of death was recorded as an occlusion of the airwaves, when a pillow came to be positioned over her face as she slept on a bed alongside her mother. (Interestingly, in 2013, Coroner Crickmore was jailed for eight years for the theft of over £2 million from clients of his solicitor's practice. Much of the money he stole was from living clients, but some was also taken from the estates of dead people, including one who suffered as a Second World War prisoner of war.)

Despite the ruling that baby Martha had died an accidental death, this was not the last time the issue would rear its head in Samantha's life. As she walked out the doors of Shire Hall on that April day in Gloucestershire, little did she know the circumstances of her daughter's death would follow her into courtrooms across the UK and Ireland for years to come.

3

THE SURROGACY SCAM

Samantha Cookes' story shifted irrevocably with the loss of her daughter. Martha's death, a cruel theft of innocence, carved through her mother's very core. She was never again the young woman who had once balanced her studies at York University with hopeful ambition. Reeling from the death of her daughter, her academic career had dissolved. The lecture halls, the textbooks, the promise of a future degree were all abandoned. Janice Cookes mourned her granddaughter but shuddered, too, at the metamorphosis she saw in Samantha. 'She was never the same after Martha,' Janice would later state, shaken by the hollow look in her daughter's eyes.

Samantha's grief had not broken her, not in the way anyone might expect. Instead, it built a darker architecture inside her, a place where fabrications could live and breathe. She left York behind and settled in Telford, a place where she was determined to begin again. But new beginnings are sometimes not all they seem, and Samantha's was inked in deception.

It was in Telford that her lies found teeth. What had once seemed like harmless storytelling, exaggeration, borrowed anecdotes, hardened into something purposeful and predatory. She began to weave stories. Not just half-truths or altered versions of her own life, but entire worlds populated by fictional figures who moved like chess pieces under her hand. Samantha became author, director and star of her own intricate dramas, lives carefully constructed to insinuate themselves into those of others. The first to walk into her web of deceit were the Taylors.

* * *

In February 2010, Katie and Luke Taylor were young, newly married and painfully fragile with the fact that what they wanted, they could not have: children. Katie had always imagined her life filled with prams and bedtime stories, toys scattered across the carpet. But while others around her fell pregnant seemingly effortlessly, Katie's arms remained empty. She and Luke tried and tried again until hope started to taste like ash.

Late one evening, in their home in the sleepy market town of Northallerton in Yorkshire, Katie sat at her laptop as Luke slept beside her. Her fingers hovered uncertainly before she typed the words she had resisted for months. A post on a forum about surrogacy. Even writing it made her cheeks burn – it felt too raw, too exposing. But she pressed send, then closed her eyes. The sudden chime of a notification pulled her heart into her throat.

A message was waiting. Katie clicked, hands trembling, and the words bloomed onto the screen: 'Hello, my name is Samantha. I was so moved by your post. I would love to help you, to carry a child for you. I know what it feels like to long for something so deeply, and I want to make this dream real for you. Please, let's talk ...'

Katie's pulse quickened, her breath catching. Here, suddenly, was deliverance. A crack of light in the oppressive dark that had smothered her for so long. She touched the words on the screen, as if they could steady her. Hope blossomed.

Reading Katie's post filled with longing, Samantha Cookes pounced. Like a vulture circling an ailing creature, she zoned in.

The message glowed on the screen, gentle and kind. Katie reread the words a dozen times, her mind racing. Could this be real? Surrogacy had always seemed unreachable, tucked behind layers of legality and cost, a fortress she and Luke could never scale. And yet here was someone offering it, without any of that cold formality.

Her hand hovered near Luke's shoulder where he slept. She wondered if she should wake him, shake his arm and thrust the laptop under his nose. No, she decided. Not yet. This was too fragile. Too precious. She wanted to hold it for herself a moment longer, this spark of possibility, before reality could reassert itself and crush it. Still, it seemed like someone wanted to help them, to give them the family they craved.

Katie typed back, careful but emotional: 'Samantha, thank you. I don't know how to explain what this means to me. Please, tell me more.'

Back in her flat, Samantha had been waiting for a reply. When it came, Katie's yearning was clear. For Samantha, it was all too easy to take that and twist it to her own ends, to feed into the new story she was directing. It was almost too easy.

She replied swiftly. 'I've done this before ... I gave birth to a little girl for a lady called Claudia Bronwyn, it was an amazing experience. I just want to help.' The lie streaked freshly across her screen, bold and bright. Every invented syllable tightened the snare.

Back in Northallerton, for the first time in months, Katie allowed herself to imagine tiny clothes folded into drawers, faint laughter in all corners of the house, Luke's tired but joyful smile as he cradled a baby. A family, finally.

Her hands shook as she typed her response, 'We'd love to meet you.'

She pressed send.

* * *

Katie had always thought luck was something that happened to other people. Then Samantha walked into her kitchen with her soft blue eyes, a reassuring smile and a promise that sounded as impossible as it was intoxicating. For once, Katie dared to believe her turn had come.

The evening Samantha first spoke the name Claudia Bronwyn, she wove it almost casually into conversation, as though recalling an old friend. Claudia had become a mother, she said, radiant and fulfilled thanks to Samantha's help. When Katie's face lit up with hunger, the hunger only someone who had longed, pleaded, begged for a child would truly understand, Samantha pressed the advantage with an elegant flourish.

'She's just a lovely woman,' she added lightly. 'Here, I'll show you.'

Moments later, Katie sat bent over her laptop, staring at Claudia's Facebook profile as though it were a treasure chest. There she was, Claudia, blonde hair catching the sun, smiling down at her baby daughter. Another photograph showed the little girl in a white cardigan clutching a toy rabbit with worn, pink ears. These were not grainy, careless snapshots of fabricated lives, they had the glow of truth. A life captured in small frozen instants, the very life Katie had been desperate to achieve for herself.

Her chest constricted. Here was a real mother, a real child, proof that Samantha could make Katie's dream something more than a cruel nightmare. As she clicked through each image, Luke's hand rested lightly on her shoulder, as if steadying her from being swept completely away by her emotions. For the first time in months, the dark shadow of three failed IVF cycles lifted, replaced by a fragile, bright and terrifying hope.

And Samantha – clever, warm Samantha – sealed it with the simple title she bestowed on herself. She was a 'social worker', she told the young, eager couple; an honourable role that carried weight and implied trustworthiness. Who better to guide them through the labyrinth of legality, of surrogacy, of the pitiless bureaucracy that had always felt stacked against them?

Despite being only twenty-one years of age, Samantha's manner never faltered. She was gentle but measured when she asked the couple for funds. Contracts and legal processes weren't free, she explained, and neither were insemination kits or the travel required to coordinate the delicate process. Katie and Luke didn't hesitate. They quickly did a bank transfer, passing £1,200 – their entire savings – into the hands of their bright-eyed saviour.

A few days after Samantha's visit, a Facebook message popped up on Katie's laptop screen. It was from the happy new mother Claudia Bronwyn. 'I am extremely grateful to Samantha, she has an incredible heart. She has given us the wonderful gift of our daughter.' The words dripped with sincerity. Katie read and reread them until the letters blurred. If another woman could speak with such reverence about Samantha, how could she not believe in her?

But her belief soon required more financial aid. Samantha pressed again about expenses, contracts, health insurance upgrades. Her tone was still careful, practised, like a storyteller layering her plot with just enough urgency to demand agreement. Katie and Luke complied, drawing on the last reserves of their money, even siphoning from Luke's business in the desperate chase towards parenthood.

Soon the dream began to unravel quietly. Despite paying Samantha, she was yet to produce a surrogacy contract for Katie and Luke to make their plans concrete and binding. She missed a call here, ignored a message there. Days passed with excuses or silence. *Is she avoiding us?* Katie began to wonder. She tried not to hear the whispered voice inside her head, the same voice that had whispered her despair after so many failed tests and the doctor appointments where hope had evaporated.

However, in the end, it was not instinct but evidence that shattered the illusion. As weeks went by with no progress, Luke, growing frustrated with Samantha's delays and excuses, dropped into his local police station to make a concerned report. The couple had given their life savings to a woman promising surrogacy, but they were now worried it was too good to be true. Luke believed their desperation had been used against them. Could the police pay her a visit and check it out, even just to put their minds at ease?

The police arrived swiftly at Samantha's Telford home. The truth, under their scrutiny, was as stark as dawn after a sleepless night. She was no social worker. She had never been a surrogate. Claudia Bronwyn never existed. The smiling child in the photos was probably plucked from someone else's family album, an ornament on Samantha's mantle of deceit. In the recycle bin on her computer police found, among other things, an expenses document being prepared for Katie and Luke dated to the previous day.

What Katie had mistaken for luck, she realised too late, had been nothing more than another woman's duplicity, crafted not for healing but for theft.

* * *

October 2011 saw Samantha once again in court, this time in Teeside Crown Court. When the quiet settled in the courtroom, Samantha Cookes read aloud from a letter in a voice that was not the one that had charmed Katie and Luke months earlier but held, instead, a paper-thin simulation of contrition: 'I want to apologise for my mistake and the hurt I've caused. I'm truly sorry.'

The words hung in the still air.

'Now I am in intensive therapy, I can see that I never dealt with my grief after my daughter's sudden death. I am sorry this caused me to hurt other people. I hope to resolve my mental illness ... this will never erase my mistake, though. Never again will I get myself into trouble. I never want to hurt anyone else again.'

As Samantha's legal counsel informed the court that she was struggling after her baby daughter died due to cot death, Katie gasped, audibly and involuntarily. Luke reached for her hand, but she snatched it away, her face pale. They hadn't expected such a justification, the invocation of a dead child. It was manipulation, Luke thought, a sick twist in the story. Samantha was writing new plotlines even in court, shading herself in tragedy to earn sympathy.

The judge shifted heavily in his chair. 'Miss Cookes,' he said, tone clipped, 'you have admitted to a cruel and hurtful fraud. Your victims were vulnerable because their desire to have children was both profound and unfulfilled. They trusted you. That trust, you warped into profit.'

When the gavel descended Samantha was facing a suspended sentence for nine months. Instead of incarceration, she faced probation and supervision. She was also ordered to pay £1,890 in compensation to the devastated couple.

To Katie it felt as if the ground had been pulled out from under her. After everything – the lies, the humiliation, the shame of giving their savings to a fantasy – this careless girl was avoiding prison, allowed to walk home to Telford with her 'therapy sessions', a fine and a warning to never do anything like it again.

Outside the court, facing the cool autumn air, Katie told a reporter through tightened lips, 'We are annoyed she did not get a harsher punishment; it's just a slap on the wrist after all the hurt she has caused.' She meant it. Nothing felt finished. Nothing felt safe.

* * *

What neither Katie nor Luke realised, and what no one in that courtroom seemed to question, was just how flawed the story of Cookes' grief had been. Her legal counsel had stood unchallenged when citing Samantha's trauma, the supposed 'cot death' of her baby daughter Martha in November 2008. Yet Martha had not died quietly in her crib alone. Martha had suffocated, smothered by the softness of a pillow as Samantha slept beside her. Recorded as an accident, yes, but it was not a cot death, the narrative her lawyers wove into their plea for leniency. That vital detail lay unchallenged, unnoticed.

For Katie and Luke, only the aftermath and trauma remained. Katie could not shake the sense of having been enchanted by a witch whose trickery left scars long after the spell faded. And yet life moved on, as it always does.

Against the odds, Katie and Luke went on to have children of their own, filling the house with laughter where despair had once lingered. Katie, steeled by what had happened, went further still. She became a surrogate herself, carrying children for families who shared her old desperation. Each birth, each new cry filling a delivery room, felt like a personal act of defiance. Katie would give others what Samantha had promised her but never delivered. Not a lie, not a fantasy, but life itself.

For ten years, Katie and Luke lived as though Samantha Cookes had been sealed in a past life: distant, grotesque, like a shadow they refused to acknowledge. It was easier to think of her as gone; easier to believe her letter to the judge, remember that she was in therapy, assume she was recovering, putting distance between herself and the damage she had wrought.

Then, in the summer of 2024, a letter slid through their post box with the neat, cat-headed logo of Alleycats Films. Katie opened it casually at first, expecting something mundane, another circular in disguise, but the words stalled her heartbeat. The producer's tone was polite, professional. They were contacting her and Luke about a documentary project. A piece on fraud. On families deceived. Their names, the letter explained, had surfaced in connection to a figure at the heart of the documentary: Samantha Cookes.

Katie felt the paper crackle under her tightening grip. The name leapt at her and a shiver ran down her spine. Katie remembered listening as Samantha had promised in that courtroom, with scripted contrition, that she would never hurt anyone again. She had claimed to be broken, repentant, reshaped by the fire of grief and therapy. She had looked at the judge, at the world, and begged to be believed. But the letter in Katie's hands told another story.

The truth, unhappily, was that Samantha Cookes had not stopped. She had kept weaving her tales, shifting guises, ensnaring others with the same creativity Katie once mistook for kindness. More families. More victims. More heartache flooding from the pen of a woman who never stopped writing her cruel lies at the expense of those desperate enough to believe them.

Luke read the letter quietly over Katie's shoulder, his hand tightening on her arm as the words sank in. Together, they felt the old horror resurface – not a memory now, but something living, prowling again. Katie folded the letter slowly, her face unreadable. All these years she had built her family, built joy out of the rubble Samantha had left behind. She had given life to others as a surrogate, righted the balance in her own way. But there, in her kitchen again, she felt the cold truth land – the story of Samantha Cookes was not over. And somehow, impossibly, she was part of it still.

4

A DISAPPEARING ACT

In September 2011, just before her court case for surrogacy fraud began, Samantha enrolled for a Higher National Diploma in Business at Shrewsbury College. There she could pass herself off as being like any other new student, albeit in her case one trying to stitch some purpose back into her life. From her flat – a plain, narrow place overlooking the Abbey – she walked through the grey mornings to college, head held high, footsteps brisk, her now auburn hair always tucked neatly beneath a scarf. No one here whispered, no one stared. No one knew of her deceased baby, of her pending conviction for fraud. Here Samantha could breathe.

Her classmates thought of her as warm, if occasionally overbearing. Jamie Bunting, who sat two rows back from her, was one of the first to gravitate towards her. A knot of nervous habits, chewed nails, collars tugged too often, Jamie seemed to shrink in on himself with each passing day. He was kind in the uncalculated way that only the wounded learn to be, and in Samantha's presence, he found an anchor.

However, it wasn't long before Jamie started to sense something was off. Samantha had told her classmates about her bad back, a story of slipped discs and unbearable spasms. Jamie, along with other students, had been quick to help, with bags carried and car rides offered. One Tuesday afternoon, though, Jamie caught sight of her across a lecture hall. Their tutor, who was struggling with a box of journals, was suddenly relieved by Samantha's eager hands. She lifted the heavy box without a wince. Not even a frown.

Jamie blinked, unsettled, but said nothing.

During this time, it wasn't just Jamie who became entranced by Samantha. Another young man in their class was bewitched by the charming bombshell. Joe (not his real name) was a quiet young man, three years younger than her. He was captivated by her beauty and her effortless confidence. The only problem was that Samantha claimed to have a boyfriend already. A serious boyfriend – Peter, a musician, apparently – with whom she lived, along with their flatmates, Simon and Chloe. Two couples. 'It is like living in a French film,' she mused once, eyes unfocused, stirring her coffee so slowly it went cold before she'd taken a sip. She spoke of dinner parties, of late-night debates about art and politics, of Simon's dog that would refuse to settle unless Bach was playing. But when Joe asked to meet them, she smiled faintly and said, 'One day.'

That day never came. The only time she tried to organise it, a dinner party at the very apartment she'd described in such detail, she'd called him that afternoon, voice trembling, to say Simon had been rushed to hospital. A stroke, she said breathlessly. 'Can you believe it? He's only twenty-five.' Joe had said all the right things – 'Poor Simon, how terrible' – but, later, he found himself pondering what a strange coincidence it was. As he was to finally meet these people, one of them, a young – and by all reports healthy – man, was struck down by a stroke.

Still, Samantha's sweetness was absorbing. She remembered Joe's favourite brand of crisps and surprised him at college with them tucked into her bag. She'd text him out of nowhere with lines like: 'You make me feel safe in a world that isn't.' It was impossible not to fall for that. The two grew closer and closer, until one evening, after studying late at college, they fell into each other's arms outside the library. She told him she had broken up with Peter and they could now be together. Joe was elated. In the warm glow of new love, he ignored the little niggles in the back of his mind.

Christmas 2011 was one Joe recalls being filled with joy. With his new girlfriend on his arm and his studies at Shrewsbury College going well, he felt like he had the world at his feet.

The months rolled on, with their relationship gathering a rhythm. Evenings were spent with takeaway curry containers and open notebooks, Samantha sprawled across the sofa and wrapped in a knitted cardigan from the local knitting shop in which she had started a part-time job, half studying, half daydreaming. She spoke often now about the future, names for their theoretical children, quaint little cottages, dogs that would grow old with them. Joe thought it was harmless, even endearing, dreaming, though he sometimes caught a flicker in her eye when she spoke of 'someday' – a certainty that unsettled him.

That day was to come sooner than Joe ever expected.

It was April 2012 when the news came. Outside, the light had already died, and the air smelled faintly of the scent of the blossoming apple trees in the front garden. Samantha was standing by the sink, her back to Joe, shoulders tight beneath her cardigan.

'I need to tell you something,' she said.

Her tone, soft but without its usual playful lilt, made him glance up from the kettle. 'What's wrong?'

She turned around slowly. The expression on her face was unreadable, neither excited nor afraid, but suspended somewhere between. 'I'm pregnant,' she said simply.

The room stilled.

For a long moment Joe thought he must have misheard. The kettle bubbled, reaching boiling point, and the sound seemed almost comically intrusive. 'But ... how?' he managed. 'Weren't you on the coil?'

'I was,' she said, lowering her eyes. 'Something must have gone wrong. It happens.'

Something about the calmness of her voice chilled him. She wasn't frightened, not even surprised. Her hand came to rest lightly on her stomach.

Samantha had spoken often about wanting a family, about wanting to matter to someone in that irrevocable way. To be a mother. But until that moment, he had never imagined those fantasies would coalesce into something real, something they couldn't unmake with a conversation. He felt as though a door had closed behind him and another had opened onto a corridor he didn't recognise.

He tried to summon joy or at least resolve. He wasn't ready to be a father, but this brilliant, bewildering woman was carrying his child. He would do the right thing, of course he would. Yet as she smiled faintly and said, 'We'll be fine, Joe. You'll see,' he sensed, for the first time, how completely she had pulled him into her story.

While Joe came to terms with becoming a father, Samantha continued to push the boundaries with her friends at Shrewsbury College. It was a class trip to Amsterdam to mark the summer holidays that would prove to be one push too far. She had pitched it over coffee, eyes alight, words tumbling out in a rush. How good it would be, how cultural, how they all deserved it. Convinced, Joe, along with fellow classmate Jamie Bunting and other friends scraped together the money. Jamie, finding it hardest of all, still remembers his relief at gathering together enough cash to hand over to Samantha in a little white envelope. Then came silence. No tickets. No confirmation. Just Samantha's growing excuses.

As the end of the academic year approached and no sign of any concrete travel plans appeared, Jamie pressed her for answers, his voice frayed with worry. In response, she snapped. 'You're stressing me so much I'll lose this baby,' she hissed, clutching her belly. Her voice rose, accusing, shoving blame onto him until others turned their heads. Terrified he might truly do her harm, Jamie faltered.

As the date for the planned Amsterdam trip grew imminent, with no sign of tickets or plans, a tutor overheard Jamie and his classmate one morning debating whether they'd ever even get as much as a refund for what now increasingly seemed like a bogus trip.

That tutor's face tightened with unease. 'There's no trip, is there?'

'It doesn't look like it,' Jamie frowned.

'I shouldn't be saying this, but ...' he lowered his voice, 'do some research on your friend Samantha.'

Fifteen minutes later Jamie sat rigid in the glow of a college library computer screen. Words leapt out at him like fire: 'Surrogacy fraud conviction.' He read and reread the online news article in disbelief. An image was attached to it of a young woman walking from court in October 2011, the October just gone by. It was her.

When he confronted Samantha, standing square in the corridor, she tried to drown out his fury with volume. She shouted, twisted the blame, clutched her stomach again. But Jamie's voice cut through. 'I know who you are. I want my money back. I know what you've done.'

In the face of his steady words, Samantha held firm, dismissing him as crazy, deranged, a fantasist. Jamie never received his deposit back.

* * *

When Jamie told Joe, the young father-to-be, the truth about the Amsterdam trip, the words didn't land all at once. They came like loose gravel rolling downhill, impossible to grasp before the full weight struck.

'She was in the papers, Joe. Samantha Cookes. Charged. Pleaded guilty. It was some surrogacy thing. A scam.'

Joe laughed at first, a bewildered, strangled sound that caught in the back of his throat. 'That can't be right,' he said. 'You must've mixed her up with someone else.' But Jamie only looked back at him, expression grim. The kind of look people use when they wish they weren't right.

'She tricked a couple who couldn't have kids,' Jamie said quietly. 'Told them she'd carry their baby for them. Took their money. But there was never a pregnancy. She strung them along for months, then bailed. Got a suspended sentence.'

The world tilted. Joe sat very still. He could taste copper, though he wasn't bleeding.

'That's not her,' he said finally. 'You don't know her, she's not like that. She's …' he faltered. Gentle. Sweet. Honest.

'It's her name. Her photo, too,' Jamie pressed. 'Look it up if you don't believe me.'

Joe did. Later. Alone in the library. The articles were still there, a grainy photograph of Samantha outside Teeside Court, head bowed, coat buttoned to the chin. Unmistakable.

That night, he barely noticed himself walking home from college. The streets blurred past, rows of dim-lit terraces, the smell of wet brick and fried food clinging to the air. His mind replayed Jamie's words in jagged loops.

Surrogacy scam. Money. Lies.

By the time he reached the flat he shared with Samantha, something braver and colder than fear had settled in him.

Samantha was sitting at the small kitchen table, knitting half-finished in her lap, a cup of hot chocolate steaming beside her. When she looked up, she saw it instantly, the edge in his eyes, the way he stood. 'What's wrong?' she asked, her voice low.

'Jamie told me something this evening.' His tone was flat, careful. 'About ... your past.'

Her hands stilled. For a long moment she said nothing. Then, quietly, 'What exactly did he say?'

'That you took money from a couple, said you were having their baby when you weren't.'

The knitting slipped from her lap. Her expression cracked like glass under pressure. 'Joe, please, don't listen to that. It wasn't like that. It wasn't.'

'Then what was it?'

She pressed her fingers to her temples, elbows braced against the table. When she spoke again, her voice trembled, but her eyes stayed dry. 'I had a baby,' she whispered. 'Her name was Martha. She died in 2008. Cot death. I was nineteen. I didn't cope. I wasn't thinking straight after. When the couple contacted me, I thought maybe ... maybe helping them would make the pain mean something.'

She looked up at him then, the full force of her gaze landing with desperate precision. 'I didn't mean to mislead anyone, Joe. I wasn't ... right. My head was gone. I just wanted the hurt to stop. I got in too deep and then couldn't back out.'

His heart twisted painfully. The story fit, neatly enough to disarm him. And yet. 'What about the trip to Amsterdam?' he pressed. 'Jamie says you never booked anything.'

Her shoulders slumped. 'I'll give him his deposit back,' she said, her tone almost wounded. 'I lost track, all this pregnancy stuff, my mind's everywhere. Do you really think I'd scam my own classmates, our friends, Joe?'

He didn't answer. Not straight away. Her fragility hung between them and Joe noticed a tremor in her hands. She looked like someone breaking under the weight of too much truth.

He wanted to believe her. God, he wanted to. This woman, carrying his child, the one who remembered his favourite crisps and laughed with him under streetlights, how could that Samantha be the one from those headlines?

He moved to her uncertainly, placing a hand on her shoulder. 'It's okay,' he said, though it didn't feel true. 'We'll just ... sort it out. For the baby's sake.'

In the silence that followed, Samantha leaned into him, burying her face against his chest. But behind his ribs, that unsure feeling, the quiet, persistent wrongness, stirred again like something waking from sleep.

* * *

As the summer of 2012 rolled round, Joe and Samantha put all thoughts of Shrewsbury College out of their minds. The expectant young parents became wrapped up in their own bubble. Samantha couldn't realistically return in the new term as she would be heavily pregnant by then. Joe pushed all thoughts of Jamie and his deposit out of his mind. He needed to focus on preparing to become a father.

At first, Samantha seemed radiant with pregnancy: proud, indulgent, glowing. She knitted perpetually, churning out tiny hats and blankets like a woman conjuring safety through repetition. Yet as autumn crept in, that careful composure began to fray. Her phone went unanswered more often. Some days she'd seem distracted, vacant. Then came the fainting spells.

The first occurred outside the post office. A well-meaning stranger phoned Joe from Samantha's battered old Nokia. 'She just went down,' the woman said, 'right there on the pavement. We thought she was dead.'

Joe left a seminar mid-sentence, heart in his throat, and raced across town to find Samantha sitting dazed on a bench, pale but smiling weakly. 'Just blood pressure,' she murmured. 'It's normal.' But the softness in her movements that day unnerved him; she looked almost translucent, her eyes too shiny.

It happened again two weeks later, this time in the supermarket. She had been standing near the bread aisle when she simply crumpled, knocking over a display of cereal boxes. Shoppers gathered, voices hushed. Paramedics came. When Joe arrived at the hospital, she was hooked to a monitor, two nurses fussing over her like she was made of porcelain.

After that, things changed in ways he couldn't quite name. Samantha became distant. When he returned from a day of college, there were leaflets stacked quietly on the kitchen counter: Maternal Mental Health, Social Services Support Pathways.

He asked, once, what they were for. 'Oh, they just gave them to me in the clinic,' she said, waving a hand, too quick, too dismissive. 'Routine stuff.'

But it didn't feel routine.

By October, Samantha had been admitted to hospital 'for observation'. This meant 24/7 supervision, but no one would tell Joe much. The midwife said she was 'in good hands'. A doctor, when pressed, muttered something about 'complex needs'. The phrase clanged in Joe's head like a warning bell, but whenever he asked Samantha about it directly, she turned her face to the window and said she was too tired to talk.

Joe wanted to believe that everything was under control. That the system had her, and their baby, safe. But the nights stretched long and the silence between them grew heavier. Sometimes, late at night, he would dream of her wandering hospital corridors, barefoot and bewildered, while distant voices whispered behind glass.

Then, in November, the baby came. He wasn't even called until the following morning. The hospital smelled of antiseptic and coffee, its hallways too bright, too echoing. Samantha lay in her bed, pale, a nurse hovering just inside the doorway. She looked up as he entered, eyes blazing, cheeks slick with salt.

'They've taken the baby,' she said. 'They've taken my baby.'

The words hit him like a blow. 'What do you mean taken?'

Her breathing was ragged, furious. 'Social services. Court order. They said something about emergency protection, safeguarding. I'm the baby's mother, Joe. I was breastfeeding this morning, and they just, just took my baby!'

Joe's stomach turned to lead. He caught fragments – concerns for welfare, supervision order, temporary placement – bureaucratic words that meant nothing and everything.

Samantha thrashed against her blankets, sobbing into her hands. 'I didn't do anything wrong,' she kept repeating. 'They can't just take my baby away.'

Joe stood helplessly at her bedside, feeling the edges of his world collapse inwards. He wanted to believe her, that this was a cruel mistake, that soon somebody would walk back into the room with their baby and apologise. But even as he reached for her trembling hand, part of him knew those bizarre and unexplained fainting spells, those unspoken medical visits, those unreadable silences, they all led here. He just hadn't wanted to see it.

In fact, he was still not quite ready to see it.

The day Samantha came home from hospital, the winter light seemed brittle, like it might shatter on the windowsill. Joe stood by the radiator, clutching the paperwork the social worker had handed him that morning, pages stamped, signed, clinical. Somewhere among the dense lines of text hid the words that changed everything.

Psychiatric Evaluation Summary: Samantha Cookes. Diagnosed with Pseudologia Fantastica; Narcissistic and Histrionic Personality Disorders; Factitious Disorder, including Factitious Disorder by Proxy.

He read the terms again, each as foreign and complicated as her recent silences.

Some time later, a social worker would explain them to him gently, almost apologetically. Pseudologia fantastica, she said, meant Samantha fabricated stories so intricate and consistent she often believed them herself. These weren't simple lies, they were entire alternate realities constructed to sustain her emotional needs. Narcissistic and Histrionic Personality Disorders pointed to her craving for admiration, her theatrical self-presentation, her deep fear of abandonment. Attention, even negative, was oxygen to her. Factitious Disorder meant she could feign or induce illness, sometimes in herself, sometimes in others, to gain sympathy or control. The 'by proxy' was the most concerning, suggesting risk that she might create or exaggerate illness in someone under her care.

Joe remembered the tall tales about Samantha's ex-boyfriend who never seemed to exist. The bogus Amsterdam trip. The surrogacy scam. The fainting spells. And now, with those words, the picture rearranged itself into something far darker.

Social Services were clear: If you want a relationship with your child, you must fully separate from Samantha. The risk assessment left no room for interpretation. Samantha, they said, posed a threat to the baby's welfare and healthy development.

Joe had stared at the report long after the meeting ended, hands trembling slightly. He was twenty-two, too old to plead naivety yet too young to shoulder this vast, collapsing reality. He wanted his baby. He wanted the tiny, imagined family that had existed in his head, the one with Sunday breakfasts and nursery wallpaper and laughter. But it was all slipping away.

When he finally told Samantha, it was late, their shared flat dim except for the orange glow from the street lamp outside. She was sitting cross-legged on the bed, hair loose, eyes narrowed.

'They said what?' she whispered when he told her he couldn't see her anymore.

'I can't ... Sam, I can't choose you over my child,' he said quietly.

His voice felt thick in his throat. 'They're saying it's the only way I can keep the baby. I have to–'

'You have to?' she spat. 'No, Joe, you want to. You're just like the rest of them. You think I'm mad, don't you? You think I'd ever hurt my baby?'

He flinched but didn't move. 'I don't think that. I just, this isn't about what I think. It's about what's happening. They'll never let me near the baby otherwise.'

Her face contorted; she gave a sharp, bitter laugh. 'You coward. I carried your child and now you're abandoning me because some pen-pusher said I'm broken.'

'I'm not abandoning you,' he said, though the words sounded hollow in the space between them. 'I can't lose my child, Sam. I can't lose our baby.'

For a moment she was utterly still, staring at him, then she shoved the covers aside and stood, shaking. 'You have no idea what you're doing,' she hissed. 'You think they'll let you keep the baby? You'll see what it's like when they turn on you. You'll see what it's like to have everything taken away.'

Neither of them spoke again that night. She left the next morning. By the end of the week, she'd moved into a rented room in the Meole Brace suburb of Shrewsbury. Months later, he'd learn she never paid rent, that arrears stacked up like ghosts of good intentions.

Meanwhile, their baby, tiny, perfect, remained in foster care. Joe threw himself into the process of getting custody of his child back: meetings, court assessments, parenting courses, endless forms.

The six-week observational assessment he had to undergo felt like living under glass. Social workers watched as he changed nappies and bathed his child in monitored sessions, recording everything in neat handwriting. He smiled through exhaustion, conscious of every gesture, every breath, every word. At night, alone, he'd lie awake in a silent flat, replaying every visit, every raised eyebrow from a caseworker wondering if twenty-two was simply too young to carry this kind of responsibility.

The morning the ruling came, he could barely breathe. The child would be transferred to his custody. Samantha was to have no contact.

He cried quietly afterwards, not out of victory, but out of astonishment that something, at last, had gone right. He could start again, build something real. He didn't yet know that when Samantha walked away that final morning, she had already been carrying another secret; another set of lies waiting to ignite.

Samantha's recent diagnosis had triggered something more. Social Services, trawling back through the records, fixed a sterner eye on the past, on Martha, Samantha's first child. Although the case surrounding Martha's death had been officially closed, social services harboured suspicions that Samantha may have caused harm to her baby – raising questions about the accepted narrative of that tragic day.

In 2013 a judge in Birmingham was petitioned by Social Services to review the original Coroner's Inquest and a date was set. The review would be held in Birmingham High Court.

Samantha never walked into that courtroom. Before she was due to appear, she vanished. No explanations, no goodbyes. One child deceased. One child wrested from her care.

Joe was left reeling. A single father trying his best to get by, what he didn't know, what no one knew, was that Samantha was carrying another life inside her. Pregnant once again, Samantha slipped away into the shadows, leaving nothing but whispers. She fled the United Kingdom, although exactly how, no one could quite say. But after that, sightings became a thing of myth and rumour.

Joe was informed by a social worker that Samantha had disappeared. Police took his statement, fixed posters in waiting rooms and train stations, ran Samantha's name through databases. Her image, those sharp eyes, that well-kept hair, the faint half-smile, stared down from lamp posts and shop doors. An appeal even went out on the *ITV News*. The caption burned beneath: 'Missing Person Samantha Cookes'.

Despite leaving under a shroud of secrecy, Samantha still managed to throw a grenade into Joe's life before departing.

The first knock came so early that Joe thought he'd imagined it, just the old pipes shuddering as the boiler kicked in. But then the second came – firm, synchronised and followed by the hollow reverberation of knuckles on wood.

Joe opened the door to a uniform. Two more stood slightly behind, faces blank. Their presence dragged cold air into the hallway, mingling with the warm smell of baby powder and the previous night's burnt toast.

'Mr Whitfield?' The tone was polite, clipped. 'We have a warrant to search the premises.'

Joe's stomach turned over once, twice, with a slow, sinking tilt. Fear emptied him out like static; he thought of the crib upstairs, of tiny socks folded in the laundry basket, of the unopened jar of baby food still sitting on the counter.

When the words 'allegations of indecent images of children' were spoken, the room seemed to close in. He heard them, of course, could even see their lips forming the sounds, but it felt like two realities had layered on top of each other – one where he was a father, the other where he was suddenly, impossibly, a suspect.

The police moved with an eerie kind of efficiency, unplugging devices, logging serial numbers, sealing evidence bags. Joe stood frozen near the sofa, watching them lift his laptop with gloved hands as though it were toxic.

Samantha.

Her name slammed into his chest like an aftershock. For a long moment, he couldn't breathe. It made sense now, the way she had vanished, the way she had left things hanging, unresolved. This was her last touch, her fingerprint on the wreckage. If she couldn't have their child, then she would be sure Joe couldn't either.

Even when she's gone, she still finds a way to be here, he thought to himself in a panic.

He tried to speak, to protest, but his throat felt raw. One officer asked questions; another documented each device. In his peripheral vision, the baby monitor still blinked on the counter, a soft pulse in the chaos. When he imagined the social worker reading the report, the words 'indecent images of children' near his name, he thought he might be sick.

Outside, blue light bounced off the damp pavement, strobing across his neighbour's windows. Curtains twitched. The world was shrinking. Every glance would carry suspicion now.

It took only an hour, but by the end he felt decades older. When they left, the house seemed violated, stripped. He stared at the empty spaces where his electronics had been, places that looked ghostly clean, and tried to reconcile what had just happened. He could almost hear her laugh – low, intimate, cruelly playful – echoing in the back of his skull.

Some part of her always needed control, even in absence. And Joe realised, standing there in the dim light of his kitchen, that maybe she'd found her way back into power, not through presence, but through the shadow of what she'd left behind.

In due course, Joe was found completely innocent of all allegations and his electronic devices were returned to him. Samantha was charged with wasting police time, though she was still nowhere to be found.

* * *

Detective Inspector Shakesheff (sadly recently deceased) of the West Mercia Constabulary conducted a thorough investigation into the missing persons case pertaining to Samantha Cookes. It was a case that stayed with him long after it closed. He had spoken to Samantha's family, tracing her past and piecing together the trajectory of her life to that point. Everyone he met seemed normal, concerned, and had behaved as any family would when faced with the events they had endured. The family had tried to support Samantha as best they could.

DI Shakesheff described Samantha as 'a modern-day Walter Mitty', someone who lived much of her life wrapped in elaborate fantasies, a charming daydreamer whose fabrications blurred so deeply into reality that the line between truth and illusion disappeared. He was aware of the troubling circumstances surrounding the removal of her child from her care. When he discovered through his investigations that Samantha was pregnant again, the fear was palpable among the authorities that Samantha may cause harm to her child. It was assumed she fled in terror of losing another baby and there were unsubstantiated rumours that perhaps she had gone to Ireland.

If that was the case, Shakesheff knew it was not isolated behaviour. An Irish organisation called the Ectopia Network claimed that between 2013 and 2015 around 270 parents and families from the UK, fearing intervention and forced adoption by British Social Services, had fled to Ireland seeking refuge. Many of these parents believed Irish law to be more favourable, offering a sanctuary from what they termed 'draconian' child protection measures and forced removals by the British State. Underground networks existed across the UK and Ireland to facilitate the flight of people in this position, including providing safe houses upon arrival into the Republic of Ireland. The cultural and geographical closeness made Ireland a logical haven for those seeking to escape UK intervention, despite the fact that Irish courts work closely with their UK counterparts and take a similar approach in child welfare cases. Had Samantha availed of a similar route to evade Social Services?

Despite DI Shakesheff's lengthy investigation, Samantha's trail ran cold until, one winter morning in 2014, he received a tip-off from the Gardaí. There was a woman they believed to be Samantha Cookes living in a small community in a town called Edenderry. And what's more, she was acting extremely suspiciously.

5

SOPHIA WILLIAMSON

In the early autumn of 2013, the rain had just stopped when Samantha Cookes stepped off the bus at Edenderry, County Offaly, a soft mist still clinging to the air. The town was small, almost sleepy, with two- and three-storey terraced buildings lining the wide streets, their windows fogged from the damp, and a quiet that seemed to stretch and settle comfortably over everything. It was a place untouched by the noise and chaos Samantha had left behind, a sanctuary carved out of the everyday, where life moved at a gentler pace.

All she had with her were the clothes on her back, a worn backpack that grazed tired shoulders and, burgeoning within her, a faint, undeniable life beginning to stir. The name Samantha Cookes was already fading, lost beneath the layers of news reports and desperate appeals flickering on screens back in the UK. Here, she was someone new: Sophia Williamson.

Sophia moved through the town with studied calm, her pale fingers brushing away loose strands of chestnut hair as she searched for a place to call her own. There was a modest house tucked just beyond the bustle of Main Street, its white paint chipped and peeling, the garden wild with untamed honeysuckle and ivy. But to Sophia, the house promised refuge, a blank canvas waiting quietly for her next chapter.

Working quickly, she secured a small studio on the main street of the town not far from the house. Its large windows caught the afternoon sun and flooded the space with light. This she named the 'Honeysuckle Arts School', a nod to the garden of her new home and also the simplicity of creation. It was a humble business – just three euros for three hours per child, and to parents stretched thin beneath the weight of endless errands, care work and long shifts, it was a rare gift: a place where their children could lose themselves in glue and paint, in scissors and coloured paper.

Fiona and Karen, fun-loving sisters and cornerstones of the close-knit community, were among the first to bring their children there. To Fiona, Sophia was exactly what Edenderry needed: kind, soft-spoken and gentle in that way only a woman carrying life within her could be. She noticed, as she hurried past on busy mornings, when Sophia's belly began to curve with a subtle but unmistakable presence. It stirred something protective in Fiona, a deep-rooted trust that came without question. 'You just immediately trust a pregnant woman,' she later reflected. 'There's something about her, so non-threatening, so ... alive in a way that makes you feel safe.'

Back in the UK, flashing images and urgent voices on ITV had painted Samantha Cookes as a figure cloaked in mystery. Here, Sophia was a vision of quiet renewal. But her eyes missed nothing: the ebb and flow of small-town life, the relieved sighs of parents dropping off children, the secrets concealed by everyday smiles.

The days bled into one another with the soft, steady rhythm of small victories, kind words and tiny hands dipped in paint. The honeysuckle in the garden bloomed late that year, its delicate tendrils curling towards the sun as if reaching for the future Sophia was quietly weaving around herself. But beneath the gentle surface, beneath the calm and the kindness, the storm stirred: quiet, distant, inevitable.

Sophia's presence in Edenderry rippled gently through the town, and she became absorbed into the community. Each week, the Honeysuckle Arts School blossomed with new energy, not just from paints and paper, but from the magic of her added touches. Chocolate-making workshops quickly became a highlight for the children, the rich scent of melting cocoa filling the air, sticky fingers eagerly shaping sweet delights, whispers of joy and surprise spreading like wildfire. The children adored her, their hesitant steps gave way to eager runs, their shy glances to bright smiles, all drawn in by the warmth and creativity Sophia offered.

The town began to find in her not just a friendly new face, but a story that inspired trust. Sophia was married, she said, to a gentle pastor, a quiet man who, alongside her, devoted his life to running a refuge for women escaping domestic violence. It was a story that wrapped itself around the community like a comforting shawl. No one had ever seen the pastor, but Sophia explained he was frequently abroad doing charitable work.

Then, just as the town settled fully into their trust, Sophia unveiled her next surprise. 'We're organising a trip to Disneyland,' she announced softly one evening at the community hall, eyes shining with quiet excitement. The room stirred. Disneyland Paris was a distant dream shimmering on a horizon far beyond the Irish fields and stone walls. She explained how through both her and her husband's work at the women's refuge they were bringing a group of orphaned children from Israel on a magical trip there. They had secured some extra discounted places and, as a gesture of goodwill, she was offering those places to the local families.

Sisters Karen and Fiona exchanged glances, hardly able to believe it. The chance to take their children to such an enchanted, unforgettable place was impossible to ignore. Without hesitation, they reached for their purses, jumping at the chance to pay their deposits. This was a promise of wonder, a story they would tell for years to come. Then came an announcement about the expansion of the trip:

> From: Sophia Williamson
> Date: 11 December 2013 12:56:15 GMT
> To: Karen ________
> Subject: Disneyland paris [*sic*]
>
> April 18th–21st
> Disneyland Paris Trip
>
> As some of you know we are having a group of children over from Israel in February who have been orphaned and as part of their visit we have lots of activities lined up, including a trip to Disneyland in Paris. While booking this, if we booked two separate trips we were able to get BOTH at a far better deal.
>
> Therefore we are opening it up to all parents for the second trip.

The total cost including: coach, Eurotunnel, hotel for the 3 nights and park tickets will be:

Adults 103 euro

Children 95 euro

PLEASE NOTE: this DOES NOT include food. We can organise a group food voucher which does work out a lot more economical but this would be charged separately.

To secure your place we are going to have a 'first come first served basis' and take deposits. You are welcome to pay the remainder weekly.

Also, there are a few inter-connecting rooms so if anyone wishes to have these please let me know ASAP – for instance if there are any family groups going.

See you soon,
Sophia

Weeks passed, and the once-bustling chatter around Sophia Williamson began to fade into something quieter, something uneasy. Once deposits were paid, emails from her stopped; her phone went to voicemail. The posters about the Disneyland trip still fluttered in the arts school window, their glossy promises beginning to curl at the corners. No one knew where she'd gone, or why she'd suddenly gone silent. After the Christmas break, the art classes did not resume.

As January drew to a close without any updates from Sophia, Karen and Fiona, on impulse, decided to call to her house. Karen brought a basket, flowers and a card they'd both signed. Fiona brought curiosity disguised as concern. Karen tried to reason away their growing fears – maybe the baby had come early, maybe

Sophia needed rest. But Fiona's nerves had a sharper edge. 'It's odd,' she whispered, eyes darting towards the window of Sophia's rented cottage. 'She never said when she was due. Not once.'

The air was thick with tension when Sophia finally opened the door. She stood there, thinner than either of them remembered, her skin pale and translucent, eyes circled with bruised shadows. In her arms, a newborn stirred, a small sigh escaping from the folds of a white blanket. For a heartbeat, everything else fell away.

'You've ... had the baby,' Karen said softly, though the words came out more like a question.

Sophia smiled, tired, strange, unreadable. 'A week ago,' she murmured. 'It was quick. Easier than I expected.'

Fiona's eyes dropped to the child. As they stepped inside the front door there was something haunting in the silence of the house, no bottles, no nappies in sight, nothing that spoke of new life apart from that tiny, sleeping form. They stayed only a few minutes, polite talk skimming over the surface of something deeper, something Karen couldn't name. When they left, Fiona kept glancing over her shoulder, as though expecting Sophia to call them back, to explain everything. But the door stayed closed, and behind it, the faintest sound, a lullaby, or maybe just the wind through the cracked shutters.

As the sisters got into their cars and drove back home, they had no idea of what was unfolding behind Sophia's closed doors, but they knew with certainty in their hearts that there was something off with this young woman and there would be no trip to Disneyland. However, not wanting to cause the new mother any additional stress, they left it be.

* * *

On the morning of 27 January 2014, a soft drizzle hung over the Social Services office building in Tullamore when the call came in. An anonymous neighbour, polite but nervous, told Social Services she was worried about a woman named Sophia. Sophia had said she'd given birth alone on the bathroom floor, without a doctor or midwife in sight. Sophia had spoken of her husband, an accountant from Dublin (differing from the story of the pastor husband she told the families engaged in Honeysuckle Arts School), but in all the months the neighbour had watched her come and go, no such man had ever appeared. There was something off about her story, and now the worry had taken root.

When a public health nurse checked the records, the unease deepened. There was no record of any birth to a 'Sophia Williamson'. Within hours, a social work team was at the door of the small, rented house in Edenderry. Sophia answered with the brisk poise of someone used to improvising under pressure. Her manner remained outwardly calm.

She explained that she and her husband were from Liverpool and identified as Jewish. She claimed to hold an Israeli visa and said she was arranging one for her baby as well. When asked about the birth, her story, which differed from what she had told her concerned neighbour, faltered. She said couldn't recall the hospital's name, or that of the doctor who had supposedly delivered her child. Her partner, she said, was in Paris, but due to return soon to Edenderry, and she herself was about to begin a course in Cave Archaeology at Trinity College Dublin. (No such course exists at any Irish university.) It was a patchwork of claims stitched together with unnerving confidence. The Public Health Nurse, who was part of the team, urged Sophia to register the birth with her GP as soon as possible, so as to have the birth notification form filled in, as required by law. That afternoon, Sophia called the social workers to say she couldn't register the baby at her GP's office because the surgery had burned down. When this was checked, the clinic, of course, was found to be perfectly intact, contrary to Sophia's claims.

A follow-up visit the next day brought a fresh set of contradictions. Sophia was now claiming that the baby had been born in Paris and held a temporary French passport. The supposed father, she added, was in Israel arranging an Israeli passport so they could travel there in seven weeks to be married. Each lie stacked upon the next, implausible, contradictory and yet delivered with the conviction of a practised storyteller.

By 31 January, suspicion had hardened into alarm. The Social Services team called the local Gardaí, who soon uncovered the truth. 'Sophia Williamson' did not exist. The woman occupying the house was Samantha Cookes, a missing person from the UK and a convicted fraudster.

When brought in for questioning, Samantha denied everything, at first. But the façade eventually cracked and the truth surfaced, strange and sordid. She already had two children, one removed from her care, the other, a daughter named Martha, dead under circumstances being reviewed by authorities in the UK. She had left the UK before that inquiry could conclude.

Samantha's baby was removed from her care by a court order and placed into the care of a foster family. Samantha herself never returned to Edenderry, leaving behind her a house with its rent unpaid.

Fiona, Karen and the residents of Edenderry were none the wiser about any of this. To them the woman they knew as

Sophia disappeared into thin air, taking with her their deposits and hopes for the bogus trip to Disneyland. Fiona later expressed how she wasn't angry at the time, she just knew something was very wrong with Sophia and hoped she'd get the help she needed. They chalked the experience up as an odd one and moved on with their busy lives.

Detective Philip Shakesheff, who had led the missing person case in the UK, felt a grim sense of relief upon hearing Samantha had been found and the baby removed from her care. When being filmed for his interview for the documentary *Bad Nanny*, he later mused, 'I thought I'd hear about her again one day.'

* * *

Back in Shrewsbury, Joe and his now one-year-old infant had formed a rhythm, the kind built through exhaustion and steady love. Mornings meant cartoons and toast fingers. Daytimes were filled with juggling study, a part-time job and childcare. Evenings, bottles and lullabies whispered half-asleep. The flat still bore scars from those first chaotic months – unwashed cups, a stack of bills near the kettle – but, lately, it had begun to feel like theirs. Just him and his child against the world.

He'd stopped expecting to hear from Samantha. Once or twice he had typed her name into the Google search bar late at night but nothing new ever appeared. Always the same void staring back. Sometimes he wondered where she'd gone; other times he preferred not to know. His life was too full of immediate needs – lectures, late shifts, nappies – to stare too long into that black hole of what-ifs.

Then came the knock.

It was a grey afternoon, the sky pressed low, the baby napping in the cot. The sound wasn't hurried or violent, just firm enough to make him pause halfway through washing a bottle. Through the frosted panel he glimpsed two silhouettes, a uniformed policeman and a woman holding a clipboard. Joe had become accustomed to these unannounced knocks, yet still they drew shivers down his spine. They never meant something good.

When he opened the door, the air seemed to shift.

'Mr Whitfield?'

'Yes.'

The officer's voice was gentle, but formal. 'We're here about Samantha Cookes.'

His breath caught. The name had become almost mythic, something he half-believed he'd invented.

'She's been found,' the officer continued. 'In Ireland. County Offaly.'

Joe blinked, struggling to process. 'Found? What do you mean found?'

The social worker stepped forward, her tone careful. 'She's safe. Don't worry. But Mr Whitfield, I'm afraid there's more. She's had a baby. We believe the child may be yours.'

For a moment, sound drained from around him. The only thing he could hear was the blood rushing through his ears, the faint coo of the baby monitor behind him. 'That's not ...' he managed. 'That can't, she'd have told me, she ...'

'She gave birth at home,' the officer said softly. 'No medical assistance. But the baby survived, thankfully. Healthy. The infant has since been removed from her care due to concerns for both.'

Joe gripped the door frame. It felt like someone had reached inside his chest and twisted his insides. Another child? His?

The social worker nodded toward the briefcase at her side. 'To confirm paternity, we'll need to take a DNA sample.'

He did not resist. He sat numbly while the police officer swabbed the inside of his mouth. The sterile, cotton smell of it clung to the air. The baby began to stir in the next room. As the two officials thanked him and left, he stood in the doorway watching as their figures receded towards the gate and out of sight. The world had tilted again, quietly, without warning.

The days that followed unfurled in a haze. He went through motions – college, work, bedtime routines – while his mind knotted around the same question: Could it be true? Each hour seemed simultaneously too fast and not fast enough.

Then, one damp Wednesday morning, the call came. The test was positive. The baby in Ireland was his.

He was given a choice. The words sounded clinical, like something drafted by a committee rather than a human being: Do you wish to assume parental responsibility, or consent to adoption proceedings?

He didn't hesitate. 'It's my baby, I'll take care of it.'

On 12 February 2014, the High Court issued its formal order: the infant was to be placed in his custody, reunited with its sibling. He was to travel to Ireland to collect his child within days.

The morning of the flight, Joe left his elder child with his parents, his mother's eyes full of worry, and boarded the plane alone. The hum of the engines filled his head. Through the oval window, he could see the clouds rolling, thick and endless. When the plane finally dipped through the layer of cloud, Dublin sprawled below like a mosaic of light and rain. Joe pressed his forehead to the window, the world outside too vivid to absorb.

Ireland. He'd never been before and hadn't expected to visit under these circumstances.

He thought of the child he hadn't met. The idea barely fit inside his head. He was twenty-two, now a father twice over, shoulders braced beneath more responsibility than anyone his age should have to carry. At college, other students were talking about jobs, internships, new cities. He was flying between countries to collect the baby he hadn't known existed until a few weeks ago.

The air inside the terminal smelled of coffee, perfume and floor polish. He moved through Customs in a daze, following the small crowd toward Arrivals, his envelope of documents clutched so tightly his fingers ached. Outside, spring rain spattered the glass. The signs, Slí Amach, Bus Átha Cliath, looked almost dreamlike, as though he'd stepped sideways into a parallel version of his life.

An Irish social worker had emailed him directions to the building where they would meet: an unremarkable childcare centre in the southern suburbs, pink hyacinths blooming around a low fence. The taxi driver was chatty, but Joe barely heard him. Every mile brought him closer to what felt like both a miracle and a reckoning.

When the car pulled away, leaving him alone on the quiet street, Joe's hands trembled as he fixed the strap of his bag. The sky hung slate-grey above him, the air thick with the smell of damp tarmac. He'd just started toward the entrance when a figure stepped out from beneath the shallow awning. For a moment, his mind refused to catch up with what his eyes were telling him.

Samantha.

She stood there, a pale scarf wrapped clumsily around her, hair flattened by the drizzle. She looked different now, fuller in her face and body, a hint of tiredness beneath her beauty, her once light auburn hair now a deep brown, yet unmistakably her. Even before she turned towards him, he knew. His heart stumbled; his jaw slackened. Every muscle seemed to forget what it was for.

'Joe,' she breathed in a hushed tone.

He froze. *She shouldn't be here*, he thought. The court order had been brutally clear: no contact.

'I … I didn't expect …' he began. The tears came suddenly but were unnervingly convincing, sliding down her cheeks without the theatricality he remembered.

'I'm so sorry,' she said, voice breaking. 'For everything. For what I put you through. For what I did. I was sick, Joe, and I know that doesn't excuse it, but I've been trying, really trying, to get better.'

He stood helpless, shifting between fury and pity. The last year of madness pressed behind his ribs like a bruise. Yet looking at her now, rain in her hair, cheeks blotched, eyes raw, something in him softened. Against his better instinct, empathy flared. She wasn't the monster the reports made her out to be. She was human. Flawed, chaotic, frightened.

'Maybe I could still put things right,' she whispered. 'If they could just see I'm not dangerous anymore. If they let me see my children.'

Joe swallowed. Somewhere deep down, a voice screamed, don't engage, but another voice, quieter and more persuasive, murmured that kindness couldn't hurt. Maybe hope would steady her, maybe even help Social Services see improvement later. Wasn't it in everyone's interest that she recover?

He told himself that.

'I think you can change,' he said finally. 'I think it's possible. But we have to be careful, Sam. The court–'

She reached out, fingers trembling. 'I just want to talk sometimes. To know they're okay. Please.'

Maybe it was his nerves, or the misplaced kindness that had always undone him, but he nodded. 'Fine. We can talk.'

He took out his phone, opened Skype, and watched as she typed her name into it. A modern rebellion, sterile, silent, seemingly harmless. Two taps of a finger, and the forbidden line between them existed again.

As he pocketed the device, Samantha slunk away and the childcare centre door opened. A woman in a navy coat called his name. Joe turned towards her, pulse racing. This was it. Inside waited his new child, another tiny heartbeat tethering him to Samantha Cookes.

* * *

Joe didn't mean to break the rules. At least, not in any way that felt like he was breaking them. After returning from Ireland with his new baby he was too busy surviving to think about much else. Life became a loop of nappies, formula bottles, midnight crying, washing that never dried properly. He was exhausted, unshaven, yet fiercely proud. Every small giggle, every gummy smile, every time his children fell asleep on his chest, it made the chaos tolerable.

Money was tight. Welfare payments barely covered the rent, so family stepped in where they could: a second-hand cot from his sister, a pair of mismatched prams from his father's garage, baby clothes that smelled faintly of another family's washing powder. Still, the flat thrummed with life. It was messy and loud and right.

And then there was Samantha.

At first, the Skype calls were awkward, brittle things – careful smiles, long silences. She asked about the children, voice trembling just enough to sound sincere. Joe answered cautiously, keeping the details vague, but he couldn't ignore the way her face softened at the mention of them. It reminded him of someone he wanted her to be. He told himself they were helping her, these calls; that a little kindness could steady her footing. After all, wasn't it what decent people did?

Weeks passed. She messaged more often, short notes, photos of sunsets, Bible verses. Then came the request: Please, Joe. Come to Ireland again. Just once. We need a proper talk.

He read the message again and again. The right answer was obvious: no. But the nights were long, his thoughts crowded with questions that had no end. Why had she done it? Why had she reported him to the police for having indecent images of children? Why did she lie so consistently? Could she really have changed? Did she ever really love him?

He told himself it was one meeting, closure, peace, a line drawn under everything. He would leave the children in the UK, safe, boundaries firm. Just a conversation. Nothing more.

So, on a cold April morning in 2014, he booked the cheapest Ryanair ticket he could find.

Ireland again. The same metallic rain, the same unfamiliar signs. He was nervous, jittery, hopeful even. The hotel lobby was cavernous and too bright; Samantha waited near the adjoining restaurant entrance, wearing a soft cardigan and a tremulous smile.

She looked healthier, fuller, calmer. They talked for hours, about the children, about church, about the job she said she'd started in a charity shop.

'I understand why you did what you did,' she said quietly. 'Breaking up with me. Taking the baby. You had no choice. I was unwell. But I'm better now.'

Joe wanted to believe her. He wanted that peace, that sense of some order being restored to his universe. She spoke of hope, of someday, far in the future, being trusted again. He left Dublin that evening feeling lighter than he had in months, picturing a version of the future where his children might one day know their mother in a safe, supervised way.

But fate, as it turned out, had other plans.

Days after returning to Shrewsbury, there was another knock. This one was sharp, official, destructive. When he opened the door, the sight chilled him: a uniformed police officer and a social worker he recognised from old case meetings.

'Mr Whitfield,' the officer said. 'We need to ask, have you been in contact with Samantha Cookes?'

The question hung like a blade. He opened his mouth, tried for denial, but the truth spilled out before he could contain it. 'Yes,' he said. 'I went to see her.'

It happened fast after that. Devices confiscated. Skype history exposed. Message logs printed as evidence. He'd been reported. Someone, somewhere, had tipped them off. Someone Joe had trusted. The betrayal burned deep. He had his suspicions as to who was responsible but Social Services would never confirm this.

That night, borrowing a friend's phone, Joe sent one final text: 'They know. We can't ever do this again.'

He never heard back.

Then, Social Services and the courts took an action Joe never expected. This time, there were no appeals, no second chances. The court decreed that both children were to be placed for adoption: the risk was too great; the breach too severe. They deemed Joe to still be under Samantha's spell, to be unreliable in his vow to keep the children from her. On 19 May, the day before his twenty-third birthday, Joe said goodbye to his children forever. Two car seats left his flat, two tiny lives bundled away by strangers into the machinery of the State. He stood at the window as the car disappeared, the street unnaturally quiet, the walls around him hollowing out.

'That's it,' one of the officials said gently. 'You'll receive notice when proceedings close.'

He didn't move. He couldn't.

Weeks passed. Letters stopped. The flat turned cold despite summer sun. Just seventeen years, he kept telling himself. Seventeen years until they were grown. Until they became adults. Until they might find him.

He used to believe that anger was the loudest emotion. Now he knew it was the silence of loneliness.

Samantha vanished again, leaving behind nothing but a birthday card postmarked from somewhere in the midlands of Ireland. Inside, her handwriting looped loosely across the paper: *Tell them I still love them.*

He tore it in half, then tucked the pieces into a drawer he could not open again. Broken and shattered by his experience with Samantha Cookes and the British social welfare system, Joe's life was left upside down. Years passed, yet he never forgot his two children. He went on to marry but was never to become a father again.

Meanwhile, in Ireland, Samantha, with her fragile lies in tatters and her children gone, was already immersed in her next move, ready to charm, deceive and infiltrate yet more unsuspecting lives. This time she would find her way into the heart of a family with young children, carrying with her that same disarming smile and the endless appetite for invention that made her so dangerously believable.

6

LUCY HART

Layla DeJagger sat at the kitchen table after midnight, her laptop screen casting a bluish light across the piles of bibs, bills and half-folded laundry. The four children were finally asleep upstairs – three of them under ten – a chorus of tiny needs and endless movement that began before dawn and finished only when the house itself seemed to sigh into silence.

Childcare in Ireland, she had discovered, was almost a luxury. Every quote she received seemed impossible. The family was struggling to make ends meet as it was, so adding the additional cost of childcare seemed impossible. She'd said it so often lately it had become a family mantra: 'No family nearby, no options but to make it work.' Layla was English, her husband Pieter (not his real name) was South African, and although they both loved their life in Tullamore, sometimes it felt like being adrift on a boat with no engine. Hiring an au pair or a nanny wasn't so much an indulgence as a matter of survival. When an old school friend had teased Layla only the week before, 'An au pair? Oh, very posh!', she had laughed. 'It's not posh when it's cheaper than a crèche. You give them a room and a place at the dinner table; it's the only way we can manage.'

Scrolling through yet another childcare website, her gaze landed on a neat, reassuring profile: Lucy Hart. English, early thirties, professional nanny. She loved children, spoke warmly of art projects and outdoor play, and the grammar in her profile was impeccable – always a comfort. The photograph showed a friendly, open smile framed by tidy hair and a simple cardigan. Ordinary in the best way.

Layla wrote. Lucy replied. Within a day, they had agreed to meet at a hotel lounge in Tullamore.

Samantha Cookes had spent the previous three weeks building her new persona from nothing but fragments of memory and imagination. She'd learned to snip and reshape her life like a seamstress altering a borrowed dress, using just enough truth to make the lies fit. She had a backstory and a CV lifted and edited from an old nanny agency template. And she had a name: Lucy Hart. It sounded trustworthy, almost tender.

She had chosen Tullamore for her new start. It was only a half-hour drive from Edenderry, but it seemed to her like the sort of town where people smiled easily and didn't ask too many questions. Her last identity had burned itself out in chaos and exposure. This one would be softer, safer, she told herself each time she looked in the mirror and practised her new name.

* * *

Layla and her husband arrived ten minutes early to the hotel, and Layla was nervous enough to wish she'd worn something a bit less mum-like. She ordered tea, clutching the cup for comfort. When Lucy appeared, smiling, poised and gently apologetic for being late, Layla liked her immediately. 'She was like Mary Poppins,' she would say later, slightly embarrassed at how quickly she had been charmed.

Lucy asked about the children, listened with bright attention and laughed in all the right places. She said she adored crafts, that she'd worked with families all over England, that her previous employer still sent her Christmas cards. She even claimed to be writing a children's book in her spare time. There was nothing showy about her, she just radiated warmth and calm. Layla started to relax for the first time in months.

Across the table, Samantha studied her carefully. Layla came across as harried but kind, and her accent carried that gentle northern English edge that made her sound almost musical. It must have seemed to Samantha that it would be easy to make this woman trust her. Easy, if she played the part right.

By the time Layla rose to leave, she was glowing. 'She seems so perfect,' she would say to Pieter as they walked back to their car. He laughed, shaking his head. 'I couldn't get a word in,' he said, and that settled it. Their minds were made up. Lucy Hart was hired.

The next morning, in the quiet hour before dawn, as Samantha packed her modest suitcases, she must have allowed herself a small, satisfied smile. By that evening she would be under a new roof, with a new family and a fresh beginning.

And she desperately needed a place to live. Between 26 March and 6 April 2014, she had stayed at the Central Hotel in Tullamore, where she availed of the hotel's choice of breakfasts, running up a bill of €698.85. These costs went unpaid. When supplying her card details on check-in, she had cunningly left off the expiry date, meaning no transaction could ever be processed before she disappeared for good, never officially checking out. Luckily the

DeJaggers lived outside the town, so no one from the hotel ever realised she was still in the vicinity.

* * *

When Lucy Hart moved into the DeJagger home that April, it felt, to everyone, as if the missing piece of a puzzle had finally clicked into place. Layla remembered their first evening vividly. Lucy arrived with two neat suitcases, a basket of craft supplies and an easy smile. She was polite, unassuming and quick to laugh. The relief Layla felt was immense.

'Looking back,' Layla said years later, 'I can't believe I never checked her references. I just didn't. She seemed so perfect and we were desperate.'

Four children, two jobs, rent they could barely manage, and no family in the country. 'We were hanging by a thread,' she admitted. 'We needed her.'

At first, Lucy was wonderful. The house felt lighter, calmer. She had the sort of energy that drew the children to her as if by a magnet. Their eldest girl, Charlie, adored her. 'I bonded with Lucy so quickly,' Charlie remembered. 'She was like the older sister I always wanted. She was big into arts and crafts, she always had something fun for us to do every day.' Layla would often peek into the playroom to find them huddled over paints, or find them baking together in the kitchen, giggling like old friends. 'It felt almost too good,' Layla later said. 'For the first time in years, I thought maybe things were turning around.'

But after the first few weeks there were hints, small, almost invisible threads of inconsistency, that began to tug at her confidence. Some of Lucy's stories were ... strange. She told

Layla that her mother was a millionaire who 'made sandpaper for B&Q'. Layla laughed awkwardly when she heard this, thinking it sounded oddly specific. Then came tales of Lucy's time working with special needs children in Dubai, where she supposedly had managed an entire programme herself. Layla wondered why a woman qualified to deal with such children, in Dubai of all places, would agree to be her au pair in Tullamore for the small amount she could afford to pay. 'They were the kind of stories that were so outrageous you didn't know whether to be impressed or concerned,' Layla said. 'But she told them so sincerely. She looked you straight in the eye.'

One evening, after the children had gone to bed, Layla and Lucy were watching *The Shawshank Redemption* together on the sofa. When the scene appeared of Brooks, the elderly inmate released on parole, taking his own life, Lucy suddenly leapt from her seat and ran from the room. Layla froze, surprised at the sudden outburst. When Lucy returned, she was trembling and crying. Through the tears, she choked out a tragic tale. Her fiancé, who had suffered from motor neurone disease, had killed himself to spare her from the burden of caring for him. 'She said she came home to find him hanging in the hallway,' Layla recalled softly. 'I believed every word. I mean, who would make up something like that?' Layla comforted her for the rest of that night. They sat in silence for a long time, two women bound momentarily by grief.

Pieter was less sympathetic and was starting to feel uneasy about how every story Lucy told seemed to stretch the bounds of likelihood further than the last. Still, he bit his tongue. They needed the help and their finances were already on the brink. With both parents needing to bring money in to get by, they couldn't afford to lose their childcare.

It was Lucy who suggested the 'solution' to the couple's money woes. She told Layla one afternoon over tea that she was a Jehovah's Witness and that her church had a house 'going spare'. 'It would be perfect for you,' Lucy said brightly. 'The church would just be delighted to have a lovely family in there!'

It was almost too good to be true – a much more spacious home at a rent far below what they were currently paying. 'Because we were at our wits' end,' Layla said, 'I wanted to believe it.' Although they had suspicions about Lucy's dramatic stories, they were desperate enough to look past their niggling doubts. She was so earnest and believable, and why would she lie about this? After all, she lived with them too.

They drove by the house several times with Lucy. It was whitewashed, tidy, with neat hedges and a wide driveway. Layla was eager to view the inside, but Lucy always had a reason why they couldn't. 'The church elder's away,' she'd say. Or, 'They are painting it before you see it, they want it to look its best for you!' Despite this, the DeJaggers gave notice to their landlord and started packing boxes.

Layla's doubts grew, but she smothered them. 'When you're desperate, you convince yourself,' she would later explain.

The moment of truth came on an otherwise ordinary afternoon. Driving past the house, with the children in the back seat, and Lucy humming along to the radio, Layla spotted a man outside mowing the lawn. 'Perfect!' she said. 'Maybe we can ask him for a quick look inside.'

Lucy went completely still. Her face drained of colour. 'Oh, could we stop somewhere?' she stammered. 'I need the loo. Please, just for a moment. It's an emergency!'

Irked, but wary of how desperate Lucy sounded, Layla drove

to the nearest bathroom she could think of. They pulled into the Tesco car park nearby. Charlie followed her nanny up to the toilets in the store. Minutes later, Layla, waiting in the car, saw her daughter sprinting back through the car park, her little face white with panic.

'Mum! Mum! Lucy's fainted!'

Layla's first reaction was shock, then a sudden, chilling certainty. 'It was like a light bulb went off,' she said. 'Right there in the car park, I just knew, none of this was real. No house. No church. No truth.'

She sat in the car after paramedics were called, her youngest crying in the back seat, her mind whirling. Every story, every tear, every smile, it all fell away in an instant, leaving only a knife-edged dread. 'I was staring out that window, thinking, who have I brought into our home? Who is this woman who's been around my children?'

The answer, she would soon learn, was far worse than she could have imagined.

For a few days after the Tesco incident, the household co-existed in uneasy silence. Lucy seemed pale and withdrawn, moving slower, speaking less. She claimed she'd fainted from low blood sugar, that it was nothing serious, but something unspoken had shifted. Layla couldn't shake the sense that the atmosphere in the house had changed, filled with that peculiar, heavy quiet that comes when trust begins to drain away.

Pieter said it first, late one night. 'She's hiding something,' he murmured, half-whispered into the pillow.

Layla didn't answer, though she knew he was right.

The following Tuesday, 12 January 2015, they realised she was gone. The morning light fell across the bed of their youngest as Layla came down the hall, knocking on Lucy's door to tell her breakfast would be ready soon. No answer. She knocked again, then turned the handle. The door was locked. This was odd, but not alarming. Lucy valued her privacy. Still, something didn't sit right with Layla. She made her way to the kitchen and there she found, on the table, a single folded note in Lucy's rounded handwriting.

'Gone to a writer's retreat. Needed to clear my head. Back soon. L x'

Layla stared at the paper as if it might explain itself. 'I thought maybe she just needed space,' she said later. 'But as the hours passed, I just knew she wasn't coming back.'

Charlie put it most simply. 'We never saw her again,' she said. 'One day she was there, the next she wasn't.'

That night, while the children slept and the wind rattled the eaves, Layla and Pieter sat in the living room not speaking. The note lay on the coffee table between them like evidence. They both knew what had to come next.

The following morning, Pieter forced the lock on Lucy's bedroom door. It gave with an echoing crack. The room was tidy, impersonal, with a few clothes folded on the bed, toiletries lined up, the kind of order that looked intentional. On the small desk near the window lay a spiral-bound notebook with a patterned cover. Layla picked it up, expecting recipes or childcare notes, maybe sketches the children had done. But when she flipped it open, her breath caught. The first page was blank. On the second, written neatly in blue ink, were the words: 'I stand shoulder to shoulder with the coroner. I did not murder my daughter. May she rest in peace.'

The words seemed to tilt and blur on the page. 'I did not murder my daughter.'

Layla said later, 'I just froze. My hands went cold. I didn't even understand what I was looking at. She'd never mentioned a child.'

She sat on the edge of the bed, unable to turn to another page. The faint scent of Lucy's perfume still hung in the room, something floral, faintly powdery. It felt obscene, suddenly. All those moments Lucy spent alone with Layla's children, entrusted into her care, the tearful night in front of the television where they bonded over Lucy's grief – it all collapsed into something grotesque.

'Who is she?' Layla whispered aloud. 'And what did she want with us?'

There was no answer. Just the quiet ticking of the clock and the sound of wind pressing against the windows. Outside, the early morning light dimmed as clouds rolled in, leaving the house subdued.

Layla's mind spiralled through impossibilities. Without childcare, they couldn't work; without work they couldn't pay rent; and without this supposed new house, they had nowhere to go. But worse than all of that was the dawning horror that she had invited a stranger, perhaps something far darker than a stranger, into her home to look after her children.

That night, she locked every door before going to bed, double-checked every window. 'I kept thinking she might come back in the dark,' she admitted later. 'I didn't know what she was capable of.'

It came as a relief to them that Lucy never returned. Layla

often wondered afterwards why she had suggested the new house for them that didn't exist. She had a roof over her head, money in her pocket every week, she seemed happy and content. Why would she jeopardise it all? It was always going to come to light that the house wasn't real. It just didn't make sense.

What Layla couldn't have known is that people like Samantha, diagnosed with Narcissistic and Histrionic Personality Disorder, crave the admiration and attention that comes with being the clever, indispensable helper. Even the lurking knowledge that the perfect house was a fabrication wouldn't necessarily faze her. It's possible that, in her mind, the risk of being caught was secondary. What mattered was the story, and the role she played at the centre of it – the hero Layla's family so desperately needed.

It wouldn't be the last time Samantha's unnecessary lies and embellishments would trip her up.

7

LUCY FITZWILLIAMS

For years Layla DeJagger ran her fingers over the strange words in the notebook her au pair had left behind, wondering what had become of her. To Layla, she had vanished into thin air. In truth, however, Samantha Cookes had already moved on to her next life.

In the days before she fled Layla's home, Samantha had been writing letters. Drafts were scratched into that same notebook, addressed to the Irish High Court. In her looping, erratic handwriting, she argued that her baby had been unjustly taken from her, that she was misunderstood. Although she had told Joe at their fateful meeting in Dublin that she understood the court's decision, she in fact wanted to fight it, to appeal it. It was in this context that she had written that she 'stood shoulder to shoulder with the coroner' over the death of her daughter Martha. She insisted she had done nothing wrong and that she should be reunited with her living children.

In the meantime, however, after disappearing from Tullamore, she needed a new place to stay and a new persona. It's not clear where she went next, but when Samantha Cookes finally reared her head again in a new community, Lucy Fitzwilliams was born.

* * *

Lorraine Bolger was a hairdresser from Dublin, chatty, warm and quick to laugh. People loved sitting in her chair because she made them feel like friends, not clients. But, in late October 2016, when a strange number lit up her phone and a panicked voice from Mayo started telling her about a young English nanny called Lucy Fitzpatrick, Lorraine's hands began to shake.

'That was the moment I knew it was happening again,' she said. 'Samantha had struck again.'

Lorraine had hoped that it was over, that Samantha, Lucy, or whoever she was now, had finally stopped. But deep down, she'd known better. 'She doesn't stop,' Lorraine said, 'she always finds someone new.'

The damage Samantha Cookes had done in Dublin still echoed through the people whose lives she had touched. Lorraine described it as a scar on the community. 'You don't expect evil to brush past you in everyday life,' she said. 'Not in your salon, not over a haircut.'

She had met Samantha Cookes in February 2016, on one of those ordinary Saturdays when the shop was full of chatter, the sound of scissors and the faint smell of coffee. Samantha walked in under the name Lucy Fitzwilliams, friendly and effusive, dressed neatly with a gentle smile.

'I remember thinking she was so sweet,' Lorraine said. 'She was bubbly, interested, kind. She told me she was an evangelical Christian, that she was marrying a pastor called Ross from a church in Dún Laoghaire. She spoke about faith and purpose, but never in a pushy way, just like someone with a big heart. She didn't live with Ross as they were waiting till marriage for that because of her strong faith. She was renting a room locally from an elderly lady, as a lodger.'

As Lorraine trimmed her hair, the girl talked about her work with special needs children. She said she'd trained in England and that she had specialist experience in autism. Her voice softened whenever she spoke about the children she supported.

It was a topic close to Lorraine's heart. 'I have a lot of friends with kids who have additional needs,' she said. 'They're all fighting a system that barely acknowledges them.'

And it was true. In the Ireland of 2016, as is still often the case today, waiting times for autism assessments could stretch for years. Families across the country were often left without speech therapy, educational support or respite services. According to advocacy groups at the time, thousands of children were 'lost in the system', with parents forced to pay privately for assessments and interventions that public services failed to deliver. Many parents described the process as 'begging' for help.

'That's why I thought Lucy was such a godsend,' Lorraine said. 'Someone trained, someone kind, someone who wanted to help.'

When Lorraine mentioned that her close friend Hillery was struggling as her son, Reese, then five years old, had recently been diagnosed on the autism spectrum, Lucy leaned forward, eyes bright. 'I'd love to help,' she said. 'It's what I'm here for.'

Lorraine believed her. 'I thought, she's an angel, what luck for Hillery!'

So Lorraine rang Hillery that afternoon, all enthusiasm, telling her about this wonderful English girl, this specialist with a mission to help children with special needs. 'You'll love her,' she said. 'I swear, it's like God sent her to you.'

What none of them could have known then was that, in opening that single door, they were stepping into Samantha's pattern of lies and manipulation. The same kindness she'd used to win Layla's trust in Tullamore, it was on show again here, in a Dublin hair salon, with a story too good to question.

Lorraine's voice broke when asked about her first impression of Samantha. 'She seemed harmless,' she said. 'She seemed ... good.'

She paused, then, the weight of hindsight heavy in her silence. 'If I'd known what she really was,' she whispered, 'I'd never have let her anywhere near Hillery's son Reese, or any child at all.'

By the time Hillery first heard the name Lucy Fitzwilliams from her lifelong friend Lorraine, she was reaching breaking point. Reese had been expelled from more classrooms and crèches than she could count.

The first time it happened still burned in her memory. The crèche manager had pulled her aside one afternoon and said gently but firmly, 'There's something wrong with your son.'

Hillery remembered blinking at this statement, unsure how to respond. 'What do you mean, there's something wrong?'

'He's not behaving the way he should,' the woman explained. 'He needs to be assessed by the HSE [the Irish State Health Service].' Then, in almost the same breath, she added, 'We can't keep him here. He's too dangerous.'

Hillery stood there, numb, hearing only her own voice replying: 'But I have to work. I'm a working mummy. I have to work.' The woman's expression failed to soften; Reese was no longer welcome.

And so it began, the endless cycle of schools that wouldn't take him, assessments that never came, and an invisible system that seemed to exist solely to delay her son from getting the help he needed.

Reese was born in 2011. By the age of two, his behaviour began to change, becoming more difficult, with violent meltdowns, self-harm and the silent agony of a boy who couldn't make himself understood. 'He was non-verbal,' Hillery later said. 'He couldn't tell me what was wrong.'

When the HSE finally did get involved, they recommended an autism assessment, but nothing happened. 'It felt like papers had to sit on desks for nine months and then move to another desk for another nine months,' she recalled. 'That was the waiting list, just a piece of paper sitting somewhere.'

Each letter from the experts he had seen repeated the same words – that Reese needed services urgently, that he needed occupational therapy, speech and language therapy, developmental support. Every word was stamped with the word 'immediate', yet nothing ever arrived.

'It wasn't urgent to them,' Hillery said later, 'but it was urgent in my house.'

One weekend, after yet another crisis, she broke down completely. Reese's meltdowns were growing ever more violent. She'd locked herself in the bathroom while he banged on the door, screaming and sobbing. She sat on the floor and cried, feeling hollowed out.

That was when Lorraine's voice came back to her. Lorraine, her close friend, had been gently urging her to contact a young woman whose hair she had cut. A kind English girl called Lucy Fitzwilliams. 'Lucy,' she'd said, 'is an occupational therapist, just back from Chad, where she worked with people in need. She's marrying a pastor from an evangelical church in Dún Laoghaire. You'd love her, she's wonderful.'

Each time Lorraine brought her up, Hillery had brushed it off. She wasn't ready. It felt impossible to hand over her son's care to a stranger. But that night, she'd reached the end of her tether. She called Lorraine the next morning, her hands still shaking. 'I said, "I need help. I can't do this anymore."'

Lorraine's relief was clear. 'Finally,' she said, 'you're going to listen to me. You call her. I'll let her know you're ready.'

And that was when Lucy entered Hillery's life, first as a comforting voice on the phone, then as the promise of salvation.

'She answered right away,' Hillery said later. 'And the first thing she said was, "Hi Hillery, I've been waiting for you."'

The words made Hillery's heart lurch. 'I said, "Oh my God, you know who I am?" And she said, "Yes, Lorraine's told me everything. I've been waiting for your call for a long time."'

Lucy spoke with warmth and confidence. She said she could come to the house that very weekend. Saturday morning, ten o'clock. 'Can you pick me up? I don't drive,' she said. 'We'll start from there.'

Hillery could hardly believe it. The public system had left her waiting nearly two years for support, yet here was someone willing to show up within days. 'She made it sound so simple,' Hillery remembered. 'I thought, *how lucky am I that someone like her exists?*'

She spent the rest of the week feeling, for the first time in years, something that resembled hope. On Saturday morning, she drove to collect the woman who promised to change everything, unaware she was bringing into her home one of the most accomplished con artists Ireland had ever seen.

* * *

Hillery told herself not to be nervous. After all, Lucy Fitzwilliams had come highly recommended. Lorraine trusted her, and Lorraine had never steered her wrong. Still, as she drove through the quiet, tree-lined streets of Glenageary in Dublin that Saturday morning, her stomach fluttered with nerves.

The houses there were beautiful. Wide driveways, high hedges, pastel-painted doors. It was the kind of place where people's lives seemed organised, predictable, safe. She stopped at a neat semi-detached house on Avondale Road, checked the address and rang the bell. No answer. She called. Nothing.

For a moment, she wondered if she'd been stood up. Then, just as she was deciding whether to wait or leave, a taxi swung into the driveway. Out stepped a petite woman, neat, with shoulder-length hair and a bright, unfaltering smile. 'Hillery! Is that you?' she called out, breathless. 'I'm so sorry I'm late, you won't believe the morning I've had.' Lucy was barely seven minutes behind schedule, but she spoke as though she'd kept Hillery waiting for hours. Without pausing for breath, she said she needed to 'run inside and grab my box of tricks, it's what I use with children during sessions'. She darted through the gate and disappeared for less than a minute before returning with a clear plastic storage box filled with toys, paints and little tubs of glitter.

'She was just so alive,' Hillery recalled later. 'Energetic, friendly. I thought, wow, she's exactly what we need.'

They settled into Hillery's car and began the forty-minute drive back to her house. Once on the M50 motorway, conversation flowed easily. Lucy was funny, articulate and immediately impressive. She claimed she'd spent the morning helping a little girl whose tracheostomy tube had fallen out. A tracheostomy tube is a medical device inserted into a surgically created opening in the windpipe to keep the airway open and assist breathing by bypassing the nose and mouth, delivering air directly to the lungs through the tube. Hillery knew this well from her work as a caregiver in nursing homes.

'I had to replace it myself,' Lucy said, eyes wide but calm. 'Hospitals won't touch those cases on weekends. Nurses are terrified because of insurance, but I'm trained, so it's fine once the mother approves.'

Hillery didn't know what to say. 'It seemed unlikely, but I remember thinking, *who am I to question her?*' she said later. 'She spoke like a professional. Like someone used to saving the day.'

When they arrived at Hillery's house, Lucy carried her 'magic box' into the living room. Five-year-old Reese was immediately captivated. He tilted his head, scanning her calmly, but his gaze kept darting to the transparent box.

He reached for it.

'No, no, no,' Lucy said softly. 'You can't touch that just yet.'

Reese melted down quickly. Hillery tried to smooth things over, anxious not to upset the one person in months who had offered to help her. 'Lucy just stood there, smiling a little,' she remembered. 'It felt like a test. And suddenly I realised, I was siding with her, not my son.'

It took nearly forty tortuous minutes before Lucy relented and said Reese could finally look inside the box. The contents were simple: a few paints, glue sticks, glitter, coloured paper. Nothing technical, nothing therapeutic. But Lucy introduced each item with hushed reverence, as though performing a ritual.

'She opened the glitter,' Hillery said. 'And I thought, finally. She's going to do something with him.'

Lucy guided Reese's hand towards the paper. 'We'll make a picture,' she said kindly. Reese resisted, reaching for the tub of silver glitter. She took it away, he grabbed for it. When she took it again, he started to cry. Finally, she pushed the tub back towards him. 'Okay,' she said gently. 'You can have it now.'

Reese poured the glitter all over his head.

It was everywhere: on his scalp, in his lashes, over the table and floor. Hillery gasped. Lucy laughed softly. 'No, no, it's fine,' she said. 'We'll clean it up.'

She knelt and began scooping up handfuls of glitter mixed with dog hair and crumbs. Then, to Hillery's horror, she tipped it all back into the tub. 'We don't waste things,' she said. 'There's enough waste in the world.'

'I just stared,' Hillery said. 'She planned to use that same dirty glitter with other children.'

By the time the clock hit three, Lucy had been there for five hours. The session had veered from crafts to chatter, and she spoke about herself, about her pastor fiancé in Dún Laoghaire, about her faith. Yet she didn't ask many questions about Reese and she deflected whenever Hillery brought him up.

'It was strange,' Hillery said. 'Five hours and not a single piece of paperwork. No notes, no assessment. Just talk.'

When Reese grew restless, she suggested they go outside so she could 'do an outdoor assessment'. Hillery agreed.

Reese hopped on his scooter, zooming down the cul-de-sac, and Lucy insisted on following him. 'You stay there,' she said. 'I'm the therapist, I need to observe how he moves.'

Hillery watched in bemusement as the supposed occupational therapist ran up and down the street after her five-year-old. 'I remember standing there thinking, *what am I actually looking at?*'

When they returned inside, Lucy lingered for another half-hour, sipping tea and talking about faith and morality, how she and her fiancé couldn't live together before marriage, how their beliefs set them apart from most couples.

'She barely mentioned my son again,' Hillery said. 'It was all about her. But at that point, I was so drained, I couldn't even process how odd it was.'

As evening fell, Hillery finally stood and thanked her. 'If there's nothing else, maybe we will wrap it up for today?' she said politely.

Lucy smiled. 'Next Saturday then.'

An hour and a half later, Hillery pulled back into her own driveway after dropping Lucy home to Glenageary. She sat in the car for a long moment, mentally and physically exhausted, glitter still clinging to her jeans. 'I remember thinking, *I don't even know what just happened today*,' she said softly. 'But I believed she had helped us. In my exhausted state I felt like something positive had happened that day, when in fact, in reality, in hindsight, nothing had been achieved. No one else was coming, so I clung to the help I was being offered.'

Hillery didn't yet realise that she'd just spent an entire day in the company of a woman whose skill was not therapy, or education, or care, but deception.

8

THE WOMEN'S REFUGE

Hillery, grappling with the everyday battles of caring for Reese, brought Lucy Fitzwilliams into her orbit. Lucy's kindness and apparent expertise were a ray of hope. The Saturday sessions continued twice monthly on Hillery's only day off from work. Despite not noticing much improvement in Reese's behaviour, Hillery heard from Lorraine, who continued to befriend Lucy as well as do her hair, and other women in their network that Lucy was doing great work with other children, and they encouraged her to just give it time for Lucy's magic to start to work. Juggling childcare and a busy job, Hillery didn't have the time or headspace to dig out any more information, so, against her better judgement, she stuck with Lucy.

In the meantime, Lucy expanded her web. Her next mark was Lynn, Hillery's childhood neighbour and lifelong friend, whose resilience masked an unbearable struggle. Lynn's daughter, Daisy, was afflicted by an extreme form of Rett syndrome, a devastating genetic disorder predominantly affecting girls. As Daisy's nerve cells deteriorated, she lost skills she had once mastered, such as the simple act of holding a toy or uttering a word, and her lifespan would be tragically limited. As a single mother, Rett syndrome's cruel reality shaped Lynn's daily life, demanding every ounce of her strength.

Ellie, Lynn's elder daughter, was often pushed into the shadows as Daisy's needs overwhelmed the household. Ellie's childhood was punctuated by quiet moments of loneliness, the kind known only to those who grow up too quickly as carers themselves. When Lucy presented herself as an art therapist as well as an occupational therapist, promising sessions with Ellie to 'lift the weight off Lynn's shoulders', she did not just offer help, she offered relief from despair. Then came the biggest surprise to the overstretched and overwhelmed Lynn. Lucy offered to carry out these therapy sessions for free. 'I just want to help you, you've been so let down by the system.'

From the outside Lucy may have seemed just too good to be true, yet Lynn was in no position to turn down any offer of desperately needed help. What Lynn didn't know at the time was that this invented persona of 'Lucy', a self-sacrificing art therapist, was likely serving the deep psychological need for spotlight and validation so common in those diagnosed with pseudologia fantastica. Casting herself as both a hero and saviour, money was not Samantha's motivator here; it seems it was something far deeper.

There was magic in Lucy's presence, Lynn recalls: 'She had this kind, calm face. I thought, here is someone who can see Ellie ... someone who understands.' Lucy insisted on confidentiality in her sessions with Ellie, a boundary Lynn accepted, trusting the professional air that masked her deep deception.

Ireland, in 2016, was making some strides in disability and mental health care, but vast gaps remained. The HSE was overburdened by bureaucracy and underfunding. Parent carers like Lynn and Hillery bore a disproportionate share of the burden of care, often receiving insufficient State support. For families with children affected by conditions like autism or Rett syndrome, access to therapies was agonisingly slow. Respite services were minimal, financial grants patchy. Many described a relentless isolation, feeling abandoned at a time when community mattered most. The emotional toll, chronic fatigue, anxiety and financial strain was woven into every aspect of daily life. Lucy entered this precarious world like a breath of fresh air, a professional promising care where none had existed. The women's fragile hope became her playground.

* * *

Once she was fully immersed in Lorraine, Hillery and Lynn's lives, as a friend to Lorraine and a supportive caregiver to the others, Lucy's focus shifted. No longer content with just giving private care, she announced an ambitious plan – a refuge for women fleeing domestic violence, to be sited in Dún Laoghaire. The idea struck a profound chord with those around her.

Hillery was haunted by memories of refuge life from her own youth, having spent time in such places with her mother as a child. Lynn had once fled from violence to safety as a single mother. They knew only too well how women's refuges were lifelines, symbols of survival amidst heartbreak. So for the three women, who had long shared a bond forged through charitable work, including time spent working together in a children's orphanage in Uganda, Lucy's cause felt sacred.

They threw themselves into helping Lucy, gathering donations of buggies, toiletries, baby clothes, baby food, tins of chopped tomatoes, every item she requested. One morning, word came that a woman had entered the refuge in crisis with a support dog, and so there was a rush to procure tins of dog food. Their network of friends, local businesses and community groups moved mountains to support what they believed was a vital sanctuary.

Over time, however, Lucy became relentless. Her demands multiplied and more and more items were requested for the refuge, for the women, for the children. Lucy's presence in their lives grew suffocating. Hillery reflects, 'Before Lucy, there was nothing but the usual struggle. Then Lucy swallowed everything – our time, our energy, our hearts.' Slowly, the needs of the refuge swallowed up the time required for the care of Reese and Ellie. Lucy's intoxicating influence eclipsed the real needs she had once sought to ease.

Lynn later reflected that none of them knew the exact location of the refuge, other than that it was in a property on Northumberland Avenue, a largely residential street not far from the sea. 'This didn't bother me at the time, I knew refuge locations were kept secret to protect the women and children in there, so not knowing exactly its address didn't give me any cause for concern.' However, time would tell and Lynn's lack of concern would not last.

First there was Lucy the therapist, a light in the dark. Then there was the women's refuge, vital work saving lives. Next came the wedding.

Lucy's announcement came like a sudden gust of wind. She was to marry her pastor, a man, according to her, whose gentle demeanour and steady faith made him seem like a rock amid turbulent seas. Although the women had never actually met the pastor, they felt they knew him well from Lucy's romantic tales. The community whispered about the couple with a mix of curiosity and admiration. To Lorraine, Hillery and Lynn, Lucy's upcoming nuptials felt like the dawn of something new, an event that would bring joy not just to her, but to all who had rallied behind her cause. Lucy spoke of a wedding 'like no other', a grand occasion designed to dazzle Dún Laoghaire and beyond. A spectacle on a scale never seen before amongst the locals.

The plans unfolded rapidly. Invitations were discreetly extended, venues scouted with meticulous care. The vivid details of her wedding plans, shared over cups of tea and hurried phone calls, were intoxicating. A celebration with the elegance of forgotten fairytales, layered with the promise of hope and new beginnings. Samantha Cookes was no longer content with idle daydreaming and chit chat about her big day, which she had often engaged in during her earlier life in the UK with ex-boyfriends. This time she really would plan the day of her wildest dreams at the expense of those drawn into her web.

A new player was now pulled into Samantha's story. One sunny Dublin morning, wedding planner Collette O'Leary's phone rang unexpectedly. The caller was a young woman with a polished British accent, excited, eager and unmistakably charming. She introduced herself as Lucy, and her voice shimmered with enthusiasm. She explained how she wanted Collette's help to craft the most magical wedding in Dublin, a day that would be remembered forever. Collette, always professional but also a people person, immediately signed on, delighted to be part of such a special event. Within minutes, she was behind the wheel, headed to collect Lucy for what would become a months-long journey through fittings, taste tests and secret plans.

As they drove to their appointments, the young bride-to-be shared her dreams, each story more captivating than the last. Lucy described her fiancé, Ross, a missionary currently serving in Syria, working with children scarred by war. She told Collette that her family was wealthy, supporting her lavish wedding, and that her mother lived in America with her stepfather. It all glided effortlessly, an enchanting story that wrapped Collette in a warm glow.

Lucy's chatter was magnetic. She spoke of her desire for the wedding to be *Star Wars* themed, with the officiant dressed as Princess Leia – an odd detail, but one that seemed innocent enough at the time. She asked question after question about possible venues, about ways to make her dream a reality, and she described her penchant for the dramatic in vivid detail. The venue chosen was to be none other than Dublin's prestigious Shelbourne Hotel. With its old-world grace, marble floors and soft lamplight, it is one of the most exclusive and expensive wedding venues in the country. Collette joined Lucy on an unforgettable walk-through of the famous Dublin landmark.

The bride-to-be's visions of her big day included a bridesmaid who was a 'little person', a dear friend of hers. She enquired at length whether a carpenter could build a bespoke platform on the top table to accommodate this bridesmaid. Her voice trembled when she spoke of her favourite flowers, sunflowers, which she wanted to adorn the entire wedding room. Behind this choice was another story, one rooted in silent sorrow. Lucy recounted to Collette how her first husband and infant daughter had died in a tragic car crash caused by a drunk driver. Tears streamed down her face as she described how she used to sing 'You Are

My Sunshine' to her daughter every night, and how sunflowers symbolised hope and her lost loves. The raw pain in her voice was so genuine that Collette felt her own throat tighten and her eyes blur with unshed tears. 'My heart just broke for her; so young and to have experienced so much tragedy, I wanted to make her day extra special,' recalled Collette.

Weeks passed. The fittings, tastings and countless phone calls continued. Collette found herself drawn into Lucy's world, enchanted by her vivid stories but increasingly troubled by her outlandish demands. And there was one glaring problem. Lucy had yet to pay her deposit, a significant sum normally required upfront. When Collette gently reminded her, Lucy always came up with some excuse: Ross, her fiancé, was overseas, her family was waiting for an inheritance, or she was in the middle of 'personal emergencies'. Collette, ever-trusting but cautious, pressed gently more and more, until it became clear that Lucy was dodging her.

Finally, Collette made it explicit. To continue working on the wedding, she needed payment. Lucy agreed without hesitation, but then dropped a bombshell. She claimed that her stepfather, who had agreed to foot the bill, was dining at the White House with Barack Obama and thus unable to pay there and then. It was such an outlandish lie that it hit Collette with the cold weight of betrayal. Her stomach sank. Who was this woman? What was she really after?

In that moment, Collette's instinct told her everything – she would never see a penny. But what troubled her far more than her own loss of time and income was the purpose behind it all. The perception that Lucy's scam had no material gain deeply disturbed her. No hefty payday. Instead, she believed Lucy just thrived on the buzz, the rush of living in falsehoods. The same question echoed in Collette's mind over and over again: 'What did she really want?'

Realising she had been duped into becoming a part of some elaborate illusion Lucy was creating, Collette abruptly severed ties. Yet, despite cutting all connection and revoking her services, Collette was bombarded by calls from Lucy, so much so she blocked the number. She chalked the experience up to bad luck, an unfortunate encounter with a woman who was clearly unwell, if not completely unhinged.

However, a phone call from the Gardaí some weeks later sent chills down her spine and stopped her in her tracks. The officers had found a burner phone in the possession of a woman named Samantha Cookes. Collette's number was in the phone. More disturbingly, attached to the back of the burner phone on a Post-it note were handwritten details on Collette's life, including the name of her son and the fact he had recently played the lead role of Hamlet in his school play. Little nuggets of information that Lucy had garnered through chats during their time together. She had been keeping small details of Collette and her family recorded. Why?

Unbeknownst to Collette, as the woman she knew as Lucy was planning her wedding, she was simultaneously planning another bogus adventure elsewhere in Dublin that would out her as a fraudster once again, bringing the Gardaí to her door.

* * *

Samantha moved fast as Lucy Fitzwilliams, moving through narratives at a breakneck speed, entrancing those around her. As the summer of 2016 flew by, she moved through the city like a shadow, draped in charm and deception. Her influence spread like a subtle poison, twisting the lives of those who thought they were helping her, themselves and others.

Lynn, Hillery and Lorraine, a trio tethered to their own private struggles, had become puppets in Lucy's sprawling fantasy. They rushed ceaselessly through the streets and markets of Dublin and beyond, fetching supplies for the women's refuge in Dún Laoghaire, something that existed only in the elaborate tales Lucy concocted, a fabrication built from their desperation and goodwill.

'She had us run ragged,' Lorraine confessed quietly. 'There were days when I questioned why we were so invested. But she told the kind of stories that made you forget your own doubts. She was like a magician pulling you deeper into the illusion.'

During her industrious days in Dublin as Lucy, Samantha's energy appeared boundless, her ambition matched only by her resourcefulness. This was a woman who moved through the city and its bright-eyed community groups with ease, never the same person for long, yet always persuasive, always authentic. Long before her name would become part of scandalised whispers, Lucy Fitzwilliams' presence lit up online notice boards and classifieds. Her personal statement was everywhere:

> I am a compassionate, reliable 26-year-old woman experienced in providing high quality care to enable individuals to remain in their own home. I am committed to person-centred care and pride myself in CPD [continuing professional development]. I am seeking part-time work, evenings and weekends. Key Skills: Strong communication skills including sign language. Good time manager. Organised and self-motivated. Good record keeper.

Her CV sketched a life both exotic and altruistic. Years as a support worker in Dubai for a deaf family, sole carer for ailing relatives, ABA-trained (Applied Behaviour Analysis, a research-based therapy that helps build social, communication and learning skills) for children on the autism spectrum. She was, in her words, 'passionate about people, [I] work well under pressure and strive to provide high quality care at all times. I believe it is a privilege to support people to remain independent which is my motivation to work in this sector.' One could almost hear the earnestness humming through her words.

Lucy positioned herself as a versatile pillar of good within the city. In her assumed new identity, she answered online ads and posted her own for work in elderly and respite care, always available 'after 6:30 p.m. and on weekends'. She offered babysitting services rooted in British professional training: 'I trained in the UK as a professional Nanny and am offering my services as a Babysitter. I am first aid trained and food safety trained.' Her ambition didn't stop there. She also introduced herself as a proofreader and editor for hire: 'I am a professional writer with over 5 years' experience as a proofreader/editor. I offer competitive rates.'

The qualifications listed always matched whatever role she was seeking. She cultivated the story of a tireless learner:

> I am currently studying at night school towards a SNA [Special Needs Assistant] course to enable me to gain further skills in sensory development and am also taking my Irish conversion course in sign language ... I know I do not fit into a typical box, but I am passionate about people ... I am involved in a bereavement support group which aims at supporting parents who have lost a child. I am qualified

> in counselling and psychology skills, which I believe is an important transferable skill for working with elderly people.

In every role, Lucy charted a careful path between truth and invention. She knew just how to make herself invaluable. Typical of people diagnosed with pseudologia fantastica (pathological lying), her stories were elaborate yet consistent, her identity constructed from the things people wanted to hear. She became the answer to every need: a care worker, nanny, confidante or editor, absorbing other people's pain and secrets with deft and subtle grace.

It is not known exactly how many lives she touched through work gained from these online advertisements, but her unending industriousness was more than simple ambition. It was practice. For Samantha, each response to a real ad or demand in the city built something greater – a resumé of trust, a string of references, groundwork for the most convincing scam yet to come. Each lie sharpened her skill, each success made the legend of Lucy Fitzwilliams more difficult to untangle from the reality of Samantha Cookes. Behind each message, every 'Kind Regards, Lucy', Samantha was learning just how far a perfect story could carry her.

9

THE FIRST CRACK

While Samantha, in the guise of Lucy Fitzwilliams, was openly offering her services to the wider Dublin area, she carried out her most delicate con behind closed doors. Lynn's eight-year-old daughter Ellie, a quiet and sensitive child overshadowed by her sister's grave illness, was visited weekly by Lucy, her self-proclaimed art therapist and occupational therapist, titles she had earned only in her own fantasies. Lucy would arrive and escort Ellie down the garden to a bench hidden by trees for their secret sessions. Lynn could only guess at what happened in those private chats. Ellie seemed to adore Lucy, looking up to her like the older sister she never had, excited before their sessions. Lynn also noticed in quiet moments the sometimes heavy silence that could on occasion follow Lucy's visits. Wanting to respect the boundaries of her child's therapy and bond of trust with Lucy, Lynn never pushed too deep to uncover what they had spoken about each day. It's something she now deeply regrets.

Then there was Reese, the first focal point of Lucy Fitzwilliams' charade. Despite weeks of therapy sessions, no progress seemed to have been made. 'I wanted to believe,' Hillery admitted, 'but I saw nothing changing. She had us convinced, but it was like watching a mirage. Beautiful promises that never quite reached the shore.'

Just as the women began to catch their breath as requests for items for the refuge slowed down and the wedding talk slowly petered out, Lucy brought up her latest dazzling distraction: a trip to Lapland for the women and children supposedly using the Dún Laoghaire refuge. The very notion – an enchanted escape to a winter wonderland filled with elves, reindeer and the promise of magic – enchanted everyone immediately. 'This wasn't just some holiday pipe-dream,' Lynn said, her eyes lighting up even when discussing it much later. 'She made it feel like a gift for the families in the refuge, those women and children who needed a sliver of joy. And then, as if by grace, she said they had some extra available seats at a much reduced rate from normal. That's when Lorraine, Hillery and I signed up without a second thought.'

Lorraine was the first to hand over her deposit, €1,500 upfront, with the conviction that she was going to be part of something truly special. And Lucy was the gift that never seemed to stop giving. The women found themselves recruited to find more families, more children with additional needs who 'deserved' this once-in-a-lifetime escape. They worked round the clock to help Lucy fill extra seats coming up daily. 'We joked there would be enough seats to fill five planes,' Hillery laughed darkly, 'an endless sea of tickets, each one sold with a smile and a promise.'

Emails rolled in, glittering with careful details of flight itineraries and meticulous requests for passport information and deposits. On 25 July 2016, at 10.16 p.m., Lucy emailed all attendees:

I'll give you the brief history – basically we opened the women's refuge and I really felt that I wanted to organise some holidays for the refuge. I'd inherited some money and just got a bee in my bonnet and decided I would keep trying until I could get a trip that was affordable. Lapland were [*sic*] amazing, but we had to book 5 different trips. I only needed 4 of them, but the price was so good we decided to book all 5. I honestly thought we would be left with the 5th trip!

We decided to just see if anyone we knew would be interested in a group trip and the rest is history!!

I don't have charity status yet (paperwork has been done, just waiting to hear back but have been warned that it can be a slow process) and we are Christians, so the price everyone is paying is exactly how much we have paid. So there really is no pressure. We are blessed to be able to take the women in refuge on these trips and are so thankful that the 5th trip has proven so popular. I had thought we would have to just write that trip off, whereas now we have people attending that trip we are using that money to donate back into refuge to purchase 4 new bathroom suites and a new kitchen. As long as the balance is paid at some point, I'm very relaxed. We are only taking a deposit so that I know people are definite to come.

I will confirm if the ski trip is a long drive. Off hand I think it is a 90 minute drive. Although when I was speaking with our group booking co-ordinator there was talk of a ski village further afield for 'proper' skiers. I will get back to you tomorrow ASAP with the exact answer to that. I know some people are signing up to do only half a ski day and then use the afternoon to do other activities so I'm 99% sure it is fairly nearby.

Really looking forward to meeting you and again thank you so much for your support!

Three days later, the following email appeared:

Subject: under 2 year olds

Regarding Under 2 Year Olds

This is an emailing regarding parents bringing under 2 year olds on the trip to Lapland as there appears to have been some confusion regarding travelling with youngsters.

If your child is 2 or under on the day of travelling we will assume that you are not wanting a seat for them on the plane. This will mean that for a child under 2 they will cost 30 euros, not 217 – this for children over the age of 2.

IF YOU WANT YOUR 2 YEAR OLD TO HAVE THEIR OWN SEAT PLEASE LET ME KNOW IMMEDIATELY, OTHERWISE I WILL BE ALLOCATING THEIR SEAT TO SOMEONE ELSE.

As the flight is short a lot of parents have already opted for the under 2 year old to sit on their lap, however, after numerous calls today I realised that not everyone was aware of this. As such, we are now going to have the default position that all under 2 year olds will be sitting on a parent's lap.

This also means that we have a few extra spaces, so if you know anyone still interested please let me know ASAP, particularly as the activities are only held at the low cost until tomorrow.

Kind Regards,
Lucy

On 31 July 2016, she wrote:

Please can you let me know ASAP if anyone in your group is a vegetarian or vegan?
Thanks [*sic*] you

Lucy

Another email appeared on the same day:

Hello Everyone,

Just a quick email to say that we will be confirming some very important information with Lapland regarding medical information by the end of August.

As I am running 4 other trips (for the women at refuge) alongside this I am having to deal with high levels of paperwork! This trip alone involves the information for over 120 people, so please can you let me know if anyone in your group has any specific illnesses, such as asthma, diabetes or the like.

Also, if you have had any serious breaks and a plate fitted.

This is simply [because] there are separate medical forms for people who have specific long term needs. If I know in advance it will save some work in the long run.

> Thank you for your co-operation, and I look forward to seeing some of you tomorrow at the house for an open house meeting!
>
> God Bless,
> Lucy

With Lucy in control of the details, everyone else could relax and just look forward to the upcoming trip, imagining Rudolph's red nose in the snow and the magic waiting for them at Santa's workshop.

* * *

Wrapped in the guise of trust and necessity, Lucy approached Lynn one August afternoon with a carefully crafted proposal. With the upcoming Lapland trip in mind, she wanted Lynn to sign paperwork granting her permission to take Ellie out of the country without her mother's presence.

'It's like a school trip form,' Lucy explained smoothly. 'Just a form to let Ellie experience the magic, even if Daisy isn't well enough to travel and you need to stay behind to care for her. It would make things easier, more flexible.'

But Lynn's instincts, the fierce, unyielding instinct of a mother, made her hesitate. Something intangible but undeniable twisted in her gut. 'I couldn't put my name on it,' Lynn recalled, her voice barely a whisper. 'It wasn't distrust, not exactly. But a quiet alarm rang inside me. I just knew it wasn't right.'

Lucy persisted. She asked repeatedly, putting pressure on Lynn that she wasn't expecting. Yet, despite the mounting insistence,

Lynn held firm. This single mother's quiet refusal to sign a form would mark the first crack in the flawless fantasy that Samantha Cookes had been building in the heart of Dublin.

10

THE ILLUSION CRUMBLES

Samantha Cookes built personas like some built businesses, with planning, patience and a theatrical instinct for detail. When the mask of the caring professional began to dry and crack, she simply brushed over it with another layer. The line between fantasy and fraud blurred until the two were indistinguishable.

Through patience or luck, or perhaps that uncanny ability to become precisely what others needed, as well as planning both a bogus wedding and a Lapland trip in 2016, she also found time to add the character of new student to her resumé, enrolling at Dublin City University as Lucy Fitzwilliams. This would not be the only occasion Samantha would darken the university's door under a false identity.

This period of Samantha's life was particularly industrious and successful, but the glittering illusion began to crumble the moment Hillery's friend – an astute businesswoman with a sharp eye for detail – stepped forward with the idea of bringing her entire extended family along on the magical trip to Lapland. The entire cost for the family was staggering, nearly €20,000, a significant sum to be entrusted without question. And this woman wasn't one to leap blindly into a situation on just promises, however enticing.

She requested the women's refuge's official charity number, a simple formality for her records, before signing over such a hefty cheque. The request, however, was met only with excuses from Lucy, promises to send the information 'soon' or 'once the paperwork was finalised'. Days passed with no response. Growing concerned, the businesswoman then scoured the Irish charity register online but found no trace of the refuge in question. The digital silence was deafening.

On the day the businesswoman was due to meet Lucy and hand over the cheque, she found she couldn't reach her. She was hoping that talking to Lucy in person would allow her concerns around the missing charity number to be allayed. Like the others, she was keen to not disappoint her excited children at home. However, repeated calls went unanswered. In desperation, she rang Hillery. 'I can't get through to Lucy. She still hasn't given me the charity number. I can't find any record of this refuge anywhere online. What's going on?'

Hillery's heart sank. Doubt began to trickle in, unwelcome and unsettling. A knot tightened in her stomach, but before she had time to unravel her thoughts, her phone rang again. It was Lucy. The voice on the other end was trembling with distress. 'Hillery! I've collapsed ... in Eason's ... they've taken me by ambulance to St Vincent's Hospital! Please come, please, I don't like hospitals. I need to get out of here!'

A loyal friend and quick to act, Hillery didn't hesitate. She jumped into her car and sped through Dublin's tangled streets to St Vincent's Hospital. Bursting through the automatic doors, she headed straight for A&E reception.

'I'm looking for my friend, Lucy Fitzwilliams,' she said breathlessly.

The receptionist typed the name into the database, but then her brow furrowed. 'No record of a Lucy Fitzwilliams.'

Hillery blinked in confusion. Trying possible iterations of Lucy's surname in case there'd been a mistake in the rush to A&E, she suggested, 'Maybe Lucy Williams?'

'No.'

'Hm ... Williamson?'

'No.'

The receptionist pressed, 'What was she brought in for?'

'She collapsed in Eason's and was brought in by ambulance.'

The receptionist's tone changed, almost apologetic. 'Oh, Samantha. She's in bay five.'

Shock rippled through Hillery. The receptionist had called her friend 'Samantha', but that didn't make any sense. What did it mean? She rushed down the corridor to bay five. Pulling back the curtain, she expected to see a stranger, a 'Samantha'. Instead, there was Lucy, her face pale, eyes wide with panic.

'Lucy!' Hillery exclaimed, voice trembling.

Lucy looked up.

'The receptionist called you Samantha! What's going on?' Hillery asked.

A clearly flustered Lucy burst out, 'Oh, Hillery, help me, get me out of here! I need to leave, please! I don't like hospitals!'

'Lucy, you need to stay. The doctors will have to run tests. You collapsed, you can't just leave!' Hillery insisted.

But Lucy's distress was so fierce, almost desperate, that, against her better judgement, Hillery acquiesced, helping her friend out of the hospital as nurses looked on with puzzled concern. No sooner were they outside than Lucy transformed. The frantic mask dropped. Her breath steadied, and the cool, composed, sweet woman Hillery knew slipped back into place.

'Oh, Hillery,' she smiled softly, 'it's a beautiful day out, isn't it?'

The sudden disparity between panic and poise was unsettling. Hillery felt bile twist in her throat. *What the hell is going on here?* she thought. And, more sharply – *Who is Samantha?*

Lucy said she didn't feel safe going home alone that night after collapsing and wondered if she could perhaps sleep at Hillery's house. Despite her concerns about what had happened earlier, the answer came without hesitation. Hillery said, 'Yes, of course.' What else could she do?

As twilight seeped into the narrow streets, Lucy relaxed in Hillery's living room, a fragile figure cast in the glow of the nearby table lamp. Hillery helped her settle on the sofa bed with the kind of measured tenderness only a good friend could offer. She handed Lucy pyjamas and a toothbrush, urging her to rest. Still, a gnawing unease crept through her veins, a knot tightening beneath her ribs. Knowing Lucy had been rushed to hospital just hours before, Hillery wrestled with the thought that she should still be under medical supervision, regardless of Lucy's protestations otherwise.

As night deepened and the city's hum softened to silence, sleep evaded Hillery. She had left her bedroom door ajar, allowing her to listen for any sign of movement. As the minutes stretched endlessly, each whisper of a breath, each creak from the sofa made her pulse race. Finally, unable to bear the silence any longer, she rose, padding quietly through the darkened hallway towards the living room.

Lucy was standing at the window, the curtain drawn back just enough to let a sliver of moonlight fall upon her face, casting flickering shadows. Her eyes were wide, darting fearfully, as if expecting something or someone to emerge from the night outside.

'Lucy! What are you doing? Get back to bed and rest,' said Hillery in a voice that held a tremor beneath the calm.

'Oh, yes, of course,' came the flustered reply. 'I was just ... looking at the beautiful moon.'

But Hillery's unease only deepened. A cold certainty settled over her skin like the damp outside. Something in the house, something in Lucy, was wrong.

By morning, Hillery's worry had reached such an extent that she reached for her phone. 'Lorraine,' she texted, 'there's something not right with Lucy.' Hillery was scheduled for a long day at work, so she was unable to watch over Lucy herself. It was decided Lucy would stay with Lorraine instead, presented to her as a safe harbour under the guise of medical supervision, but in truth, a holding pattern to buy time. The women circled warily around Lucy, protective yet increasingly suspicious.

When Hillery pulled into her work car park, the damp gravel crunching under tyres, Lorraine's car was already parked nearby. Hillery stopped next to Lorraine, and as Lucy slipped silently from Hillery's car, moving around the back to get to Lorraine's passenger door, Hillery leaned over, whispering with urgency to Lorraine through the open car window, 'There's something going on. I don't know what, but something isn't right.'

Lorraine looked Hillery squarely in the eye, the weight of years of friendship and hard truths settling between them. 'Don't worry,' she murmured, 'I've got this.'

Lorraine had no children of her own, but as she sat in the quiet calm of her living room, the gravity of her choice pressed down on her like a physical weight. She had brought Lucy into the inner circle, into the homes of her closest friends, into their lives, even close to their vulnerable children. The thought twisted in her mind, making her head spin in a swirl of confusion and dread. She felt a crushing responsibility to unravel the truth.

All morning, Lorraine watched Lucy like a hawk. On the surface, Lucy was as chatty and amiable as ever, her easy laughter punctuating the air, her warmth seemingly genuine. Lorraine forced herself to match her tone, to be the good host, the supportive friend, the smiling woman who welcomed a guest into her home. But beneath the façade, every fibre of Lorraine's being was taut, alert to every word, every glance, every twitch.

After lunch, the air grew heavier, with the conversation drifting towards the struggles of Lynn and Hillery's families. The two women spoke quietly about the endless battles to secure adequate care, the way exhaustion gnawed at the edges of love, the frustrations with a system that was supposed to help but too often failed. Lorraine was at the sink doing the dishes, the warmth of the soapy water running over her hands, her back turned as Lucy and she talked.

Then it happened, a moment Lorraine describes as a mask slipping. A voice emerged from Lucy unlike any she had heard before. 'Those people don't deserve their children,' Lucy said, her tone sharp and cold. 'I would do a much better job. I will have them.'

Lorraine froze mid-breath, staring out the window. Her heart slammed against her ribs, flooding her with a shock that clawed at her jaw and clenched her fists. The words echoed in the silent room, reverberating through her very soul. Who was this woman? What did she want? Frightened by what she had heard, Lorraine's survival instincts ignited, a raging blaze of clarity that crackled beneath the surface. For a heartbeat, a nightmare played through her mind. What if Lucy's intentions went beyond lies and deception? What if her presence in their lives was about to lead to something far more dangerous than deception?

But Lorraine was no stranger to hardship or fear. She swallowed the dread knotted in her throat and took a steadying breath. Calmly, she ignored Lucy's words, smiled a tight, practised smile, and changed the subject. It was an Oscar-worthy performance, the kind born of necessity and raw instinct. All the while, beneath the placid surface, Lorraine knew one thing with unbearable clarity: she had to act. The clock was ticking, and the only chance to protect her friends, and herself, from someone who was clearly not who she said she was, was to expose the truth lurking behind Lucy's perfect mask.

Lorraine sat at her kitchen table, the weight of doubt tightening like a vice around her chest. She knew she couldn't yet go to the Gardaí. What would she say? 'There's a woman, I think she's not who she says she is.' It sounded absurd, almost hysterical. And she realised that if Lucy could deceive them all the way she had, she could probably talk her way out of anything. No, Lorraine needed proof, something concrete to expose the deception. The solution was obvious – she would have to become a detective. The others needed her to expose the real Lucy, and she couldn't let them down.

The next morning, feigning a routine workday, Lorraine slipped out early. Instead of heading to the salon as usual, she drove straight to those places that Lucy had claimed were real but now seemed more like shadows in a fog. She began on Northumberland Avenue, where the women's refuge was supposedly located. Lorraine drove slowly along the street, until she found a parking spot. Getting out of her car, she went door to door, asking neighbours and passers-by if they knew of any refuge located there. 'They must have thought I was mad,' she later confessed. But every answer was the same: no refuge, no shelter, nothing on that street associated with Lucy.

The sinking realisation hit her like a blow: there is no refuge. There never had been.

And that wasn't all. She visited the site where Lucy had claimed she and her pastor were building their new home. Dusty earth and half-finished walls lingered like a ghost. It was clearly a genuine building site, so for a moment Lorraine wondered if maybe this part of the story was true. However, to make sure, she visited the local council offices and checked the planning records. There was not a single application on file under the name of Lucy or her alleged fiancé, Ross. The site belonged to someone else entirely.

No refuge, no house. None of it was real.

Lorraine's stomach turned sour. Determined to find out more, she pressed on. Her next stop was the evangelical church to which Lucy claimed to belong. The moment she stepped through the large wooden doors, her heart started to pound fiercely, a heavy weight of uncertainty pressing on her shoulders.

She hurried to the pastor's office and found there a man named Ross, who was poised and courteous. Could there be a shred of truth in Lucy's tale? Was this the real Ross? She explained why she was there and then braced herself. Ross looked at her steadily and shook his head. 'I've never had any relationship with this Lucy. I'm a married man, with children.'

No refuge, no house, no fiancé, no wedding.

The walls seemed to close in. The woman she knew as Lucy was fracturing before her eyes.

Lorraine knew where Lucy lived. She'd picked her up from there many times, a quaint, quiet house run by a kindly elderly woman. It was her next stop. Gathering her courage, Lorraine walked up to the door and knocked. The woman answered, opening the door with a warm smile. Lorraine re-introduced herself as Lucy's friend, hoping the lady would recognise her from her pick-ups and drop-offs. Luckily, she did.

'Oh, she's away, on holidays in Morocco,' the woman said casually.

Morocco? Lorraine thought, the lie sharp in her mind. Lucy was currently staying under her roof.

The old lady's tone shifted. 'Funny you called today ... Gardaí were just here, looking for Lucy. How odd,' she said with a thin smile.

Hmmm. How odd indeed.

Lorraine asked, 'Would you mind if I took a look at her room?'

The woman agreed.

When Lorraine stepped inside Lucy's bedroom, her heart sank. The room was crammed with the spoils of people's goodwill – tins of tomatoes, baby buggies, blankets – items she, Hillery and Lynn had collected for the supposed refuge. Notebooks overflowed from the desk onto the floor. She picked one up, flipping through pages filled with frantic, troubling notes. Names, 'Martha', a dead baby – words that prickled her skin.

Then, her eyes lifted to the window. Hanging from the curtain rail was a wedding dress, pristine, yet haunting. A symbol of a wedding with no fiancé, no date, no future. A cold, bone-deep chill coursed through her veins.

A moment later she spotted something else poking out of the corner of a notebook on the nightstand. It was a bank card. She pulled it out and read the name printed across it: 'SAMANTHA COOKES'. *Who is Samantha Cookes?*, she wondered, her mind racing. More importantly, what to do about the woman they called Lucy, who was still in her friends' lives and in her community? Her breath hitched as she snapped her phone open and dialled Lynn.

'Lynn, are you sitting down? You're not going to believe this.'

Lynn sat frozen, every word Lorraine spoke pounding like a hammer against her heart. She had believed so firmly in Lucy, an angel sent to rescue them from the darkness of exhaustion and overwhelming care. She had bought every last piece of snow gear for Lapland during a summer sale in Aldi, with the hope that Ellie and Daisy would soon be wide-eyed and joyful, meeting Santa beneath twinkling lights. The magical trip to Lapland was meant to be a balm, a rare gift amidst endless struggle. Could it all be a lie?

A cold trickle of fear slithered down Lynn's spine as she thought about Lucy's secret sessions in the garden with Ellie, those shared smiles and confidences that no one else saw. Even more chilling was the recollection of Lucy's warm, persuasive smile as she gently pushed Lynn to sign the paperwork giving her permission to take Ellie abroad without her. Lynn felt sick just thinking about it.

Having finished her call with Lynn, Lorraine, her mind swirling with shock and exhaustion, flicked tired fingers against the screen of her phone, composing a terse message to Hillery: 'I have the evidence. None of it's real ... let's confront her and find out what's going on.' But panic robbed her of precision. In her haste, Lorraine's trembling thumb sent the message not to Hillery, but directly to Lucy. The very woman at the centre of the web of lies.

Lorraine's heart plummeted to her stomach. She frantically tried to retract the message, but once sent, it was impossible to recall. The damage was done. By the time she returned home, Lucy/Samantha, was gone without a trace. The house felt hollow. The carefully constructed fantasy had shattered, leaving only questions in its cruel wake.

The moment the truth came crashing in on them, Lynn, Hillery and Lorraine exploded into frantic worry. What exactly had this woman, Lucy/Samantha, wanted from them? What dark purpose lurked behind her uncanny closeness to their families and vulnerable children? Talking about it afterwards, Hillery's voice trembled with disbelief as she reflected, 'It's hard to get even close family to spend time with our children, given their challenges. Yet she ... she was there willingly, all the time, like she belonged. For what?'

Lynn's reaction was more one of fear, raw and visceral. The memory of Lucy's relentless push to sign travel paperwork for Ellie haunted her. What if Lucy returned, determined to take her daughter? The thought tightened around her throat like a noose.

Lorraine had shared with the women the name she saw on the bank card in Lucy's bedroom: Samantha Cookes. Lynn hunched over the glow of her laptop, the room dim behind her, and googled the unfamiliar name with hands shaking. It was all she had to go on, since Lucy, the confidante her daughter had adored, had slipped away without a word.

A news archive popped up in relation to the search and she clicked on the link. What she saw stopped her breath. 'Surrogacy scam in Britain, 2011. Samantha Cookes convicted after defrauding a couple desperate for a child. Court hears of personal tragedy, the death of her infant daughter, from cot death.' Lynn read the words twice, letting them settle inside her chest like heavy weights.

She checked the years, the maths precise. The baby, which had died at four months old in 2008, would have been Ellie's age now. They had the same year of birth. The realisation hit her like an electric jolt. Samantha had slid so seamlessly into their lives, bonding with Ellie. Lynn wondered if she had seen Ellie as some sort of replacement for the child she'd lost.

A shiver crept up her spine. Samantha, smiling, gentle, coaxing secrets from Ellie, trying to get Lynn to sign those forms that would let her take her away from her mother. 'Just for paperwork,' she'd said. But was it just paperwork? If no trip to Lapland was ever really planned, then what was the purpose of such paperwork?

Lynn stared at the news report, eyes blurring. Maybe, in Ellie, Samantha had found a little girl who was a perfect reflection of what her daughter might have been. Lynn pressed her palm to her mouth, stifling a gasp. She didn't know what to think. Was her daughter caught in the undertow of another woman's grief?

While Lynn did her devastating research at home, Hillery and Lorraine knew they had no choice but to go to the Gardaí. Lorraine recalled later with a rueful laugh how they must have appeared, two fraught women barrelling into the Garda station in Dún Laoghaire, breathless and wired, spinning a tale so strange it teetered on the edge of disbelief. An English woman, pretending to be an occupational therapist, an art therapist, claiming to run a non-existent women's refuge, engaged to marry a pastor of the local evangelical church, to whom they'd paid deposits and with whom they'd shared their passport details for a trip to Lapland, had infiltrated their lives, and, more terrifyingly, they believed that the safety of children was possibly at risk.

At first, their fears were met with quiet scepticism. Lorraine and Hillery thought they were being branded as hysterical, their words weighed but dismissed. But then, having left the women in the interview room for some time, the Gardaí returned and produced a photograph for them to look at. The image was startling, showing a younger woman, blonde-haired, eyes sharp and intent. Lorraine's breath caught as she focused on the text above the photo: Samantha Cookes, missing from her home in Gloucester.

Samantha Cookes. The name on the bank card found in Lucy's bedroom.

Was this her real name?

The memory of the hospital receptionist stating 'Samantha' echoed cruelly in Hillery's mind.

'Oh my God ... who is this woman?' Lorraine whispered, voice cracking.

Once notified, the Gardaí placed Lynn's home on red alert, with Garda cars patrolling the area. This woman, a fantasist, posing as a therapist under a false name, who had her own children removed from her care in the UK, who had urged Lynn to sign papers giving her access to take Ellie abroad without her mother, had left behind too many red flags to ignore. That night, terror robbed Lynn of sleep. She clutched a hatchet beneath her pillow, her children pressed close beside her in the bed as she lay awake, wide-eyed, fearing Samantha's return in the shadows.

Rest would not come for Lorraine either. She was weighed

down by guilt and despair. After all, she had been the one to bring this woman into all their lives.

But from the ashes of their fear rose a resolve as fierce as fire. Lorraine, Lynn and Hillery began a relentless pursuit, their shared pain and courage propelling them forward. Samantha had messed with the wrong women. Over the coming years they traced Samantha Cookes across counties and cities, uncovering the trail of lies and heartache she left in her wake. Yet even as the Dubliners were left reeling in her initial absence, unbeknownst to them, Samantha's shadow had already stretched west, weaving its way to the quiet landscapes of Mayo. There, she ensnared another family in her web.

11

LUCY FITZPATRICK

The role of nanny had proved useful before, providing a home, food and proximity to families who would trust her without hesitation. So Samantha now used it again, simply changing her surname to Fitzpatrick.

Her new online profile was read with delight by Sinead (not her real name) from Mayo's rugged west coast, where the wind rattled the windows and the sea felt close to everything. Sinead's life was a whirl of early mornings and unfinished coffee cups. She and her husband both worked full-time, at the same time as raising three young children: five-year-old Rory and three-year-old twins, Molly and Conor. Sinead was exhausted, perpetually behind and the sort of tired that made every small kindness feel miraculous.

'Childcare's a nightmare,' Sinead later said. 'We'd had au pairs before, but they never lasted long. Rural Mayo isn't for everyone.' So, when a notification pinged from the au pair agency site announcing a new message from an English woman named Lucy Fitzpatrick, Sinead opened it at once.

The message was perfect. Lucy wrote that she was taking a break from her career to work on a children's book, that she loved baking, crafts and imaginative play. She described herself as someone who 'believes children are their most creative when allowed to make a glorious mess'.

'She sounded warm and genuine,' Sinead recalled. 'And, honestly, nobody else was applying. I thought, thank God, finally someone.'

Sinead contacted Lucy, who said she could start immediately. After a short exchange of emails, Sinead offered her the job, relieved to tick one burden off her endless list. She assumed the au pair website pre-vetted its users, giving her a mistaken sense of comfort.

As August 2016 drew to a close, one bright morning she drove to the bus stop in Westport to collect her new nanny. 'I remember it so clearly,' she said. 'There was a big crowd that day, and I spotted her right away. For some reason I just knew it was her. She had a lovely, kind face.'

Then something caught her attention. 'All she had with her was a small plastic bag and a tiny backpack. That was it. I thought it was weird, but I shrugged it off. Maybe she just travels lighter than me.'

They chatted on the drive home. Lucy was well spoken, her accent an upper-class British lilt. She asked about the children, remembered their names right away and laughed easily. At home, the children were instantly smitten. Rory, bright-eyed and boisterous, fell for her the hardest. 'He just lit up around her,' Sinead said. 'It was like he'd known her forever.'

From that first evening, Lucy seemed to weave herself into the household effortlessly. Dinner, bedtime, homework, everything felt smoother. The house, which often sounded like a small riot was occurring, fell into a rhythm.

But even on the first night, something strange happened. 'After the kids were in bed,' Sinead remembered, 'she went down to the bathroom. When she came back up, her hair was different, shorter, darker brown. I swear, it had been light when she arrived. I just stared.'

Lucy laughed and brushed it off, saying she'd 'got sick of the colour'. Sinead smiled along, though an uneasy flicker passed through her. 'It was odd,' she admitted later, 'but she seemed so normal, so polite. I told myself I was overthinking it.'

Within days, Lucy had transformed the household. She organised morning routines, got the children tidying up after themselves, even started making sandwiches for Sinead's husband to take to work. 'I nearly laughed,' Sinead said, 'when he told me she'd packed his lunch for him. She was like a dream.'

On their first Friday evening, Sinead came home to find the children sitting neatly at the table, eating together without chaos. When they finished, Rory turned to her and asked, 'May I be excused?' Sinead nearly dropped her fork. 'I just looked at my husband, and we both started laughing. I thought, *Who is this woman? She's a miracle worker*.'

But Samantha Cookes was not a miracle worker. She was, once again, manufacturing a story, one that would not end in kindness.

* * *

At first, it was nothing more than an oddity. Lucy had arrived with a tiny backpack and a plastic shopping bag, promising that her belongings would follow on 'tomorrow'. When nothing arrived the next day, or the day after, she laughed it off. 'You know what couriers are like,' she said.

Weeks later, the story still hadn't changed, but the missing luggage had become a quiet presence in Sinead's mind. No courier was this inefficient. Lucy seemed to be re-wearing the same few outfits over and over, and seemed to have very few belongings at all. 'She kept saying her things would be here "soon",' Sinead remembered, 'but after a while, I realised there was nothing to arrive.'

Lucy was full of tall tales, informing Sinead of her publishing deal with Penguin for the children's book she was writing. 'She said they were waiting on final illustrations,' Sinead later recalled, 'and that the story was about a girl who could talk to the sea. It almost sounded too poetic to question.'

Still, curiosity nagged at Sinead. One morning after the school run, she searched online for Penguin's contact number, dialled the UK line and asked to be put through to someone who dealt with upcoming books. 'I remember standing there, twisting the phone cord around my finger,' she said. 'I asked if they had an author called Lucy Fitzpatrick and they said no one by that name had ever published with them.'

'I thanked them and hung up, and that's when the dread came in,' she said. 'My stomach just dropped. I thought, what's going on here?' Sinead was acutely aware that in the desperate rush to secure childcare she had never actually received any references for her new nanny. She started to wonder if the au pair website actually vetted its candidates.

She called her mother, her voice shaking. 'I told her everything – the missing bags, the fake book deal.' Her mother's reply was blunt: 'You need to be sure who's in your house.'

Together, they devised a plan. Sinead's mother would invite Lucy over to her house on the pretence of needing help reupholstering a sofa, a chore that would keep her busy and out of the way long enough for Sinead to have a look in her room.

'When I opened that door, I felt like I'd broken into my own home,' she recalled. 'It felt wrong.'

Inside, there was almost nothing. A few notebooks stacked neatly on the dresser. One pair of shoes lined up by the skirting board. 'She'd been living with us for weeks and there was nothing there,' Sinead said. 'It gave me chills.'

Sinead sat down, leafing through one of the notebooks. One page outlined a plan for 'a class in a local hotel for children with Down Syndrome'. 'It was bizarre,' she recalled. 'I'd never heard her mention anything about teaching or qualifications.'

Panic began to mount. 'I didn't know what to think. Was she lying about everything? Or was I overreacting?' She phoned her husband immediately. 'We decided that once the kids were in bed that night, we'd sit her down and talk.'

That evening, after the bedtime stories were done and the lights switched off, Sinead found Lucy in the kitchen, humming quietly while scrubbing dishes. 'Lucy, do you mind if we have a chat?'

They sat together in the living room. Sinead's pulse thudded in her ears. 'Everything's going really well,' she began carefully. 'The kids love you. But to move forward, we'll need some identification, maybe a passport or a bank card.' Sinead described what happened next as 'like flicking a switch'.

'The kind, gentle person I thought I knew was gone,' she said. 'Her whole face changed.'

In a voice harder than her usual gentle tones, Lucy snapped, 'If there's no trust, then I can't be here.' She stormed out of the room and down the hallway to her bedroom, slamming the door. Stunned, Sinead looked at her husband. Before she could speak, he followed Lucy. 'He told her that if she didn't show ID, we'd have to call the Gardaí,' Sinead said.

That brought her back out. Lucy stood in the doorway crying, incoherent, insisting she couldn't be questioned like this. 'She kept saying we'd ruined everything,' Sinead said softly. 'I'd never seen anyone unravel that quickly.'

Through sobs, Lucy declared she would leave that night. Sinead protested. 'I didn't want to throw her out into the dark – we live miles from anywhere,' she said. 'I told her, if you still feel that way in the morning, I'll drive you to the bus stop.'

Lucy's tears subsided. She asked if she could speak to Sinead alone.

'When my husband left the room, she looked up at me with those sad eyes and said she'd fled a violent relationship, that she'd been raped. That's why she had no belongings, no identification. I felt the air leave my lungs.'

At this point, Sinead didn't know what to believe. She nodded, mumbling reassurances, but the words barely reached her own ears. 'My mind was spinning,' she said. 'I didn't know if she was dangerous, or if I was being cruel to someone genuinely broken.' It was agreed that Lucy would stay the night at least.

Later, as Sinead lay awake, a horrible realisation struck her. For weeks, Lucy had been oddly fixated on her son Rory's passport. She had mentioned helping 'sort the papers' on more than one occasion, claiming it was needed for future family travel, but her focus had been on Rory exclusively. 'I just lay there staring at the ceiling,' Sinead said. 'Why did she want my child to have a passport? Why so keen?'

Sleep never came that night. Sinead lay listening to every creak and whisper of the house, half expecting footsteps outside her door. At dawn, she rose, heart pounding, and knocked gently on Lucy's door. She half expected the room to be empty, but when the door opened, there Lucy was, seemingly bright and unbothered. 'She was her usual self again,' Sinead said. 'Smiling, calm, cheerful, like none of it had happened.'

Lucy asked if Sinead could give her a lift to Westport. 'She said she was visiting friends.' Sinead agreed. It was Saturday 22 October, and, with the children in the car, she drove Lucy to the bus stop. Lucy thanked her warmly, waving from the pavement. 'Okay, thanks, bye, see you later,' she called. Her voice floated through the open window, light as ever.

Sinead watched her walk away, the small backpack slung over one shoulder, disappearing into the crowd around the bus shelter. She sat for a long moment before turning the car back towards home. *Goodbye, Lucy*, she thought, *that's the last I'm going to see of you*.

She was right. She never saw Lucy in Mayo again.

* * *

Sinead kept repeating the same phrase to herself in the days after Lucy vanished. 'These things don't happen in Ireland. It was like something out of a movie.'

Despite the fact that Lucy was gone, she still couldn't shake the feeling of unease that had enveloped her. One rainy afternoon, she sat the children down for a talk, to try to understand what had truly happened inside their home. The little ones squirmed and fidgeted, confused by the seriousness in their mother's voice. Rory looked close to tears when she asked about Lucy. He was missing her.

'The children really did love her,' Sinead said. 'That was the hardest part.'

But as they spoke, a pattern emerged that turned her stomach cold. From the start, Lucy had shown a strange preference for Rory. The twins said that 'Lucy always wanted Rory for herself,' that he got gifts no one else did. 'Rory told me,' Sinead said quietly, 'that she used to leave him little toys under his pillow. It was her secret with him.' He kept it to himself so as to not upset his siblings who were missing out.

Then came another revelation, one that made Sinead's hands tremble. One of the twins explained, almost innocently, that when 'Mum was out,' Lucy would sometimes dress her up like a boy. 'She called me "Michael!"' the little girl giggled, oblivious to her mother's dawning terror.

'That's when I froze,' Sinead recalled. 'Something in me felt this wasn't just eccentricity.'

And still, the question of why Lucy had pushed so hard for Rory's passport gnawed at her. Why so much interest in the paperwork of one small boy?

She went back into Lucy's bedroom and began to search it properly this time. Closets, drawers, under the mattress were all checked. When she pulled open the bedside locker, her breath caught. Inside lay four mobile phones, the batteries and SIM cards neatly removed. She wondered if they were burner phones, something she'd only ever seen on TV before. 'It was the most chilling thing I'd ever seen,' she said. 'It wasn't messy or panicked. It was deliberate.'

A sick feeling coiled in her chest. Her hands shook as she struggled to put the batteries and SIMs back in the phones. When she tried it, the first didn't come on. Neither did the second. By the third, her nerves were fraying. Finally, with the fourth, the little screen flashed to life.

There was only one number in its call log. With her heart hammering, she dialled it. The line rang once. Twice. Then a voice answered, low and cautious: 'Who is this?'

Sinead's words tumbled out uncontrollably, how she'd hired a nanny called Lucy Fitzpatrick, how she now feared she was someone else entirely. The voice on the other end of the phone sounded urgent and panicked. 'I don't know who you are, calling from this number,' the woman whispered, 'but if you've had her in your house, go to the Gardaí. Go to the Gardaí and keep your children safe. Once you've spoken to the Gardaí you call me again and I'll tell you my story. Hurry.'

The line went dead. Sinead stood very still, the phone heavy in her hand. Her mind reeled. Within minutes she had thrown coats on the children and was driving, barely seeing the road. At the local Garda station, she rushed to the desk, words spilling out before she could think. 'We had this woman in our house. I don't think she's who she says she is. I don't know who she is or where she is now.'

As she spoke, her confidence began to wobble. 'It sounded mad, like something from a film,' she said later. 'I half thought they'd laugh me out the door.'

She gave them the name Lucy Fitzpatrick and the one photo she possessed from Rory's first day of Senior Infants, when Lucy had insisted on taking a group picture outside the school gates. 'It was the only clear one of her,' Sinead said. 'She hated being photographed.' She gave them the burner phone, told them of the woman at the other end of the line urging her to speak to the Gardaí.

The officer disappeared for what felt like an eternity. When he returned, everything about him had changed – his tone, his posture, even his breathing. 'He told me he couldn't say much,' Sinead said. 'But he said one thing very clearly. Keep this woman away from your children.'

Her stomach dropped. 'He gave me a new name,' she said. 'Samantha Cookes.'

Sinead drove home in silence. Once inside, she sat at the kitchen table and typed the name into Google. There it was, missing person reports from the UK, news clips about a conviction for surrogacy fraud.

'I felt sick,' Sinead said. 'She'd been sleeping under my roof. Eating at my table. Helping with my children's homework.'

The Garda had asked her to print the photograph of Lucy and give it to Rory's teacher, to make absolutely sure that Samantha, or whatever name she might use next, could never approach the school gates. Sinead did it that same day, the printer humming while she fought back tears.

'I just kept thinking, *I* let her in,' she said, 'into my home, into my family's life. I'll never forgive myself for that.'

Outside, the Mayo wind swept across the fields, rattling the empty gate where Lucy had once stood smiling, waving to the children as they left for school.

12

REBECCA FITZGERALD

From Edenderry to Tullamore, Dublin to Mayo, Samantha Cookes had moved with unnerving ease. Untouched, unstoppable and growing bolder with every lie. Each scam was more intricate than the last, and her confidence swelled as she continued to evade any consequences for her actions in Ireland. But Samantha was no longer content to linger in familiar territory. In 2017 her boldest con yet took place in the south, in the vibrant streets of Cork, where she was living under a new identity, 'Rebecca Fitzgerald', and claiming to be a fully qualified child psychologist with a specialism in autism.

Julie Lee, originally from South Africa, had long made Fermoy, County Cork, her home. A steady presence on the town's winding roads, she worked as a taxi driver, ferrying people to and fro through the ebb and flow of daily life. One day in February 2017, she met Rebecca, a charming, sweet Englishwoman who didn't drive and needed lifts to visit the homes of children with special needs, including autism, across the county. The rides stretched longer than most, and each journey was punctuated with stories of Rebecca's 'important work' helping families struggling against unseen battles.

Julie found herself drawn in by Rebecca's warmth and apparent dedication. She became Rebecca's trusted driver, her partner in the field as they moved from house to house, client to client. What intrigued Julie most was seeing Rebecca leave some homes after sessions clutching cash payments, an unspoken testament to her success.

Rebecca was living as an au pair with a local family, arranging her psychology appointments for when the children were in school. The weeks flew by and their new routine of taxi collections and drop-offs settled into a rhythm. 'She seemed so genuine, so committed,' Julie later reflected. Yet beneath the façade, crafted with effortless ease by Samantha Cookes, lay a story untold. Julie, unknowingly, was a witness to the next chapter in Cookes' ever-expanding web of deceit.

One day, out of the blue, Rebecca informed Julie that she was buying a house. When they drove past it, she pointed it out with pride – a large property with impressive, imposing gates. On multiple occasions she requested that Julie drop her there and wait while she quickly collected some post, something Julie didn't question even though Rebecca hadn't yet moved in. What she did notice was that Rebecca never returned with any parcels or envelopes, only silence and the faintest hint of something off.

Months passed and as Samantha got comfortable in her new community of Fermoy, her latest ruse in her role as Rebecca Fitzgerald began – a series of classes for children with special needs. Mothers paid eagerly, hopeful for support, but the classes fizzled out after one or two sessions. Then came a proposed Disneyland trip, by now a well-worn trope of Cookes' deception pattern. A fairytale adventure she insisted would include Julie's young daughter, Rebecca was organising a group trip, or so she claimed, painting vibrant pictures of a magical escape she never actually booked and for which, luckily, no one paid.

She spoke about setting up a day centre for children with additional needs, her gaze fixed on a half-finished building in town. 'A sensory room, everything we need,' she promised, her tone full of conviction. But the story then shifted, and the supposed centre was relocated to an abandoned site that Julie knew could not be right. Suspicion crept in. Rebecca offered Julie a job at this new day centre, in which Julie would be trained to work with children with additional needs. It was one of many jobs she offered to numerous people in Fermoy. During this time one young woman recalls an interview with Rebecca for a job as a babysitter for two disabled children Rebecca claimed were being adopted abroad by her husband. The job never materialised, and neither did the children nor the husband. In fact, the house she held the interview in was the house where she worked as an au pair, not her own family home as she had claimed.

At a training day for the new day centre held in a local hotel, Rebecca was in her element, commanding attention and basking in the admiration of the small group attending with the promise of employment. Then came a startling moment. 'I'll show you how to tube feed,' she declared. Julie was taken aback. 'Why? Would we be doing that?' she asked. 'Why would we be doing something so specialised? Shouldn't we have proper medical training for something like that?' Rebecca brushed the question off, replying breezily, 'Oh, yes, you're going to be doing that. Don't worry, it's easy when you know how.' Julie knew then, at that moment, something was very wrong. No one could learn to tube feed a child with special needs in a few rushed minutes at one training day and no unqualified stranger should be trusted with such a task. Her unease lingered as she left the training room that day, a cold certainty that something sinister was afoot.

That very evening Julie called the Gardaí. 'There's a woman here posing as a therapist. She's going into children's homes, she comes out with cash. She said she's setting up a centre for children with additional needs, but I think none of it is true. There's something not right. You need to look into her.' They promised to investigate. However, when Julie went the next day to the house Rebecca was staying in, she discovered the au pair-cum-therapist had vanished, disappearing without a trace. Yet again, Samantha Cookes was one step ahead. How she knew things had come to a head is unclear, but perhaps she had become so finely attuned to people cottoning on to her that she sensed Julie's unease during the training day. Or felt the shift in Julie's tone as she slipped out the door that evening without the usual goodbyes.

Samantha Cookes was on the run again.

Years later, Lynn, in Dublin, recoiled when she learned about the feeding tube incident in Cork. 'My Daisy had one. I used all the terminology in our house, Samantha would have learned all that lingo here, watching me and the nurses managing Daisy's care,' she said, voice tight with anger. 'It sickens me that Samantha twisted it for her own fantasy.'

For Julie, in Cork, the shock remained. How could a woman who worked with vulnerable children for so long, weaving lies, then vanish like smoke into thin air? What Julie didn't know at the time, was that some form of minor justice was about to catch up with the woman she knew as Rebecca Fitzgerald.

* * *

During her time as Rebecca, Samantha Cookes had become embroiled in the life of Tom (not his real name). Tom's world was one of waiting and worry. His child, bright and hopeful, was desperately in need of an autism diagnosis. This would be the key that would unlock access to a special needs assistant at school, essential for helping them stay in mainstream education. Without this official recognition, the path ahead was bleak and uncertain.

Into their lives stepped child psychologist Rebecca Fitzgerald. Tom was immediately relieved. Rebecca seemed perfect – knowledgeable, compassionate and eager to help – and she agreed without hesitation to conduct the assessment. She even visited the school his child attended, and Tom remembered how impressed the staff were. 'She had all the lingo,' he said, 'making suggestions that made her sound like a pro. The teachers thought she was wonderful. They were writing down some of her ideas to implement themselves.' Tom paid her €840 to both carry out sessions with his child and supply an official report on their diagnosis.

The problems began when the promised official report didn't arrive. Weeks passed and Tom chased Rebecca repeatedly, growing frustrated and anxious. Finally, with no sign of progress and Rebecca becoming distant and unresponsive, he reported the issue to the Gardaí. Their investigation uncovered the devastating truth. Rebecca was not a child psychologist. Her name wasn't even Rebecca. Her real name was Samantha Cookes and the promised diagnosis and report was a cruel mirage.

Eventually, in 2019, at Fermoy District Court, the Gardaí proceeded with action against Samantha Cookes and she was found guilty of 'Making Gain or Causing Loss by Deception' under Section 6 of the Criminal Justice (Theft and Fraud Offences) Act 2001. This related to charging Tom to supply a psychologist's report in order to access a special needs assistant in school. Notably, in Irish law, as of early 2026, 'psychologist' is not a protected term, meaning it is currently not a criminal offence for an unqualified person to call themselves a psychologist, and CORU (Ireland's regulator for health and social care professionals) cannot prosecute someone for using that title. Hence, monetary fraud was all Cookes could be charged with.

Lynn and Hillery in Dublin were not aware at the time of the conviction in Fermoy District Court that their cases of monies lost for the bogus Lapland trip had been linked to Samantha Cookes by Gardaí, and had also been brought into the Fermoy court proceedings. Samantha was found guilty in both cases of theft, contrary to Section 4 of the Criminal Justice (Theft and Fraud Offences) Act 2001. She received a fourteen-week jail term, which was suspended. Just like her conviction for surrogacy fraud in the UK back in 2011, she again evaded prison. Her victims felt this suspended sentence was no more than a slap on the wrist. It certainly did not deter her from her deceptive ways. In fact, Cookes' biggest scam of all was yet to come. This time she would go on to deceive not just vulnerable families and communities, but also the Irish State.

13

SAMANTHA BLACK AND JADE WILLIAMS

Rebecca Fitzgerald vanished from Fermoy under cover of darkness. One evening she was there, smiling, chatting, behaving as though the world owed her no notice, and by dawn she was gone. No farewell, no trail, only the faint echo of confusion and betrayal left behind.

Prior to her conviction in 2019 in Fermoy District Court, during the summer of 2017, Samantha Cookes was still living in County Cork, a mere fifty-minute drive from Fermoy. Now based in Kinsale, under yet another invented name, 'Becca', she began attending Kinsale Baptist Church, a small, tight-knit congregation that prided itself on openness and quiet faith. To them, Becca was polite and attentive, if sometimes a little withdrawn. There was nothing unusual about her. She blended in so seamlessly that no one thought to question her.

Then, one Sunday morning in late September, with Becca missing from the church service, the Gardaí arrived. They spoke quietly to the pastor first, their expressions grave. Word moved through the pews like a slow, cold ripple. Becca wasn't Becca at all. She was Samantha Cookes, a woman with a past no one there could quite comprehend. Yet she had taken nothing from them, stolen no money, uttered no clear deceit. She simply vanished that week, leaving behind a strange, collective bewilderment, as if a shadow had passed over their bright little community. It is not known what prompted the Gardaí to appear in Kinsale, or how Samantha managed to once again slip away undetected.

Weeks later, Samantha turned up at Carrigaline Baptist Church, less than half an hour's drive from Kinsale, as 'Sam', saying she worked for the Ombudsman's office in Cork. The claim sounded plausible enough, but something about her delivery made people ill at ease. She mentioned, inexplicably, that she had sat her Leaving Certificate in Irish – a peculiar lie, given that, for all she knew, any of the congregants may have been fluent and could have exposed her instantly. Luckily for her, that was not the case.

During services, Sam would sit near the back, quietly writing in a small notebook. No one knew what she was recording there – prayers, perhaps? observations? – but it unsettled people in ways they couldn't quite express. One woman wondered if Sam was secretly a journalist writing a piece on their community. However, one Sunday, both she and the notebook disappeared without a goodbye, leaving only the faint echo of her presence and a growing sense among those who had met her that they had brushed against something unknowable.

Then, for the first time in her restless tapestry of invention, Samantha Cookes did something entirely uncharacteristic. She became herself.

With a new blonde bob and a renewed air of purpose, in the late autumn of 2017 she turned up at the gates of Bessborough

Adult Education Centre in County Cork to join the local Leaving Certificate group under her real name. The Education Centre was a mere thirty-six kilometres from where she had been living as Rebecca Fitzgerald. Her presence there among students half her age was noted but not questioned. She told them, with her usual steady confidence, that her A-levels from England had 'expired'. The seventeen-year-olds, still too green to know otherwise, shrugged and accepted the explanation. After all, Samantha always sounded convincing.

Bessborough was no ordinary educational setting. The Adult Education Centre stood near the grounds of the old Bessborough Mother and Baby Home, a place steeped in tragic history. Between the 1920s and 1990s, thousands of unmarried women had been sent there, their babies taken from them, many never leaving the grounds alive. The very soil of that place held secrets, generations deep.

What is curious is that Samantha appeared not to be running any scams during this period. There were no grand deceptions, no elaborate fabrications to extract money or sympathy. Instead, she blended in, studious, polite, even disciplined. She attended classes from November 2017 until June 2018 preparing for exams she did not need. It was as if she were trying something new, rehearsing a role still being written in her mind.

When the examination season arrived, she sat each paper formally under the watchful eyes of invigilators. One later recalled her clearly, not because of her answers, but because of something oddly mundane. Samantha never handed in her Home Economics exam paper. One script short, the invigilator searched the desks in confusion, unaware that the missing sheet would remain a small but telling fingerprint of Samantha's time there, an errant detail that hinted, perhaps, at the habit she could never fully break.

What she took from Bessborough remains unknown. Yet those months, so apparently quiet, marked a turning point. In that place, within sight of the ghosts of women who had also lived under false names, something took root. A seed of reinvention that would soon grow into her most audacious performance yet.

It was after Bessborough that something in Samantha seemed to shift. The quiet months had done what years of chaos and deceit never had: they had given her time to think. For a woman who lived through constant invention, stillness was dangerous. Reflection gave rise to imagination, and imagination, in Samantha's hands, was never benign.

It would take a little while, but eventually a character emerged who appeared to have distilled all her previous guises into one perfected creation. Gone was Lucy Fitzwilliams, the honey-tongued therapist who could charm her way into any family's home. Gone were Sophia Williamson, Lucy Hart, Lucy Fitzpatrick and Rebecca Fitzgerald. In their place appeared a woman of poise and conviction, the founder of a cause so noble, so emotionally resonant, it silenced doubt before it could form. It was an identity born not merely from deceit, but from understanding what people wanted to believe.

Perhaps it was Bessborough's shadow that sparked it, the lingering ghosts of women forced to surrender their identities, robbed of their right to tell their own stories. Whether consciously or not, Samantha seemed to pluck something from that soil – a sense of injustice, of tragic narrative, ready to be repurposed. She began to weave a story of salvation and service, of resilience in the face of pain, which drew the sympathy and trust of all who heard it.

Friends, colleagues and strangers would all recall the same thing – that she spoke with such conviction they felt almost privileged to believe her. Every anecdote was calibrated, every tear strategically shed. The result was a persona both magnetic and untouchable.

Samantha Cookes, the girl who once vanished into the night, had returned with a vengeance, not merely as herself, but as something far more dangerous, a woman whose truth and lies were indistinguishable, perhaps even to her.

* * *

In May 2019, after her conviction in Fermoy District Court, Samantha left Cork behind and moved west, stepping neatly into the busy, tangled life of Claire, a thirty-eight-year-old mother of four in Galway who was perpetually balancing a cup of lukewarm coffee on the edge of a countertop and was, at that moment in time, in a quite a fix. The school WhatsApp groups were already clogging her phone with messages about summer-term projects, while her youngest daughter had developed a habit of climbing onto the kitchen island during moments of chaos.

With Claire due to return to work as a Health and Safety Officer, after being off for some time, the Spanish au pair imminently due to arrive had seemed like salvation in her online communications: cheerful, qualified and perfectly timed. But on the morning of her flight, a text in broken English arrived, an injury, an apology, no flight after all. The au pair would not be travelling to Ireland as she took time to recover. Claire had stared at her phone for a long time, as the toast burned behind her and two of the children argued about socks. Monday loomed. Work loomed. Life loomed.

By mid-afternoon, she was online, trawling discussion boards, Facebook groups and dubious listings for childcare. Her posts took on a pleading tone: Urgent, need live-in help ASAP. The responses were either automated or apathetic until, just after eight o'clock that evening, her phone buzzed.

'Hello Claire,' the message read. 'My name is Samantha Black. I'm in Ireland at the moment and can start right away. I have a decade of experience with children and references if you'd like to see them.' The name felt reassuringly ordinary, so Claire didn't question it. She simply exhaled, her shoulders dropping in brief, exhausted relief. She would later remember that moment, the quiet click of trust forming, as if it were the first domino to fall.

After a brief phone call, Claire was delighted. The woman's voice on the other end was warm, confident, precisely what she needed. Samantha spoke of years in America working as a nanny for wealthy families in Boston and New York. Trained, discreet, professional. She even offered to do a free trial for a week, to 'make sure it was the right fit'. 'I can be with you on Sunday,' she said. The calm assurance in her tone felt like a rescue line. Claire clung to it.

That Sunday morning, Claire collected Samantha from the bus stop in Galway. As the composed woman approached, a small rucksack slung over one shoulder, Claire thought it odd that someone would travel so light. Samantha explained that all her belongings from America were locked away in a storage container in Cork. She'd lost the access code, she said, but she'd sort it soon. 'And it's only a trial week,' she added with a smile. 'No sense dragging everything with me just yet.'

It sounded reasonable and Claire was eager to see reason wherever she could find it. When she asked for the references, Samantha apologised – their details, too, were inconveniently trapped in the storage unit. But they'd be sent on, of course, once she regained access. Claire nodded, reassured by the promise.

That Sunday afternoon, Claire brought Samantha straight to the family dinner at her husband's mother's house. Within an hour, Samantha Black was a sensation. She was on the lawn, running after children and cousins, laughing breathlessly, hair coming loose in the wind. 'What do you think of my new Mary Poppins?' Claire joked to her mother-in-law, pride lighting her face.

Samantha was charming, effortlessly so. She told the children stories that seemed to spill from nowhere, about pirates and lost treasures, glittering cities, enchanted woods. She had the table covered in coloured paper and glue before dessert was served. The house rang with laughter. By evening, there wasn't a soul who hadn't fallen a little in love with Samantha Black.

However, the stories Samantha told the children weren't the only ones she spun. Her 'trial week' soon became a permanent role, but, as the bright weeks of summer settled in, the tales she shared over evening dinners grew stranger, just enough to skirt the edge of believability. She told Claire that she'd been adopted from a mother-and-baby home in Bessborough, and that she was now searching for her birth family. The story carried just the right balance of sadness and mystery. Claire listened, moved, pouring another glass of wine, assuring her that she was brave to look. Then, one evening, Samantha announced she had found her birth sister in Ireland, but her birth mother had died years before. Claire's heart broke for her kind, steady nanny. What an awful twist, to come so far only to find the door closed. The mysterious sister never appeared, but Claire, polite and compassionate, didn't pry.

It seemed Samantha was finding her place in the community too. She joined a local church, and every Sunday morning Claire dropped her off at the gates with a cheerful wave. Soon there was a new friend named Theresa (not her real name), warm, devout, full of kind words about Samantha. The two women became inseparable, often disappearing for coffee or meetings at the parish hall. Claire was glad, truly glad, that her nanny had found companionship.

But somewhere along the way, odd things began to happen. Keys went missing only to reappear in the wrong place. The remote control turned up in the fridge. Claire's phone, a sleek, pink-cased lifeline, was found in the kitchen when she could swear she'd left it on the sofa. Once, she laughed it off, then twice, then three times. Eventually the laughter tightened into unease. Was she really becoming that forgetful? Was this normal?

One bleary August morning, after yet another frantic search for her car keys, Samantha gave Claire a look of quiet concern. 'Maybe you should get that checked out with a doctor?' It was said softly, helpfully, but the words landed heavily. Claire brushed it off with a laugh, but later, driving to work, she caught herself wondering. Was she really forgetting things?

Then came another announcement: Samantha was engaged, to a man named Paul, a man from a neighbouring town she'd met through church. Claire smiled at first, but the oddness of it pricked at her mind. She'd never seen this mysterious Paul, never once dropped Samantha off or seen a text flash across her phone. Whenever Claire gently asked about him, there was always a story – he worked odd hours, he travelled for business, he preferred privacy.

In September, for her daughter's birthday, Claire decided to test her doubts. 'Tell Paul to come,' she said brightly. Samantha agreed immediately. But when the day arrived, with its cakes, bunting and laughter, there was no Paul and no message, no explanation beyond a vague excuse about family issues.

'Something's not right,' Claire whispered to her husband that night. Yet even as she said it, uncertainty crept in. Samantha was good with the children, brilliant even. The house ran smoother with her there. And, truthfully, Claire was exhausted. Between long hours at work and the chaos of four children, she was forever chasing her own tail, losing things, doubting herself. She felt something was off with her nanny but hoped she was just imagining it.

By October, however, the balance had started to shift. One rainy Saturday, Claire sat down with her daughters for some painting. The girls lingered briefly, then drifted away to Samantha's room. When Claire followed, she found all four of them huddled together, reading glossy children's magazines, each one costing about eleven euros apiece. A bit expensive for casual gifts from a nanny, Claire thought. She had noticed other gifts recently too, paint sets and new shiny books. Was Samantha buying their affection? The question burned quietly, something she swallowed before it reached her lips. Perhaps she was just being unkind, stung that her children had chosen reading in Samantha's room over arts and crafts with their mother.

November came, and with it new absences. Theresa stopped

calling. Church was never mentioned again. And then, one cold evening, Claire lost her wedding ring. It had slipped off while she was driving home from work and by the time she parked at home, it had vanished. Samantha appeared outside, sympathetic, helping her search the gravel drive. The ring couldn't be found. It had been her mother's legacy, irreplaceable. Claire mourned it privately.

Two months later, Samantha delivered her most astonishing news yet. She appeared in the kitchen doorway one dull January evening and said, almost casually, 'Paul's father died this morning.'

Claire froze, shocked by the flatness of her tone. Still, at least now there was something she could verify. Ireland was small; deaths left traces. That night, she opened her laptop and searched Paul's surname on RIP.ie. Nothing. She searched again under variations. Still nothing. Unease clawed at her. Days later, she phoned the church, speaking quietly to the pastor. When she explained, his sigh came heavy down the line.

'Yes, there's a Paul,' he said, 'but his father's alive and well. Name's Ray. Would you like his number?'

When Ray answered, his voice was tentative, kind but puzzled. Claire explained everything, her voice shaking, her words spilling over one another. A pause followed, deep and echoing.

'Claire,' said Ray finally, 'I don't know you. But that woman, Samantha, she was in our church, yes. She left after a disagreement. She's not marrying my son. They were never together. And I can assure you, I'm very much alive. You need to get that woman out of your house. And keep your children safe.'

Claire's heart slammed against her ribs. The kitchen around her blurred. For a long moment, she couldn't speak, couldn't breathe.

Who was the woman sleeping down the hall? What did she want from them?

Claire was so frazzled she could hardly think straight. Every kind of thought ran through her mind, tumbling over itself like waves in a storm. Each time she misplaced her keys or lost her phone, the same question came crawling back: Was Samantha there? Was she doing this to me? The questions multiplied. Why lie about a fiancé? Why invent the death of his father? Why fabricate a sister no one had ever seen? None of it made sense, and yet the pattern was unmistakable – whatever Samantha wanted, it wasn't work or wages.

She and her husband decided to call the Gardaí. The officers listened carefully but, in the end, their hands were tied. Samantha Black hadn't committed a crime, not yet. 'You hired her willingly,' one of them said gently. 'She's done her job, hasn't she?'

Claire hung up, frustration burning in her chest. She knew. Deep in that quiet, unmistakable place that mothers keep for danger. Samantha had to go.

The next morning, mid-January, she set the table carefully: two mugs of tea, a plate of toast neither of them would touch. When Samantha sat down, all calm smiles, Claire launched into the script she'd rehearsed. 'I've been looking at the finances,' she began, her voice too bright. 'We just can't afford the help right now. I'm sorry, Samantha. I'll have to let you go.'

For a moment, silence. Then something shifted. The soft, pleasant mask cracked. Samantha's temper flared like a match. She slammed her palm against the table, voice rising in shocked fury, accusing Claire of betrayal, of ingratitude. Cupboards banged, a door upstairs shook its frame. Claire sat frozen, pulse hammering, the calm gone. When the noise stopped, the house felt cavernous.

Hours later, Samantha reappeared in the living-room doorway, composed again, her expression unreadable. 'I'll need you to give me a reference,' she said flatly.

Claire nodded at once, afraid not to. 'Of course. Whatever you need.' But her stomach twisted. She didn't want to condemn another family, yet with Samantha watching her so intently, she could not refuse. Moments later, as if the universe were testing her resolve, Claire's phone rang. A man's voice came through, polite, steady, introducing himself as a father from Dublin. 'We're considering taking Samantha on,' he said. 'Could you tell us what she was like?'

Claire could feel Samantha's eyes on her, silent and unblinking. Every word felt like walking a tightrope over something dark and bottomless. Samantha had clearly given her name as a reference before she'd even asked her permission. 'She's ... very good with the children,' Claire managed. 'They love her.' It was the truth, but only part of it. When the call ended, she felt sick. She'd handed another family into the lion's den.

That night, Claire didn't sleep. She lay in the dark listening, every sound amplified, every creak of the floorboards weighted with dread. 'It seems absurd now,' she would tell people later, 'but that night, I was certain – absolutely certain – that she might come into my room and kill me. I lay awake until morning, listening for her footsteps.'

The morning Samantha left in late January 2020 was bitterly cold. The sky hung low, the kind of washed-out grey that promised rain but never delivered. Inside the house, chaos reigned. The children were inconsolable, red-eyed and trembling, their voices breaking as they cried for the nanny they adored.

Claire, standing in the kitchen doorway, could barely look

at them. Part of her wanted to shout, to tell them who this woman really was, or rather, who she wasn't. But instinct held her back. Survival, pure and raw. There was danger in Samantha, something she couldn't name but could feel. The air in the room felt weighted, charged.

She wanted this final meeting to end well, to smooth the edges of whatever storm Samantha might carry with her. Sitting across the kitchen table, she handed her an envelope of wages, everything owed, paid in full. Then, carefully, she slid a small box across the table. 'It's from the children,' she said softly. 'A Claddagh ring, for friendship and loyalty.'

For a moment, Samantha's composure cracked. Her eyes filled, and she stood abruptly, wrapping Claire in a hug that seemed to last too long. Claire stiffened beneath it, her skin crawling. When the hug ended, Samantha smiled, wiped her eyes and carried her small bag to the car. Relief pulsed through Claire like a heartbeat. This was almost over.

Minutes later, one of the girls burst through the back door, breathless.

'Mam! Mammy! Your ring!' she cried.

The little girl held it out on her palm – the wedding ring Claire had lost months before. At first, she could only stare. The gold gleamed faintly in the light. Then the truth slammed into her. She had changed cars since that night in November when it went missing, it was a completely different vehicle. There was no possible way the ring could have been sitting in this one. The only explanation was that Samantha had taken it that night, had hidden it, and for some reason decided, before leaving, to give it back. A last act of twisted sentiment or guilt.

Claire's stomach turned. She said nothing. She simply walked out, helped Samantha load the rest of her things into the boot, and drove her to the bus stop. As Samantha stepped up onto the bus, turning to wave, Claire didn't wave back. She watched until the doors closed and the bus pulled away, shrinking into the distance, carrying the woman and her lies out of their lives. For a long moment, Claire sat there in the car, the ring clenched in her fist, the silence of the morning pressing in. Relief, disbelief, fear – all mixed together. She drove away and didn't look back.

The next morning brought the final blow. Claire was still hollow from the night before when her sister-in-law arrived at the door, breathless, laptop clutched to her chest. 'I've been up all night,' she said, pushing past her into the kitchen. 'You need to see this.'

She set the laptop on the table and clicked through to a news article, an old one, from the UK, dated 2011. The headline mentioned a surrogacy scam that had conned multiple families. Beneath it was a photograph. A woman staring straight out of the image, her expression smooth, practised, familiar. It was Samantha. The same soft auburn hair, the same composure in her eyes. Only the name beneath sent the world tilting: Samantha Cookes.

Claire's stomach dropped. She heard herself say, very faintly, 'Oh my God.' The whole thing, every story, every lie, every charm, fell into place. 'Samantha Black' was just another invention. The adoption, the fiancé, the sister, it had all been a performance.

With a dry mouth, Claire called the Gardaí again, this time with a name that felt like a weapon. She gave them everything she had. Then, terrified of what might come next, she phoned both of the schools her children attended. 'No one but myself or my husband is to collect the children,' she said firmly. 'No exceptions.'

When she hung up, her hands were shaking. *What had that woman wanted?* she wondered. *What was she really after?* The only thing Samantha could have taken from her that truly mattered were the children, and they had adored her. They would have followed her anywhere.

That evening another knock came at the door. When Claire opened it, a pale, shaken Theresa stood there, Samantha's former church friend. 'I'm so sorry,' she whispered. 'I feel so guilty. I heard what happened.' She stepped inside, wringing her hands, and began to speak in fragments at first, then in floods. Stories spilled out, about Samantha fainting dramatically in the middle of Supermac's, only to spring up moments later, perfectly well. About the mysterious fiancé Theresa had never seen. About how Samantha had told people in the parish that Claire was an unfit, neglectful mother stretched beyond her limits.

'She said your family were struggling,' Theresa said quietly. 'That the children went without. She even collected donations for toys, treats, magazines, saying it might bring them some happiness.'

Claire stared at her, numb. The expensive craft sets. The glossy magazines. It all clicked horribly into place. Those gifts hadn't come from Samantha's kindness, they were pity offerings, purchased with money from generous strangers trying to help a family they believed was broken.

Claire could hardly find her voice. 'Why?' she asked finally, her throat raw. 'Why would any woman do something like that to a mother?'

Theresa could only shake her head.

Claire was left deeply shaken by her time with Samantha Cookes. Even after the woman was gone, the house didn't feel like home. The walls seemed to hold her voice, her laughter, the strange stillness she left behind.

About a week later, the phone rang again. It was the man from Dublin, the one she'd spoken to under Samantha's watchful eye. Claire had been afraid to call him, afraid to out Samantha in case she would return to Galway in a fury. His voice was strained.

'We hired her,' he said. 'Samantha. She started on Monday ... but she's gone.'

Claire felt her chest tighten. 'Gone?'

'Vanished,' he said. 'Left without notice. The Gardaí came round after she disappeared, left a card, asking if we could tell her to contact them.'

Claire closed her eyes. The pattern was repeating. Another family fooled, another escape.

'I'm so sorry,' she said quietly. 'I wanted to warn you, I just couldn't.'

There was nothing else to say. After she hung up, the silence settled heavy around her.

In the days that followed, Claire withdrew. She found she couldn't talk about Samantha, not properly, not without her voice trembling. Friends asked after the 'nanny who'd gone', and she'd shrug it off, change the subject. But inside, the fear still lived.

Nights were the worst. Even years later, if her husband was away for work, she couldn't bear to stay in the house alone. She would pack the children into the car, drive the short distance to her in-laws' home, and sleep there. It was irrational, she knew. Samantha was gone. But the feeling that lingered was stronger than reason, the sense that someone who had once smiled across her kitchen table, who had once tucked her children into bed, had walked a little too close to the heart of her life.

Claire never quite shook the sense that Samantha might one day walk back through the door.

* * *

In one of Samantha Cookes' discarded journals she had handwritten the quote: 'Don't close the book when bad things happen in your life, just turn the page and begin a new chapter.' She took her own message to heart as she put Claire and Galway behind her. After a short stay in Dublin she drifted south to an apartment in Bridge Street, Waterford, adopting a new identity. This time she was a self-employed Health and Safety Officer named 'Jade Cooke'. The new role was perhaps inspired by Claire, who had genuinely worked in the field.

This was to be the first, but not the last, time that Samantha Cookes would claim for her own benefit to be terminally ill. While living in Waterford in early 2020, she began communications with the Waterford Social Welfare Office, seeking to begin claiming the State disability welfare benefit. She attempted to evade having to give proof of her alleged terminal illness by claiming that the neurological condition she suffered from made it impossible to hold a pen to fill in paperwork by hand. Also unable to type, the lack of assistive technology available on the Welfare Department's online systems made it impossible for her to fill in the form and so, in turn, impossible to receive the benefit payment.

It would appear Samantha was hoping this gap in the system would allow her to pull the wool over officials' eyes. She suggested that they might make an exception in her instance and wave the submission through with no further questions asked. To her frustration, the request was denied, and so Samantha began building the groundwork required to pull a more sophisticated scam to get past the Irish State's welfare system. In this lay the genesis for her most impressive character yet – Carrie Jade Williams, the terminally ill author. However, Samantha kept this new identity close to her chest for some time, using it only in online writers' groups. She began writing ferociously, sending out drafts of her work under the name Carrie Jade Williams to see who would be the first to bite.

Her efforts paid off when she was offered a two-week residency at Cill Rialaig Writers' Retreat in County Kerry by the Irish Writers Centre. So, the autumn of 2020 saw Samantha migrating further west, to a place filled with artists, writers and opportunity. Her time there gave her a roof over her head for free and an opportunity to write without the distractions of everyday life.

Kerry is a place of wild beauty, where jagged cliffs meet endless grey sea. It has a kind of magic to it, with its storm-lashed coastlines, villages folded into green valleys and people whose trust comes slow but runs deep. It was a quieter world than the towns Samantha had known before, the sort of place where new arrivals still caused a stir and stories took root fast.

Cahersiveen lay on the fringe of that coast, a postcard town framed by the River Fertha and the dark shoulders of the mountains beyond. Tourists came and went each summer, following the Skellig Ring or catching boats to Skellig Michael, but the locals were steady folk, shopkeepers, farmers, schoolteachers, content with their own. It was there that Samantha shed her latest skin and developed the persona of Jade Williams, a version of her writer persona Carrie Jade Williams, who she was still keeping exclusively for online and writers' communities.

After moving around short-term accommodation in the area for some months, when Jade turned up to rent an apartment from Pauline Hayes, she seemed the kind of tenant any landlord would dream of. 'Polite, well-dressed, and with that lovely English accent,' Pauline later recalled, 'the sort that makes you feel like you should offer tea even before she's asked for it.' Jade claimed she was writing a book, part memoir, part research project, and doing health and safety consultancy on the side. She spoke with a quiet assurance, the kind that drew people in. Pauline was charmed. 'She made you feel like you'd known her forever,' she said. 'Smart as anything, too.'

At first, Jade seemed perfect. Months went by with rent paid on time (Samantha had begun doing odd jobs as a cleaner) and no complaints, until, suddenly, there were. It began with calls about the noise from the tenants in Pauline's other unit, downstairs. Jade complained of loud music, shouting, slamming doors. 'She'd ring at all hours,' Pauline said, shaking her head. 'Two in the morning she'd call, whispering like she was in the middle of a siege, "Pauline, it's unbearable again. I can't sleep for the racket."'

Trusting her polished, earnest tenant, Pauline acted. She spoke to the young couple in question, who insisted they were quiet; yet the calls continued. Guilt gnawed at Pauline. Finally, in frustration and against her instincts, she gave the couple notice to leave. Jade seemed relieved, even grateful. Pauline thought the matter was closed.

Then, out of the blue, in late 2021 Jade announced she was moving. Pauline explained, kindly but firmly, that she'd need a month's notice to reclaim her deposit, as was standard procedure for rentals. Jade agreed, or so Pauline thought. When she stopped hearing from her, Pauline called by the flat, only to learn from a neighbour that Jade had packed up and gone. Gone without a word, without even a forwarding address.

As she stepped inside her property, Pauline's heart sank. The apartment she remembered as pristine was unrecognisable. The carpet was filthy, the walls gouged and scratched, the curtains hacked apart as though with scissors. Jade had switched off the freezer before leaving, so a pool of water now seeped across the floor, smelling faintly of rot. 'I couldn't believe it,' Pauline recalled. 'It was like someone else had been living there all along.'

Just as she was piecing together the mess, a letter arrived. Official. From the Residential Tenancies Board, the Irish State body that mediates in landlord–tenant disputes. Jade Williams had filed a complaint. Pauline read it twice, her outrage mounting:

> I hope to achieve
>
> 1. My deposit of 500 euro being returned.
> 2. An agreement to cover my medical costs caused by the failure of the landlord to ensure the safety of the stairwell up to the property.
>
> I am being beyond fair. If this situation escalates through the Personal Injuries Board, the landlord will be facing serious scrutiny.
>
> Due to the nature of my injuries the Personal Injuries Board dictate around 85,000 euros in compensation. I literally am willing to agree to settle this as long as my medical costs of between 1500 and 6000 euros are covered.

Pauline could hardly believe it. 'Medical costs? What medical costs?' she said later. 'The only thing broken in that place was my trust.'

Jade claimed to have suffered a fall and injured herself due to the unsafe nature of the stairwell at the property.

Offered the choice between court and mediation, Pauline opted for the latter, knowing the first would cost time and money she didn't have. She entered the call determined to stand her ground. But Jade – calm, articulate, persistent – wore her down like water eroding stone. Two hours of unrelenting grievances, every complaint delivered with the composure of someone utterly convinced of her own righteousness. By the end, exhausted and defeated, Pauline agreed to pay 400 euros just to end it.

'The money didn't matter,' she said quietly. 'It was the feeling of being tricked. She knew exactly how far to push.'

Pauline has since left the rental market. 'I swore I'd never do it again,' she said. 'If someone like her could fool me, what chance has anyone?'

During this time, under the false names of Jade Williams and S. Jade W. Cooke, Samantha Cookes filed a dispute against Eir (one of Ireland's leading telecommunications companies) as a disgruntled customer with a disability discrimination complaint, and another against a company that had engaged her as a remote worker to edit short video content for them – content she never delivered – also alleging disability discrimination. Samantha took both companies to the Workplace Relations Commission, the Irish State body responsible for promoting good industrial relations and enforcing employment rights. Eir settled with Jade Williams for a figure of €3,000. The video-editing company agreed to pay Jade for the works she had been employed to do but had not produced. Similarly to the Residential Tenancies Board, it appears the Workplace Relations Commission was engaging with a woman whose identity was false, to the detriment of those she was taking cases against.

The years of deception began to shape Samantha in ways that were almost invisible to the casual eye. Alongside financial gain, her lies became part of the reward as well, a private world where she could become anyone she wished, whenever she pleased. The satisfaction of her successes created a feedback loop, strengthening her belief that she was untouchable. In Cahersiveen, Samantha refined this skill to a dangerous edge.

14

HUNTINGTON'S DISEASE

In 2020, just as the world braced for the first tidal wave of the COVID-19 pandemic, Samantha Cookes began a mission that would carry her through the next four years of her life. With the seeds sown in Waterford, she continued to develop the persona of a tragic young woman with a terminal illness – Huntington's disease.

Huntington's is a rare, inherited disorder that damages nerve cells in the brain, leading over time to uncontrollable movements (chorea), loss of coordination, mood swings and serious cognitive decline. Its early symptoms can look like depression, absent-mindedness or clumsiness, but later stages are marked by severe motor and mental disability. The illness is progressive, worsening relentlessly, and there is no cure. It almost always leads to complete dependency in advanced stages.

When the COVID-19 pandemic swept through Ireland in the spring of 2020, daily life across the country changed overnight. Lockdown regulations became the new law. There were strict limits on movement that meant even doctors and health professionals could no longer visit vulnerable patients in person. For most, these new boundaries were a source of fear and inconvenience. For Samantha, they were an opportunity.

It was then, as isolation became routine, that Samantha began to construct this most elaborate deception, pulling a wide range of healthcare professionals, Kerry County Council and the Irish State into her web. One of her most devious scams during this period focused on the work of a charitable organisation striving to support and help its community as best it can. She turned her attention to her local branch of the St Vincent de Paul (SVP) charity, known in Ireland for its community outreach and support for those facing hardship.

SVP is one of Ireland's oldest and most-respected charities. Run almost entirely by volunteers, it provides practical assistance to people in need, from food and clothing to direct financial help, advice and home visits, no matter the circumstances. They operate community resource centres, deliver day care for the elderly, run homeless shelters and offer emotional support, reaching every corner of Irish society. Their approach is deeply personal, meeting with people one-on-one, showing respect and genuine care in even the most challenging of situations.

It was this ethos of trust and compassion that Samantha, in the guise of Jade, exploited with chilling precision. In 2020 she went to them with a tragic story, saying she was battling Huntington's disease, the kind of story designed to disarm even the most sceptical. Subsequently, two volunteers visited Jade outside her apartment in Cahersiveen, keeping a safe distance. They would return on multiple occasions, each time searching for ways to help.

An occupational therapist's assessment supported by SVP soon followed, but with the strict lockdown in place, it had to take place online, over Zoom. Based on Jade's needs, and with in-person visits impossible, the therapist recommended that a Burco boiler would make her life easier to manage. A Burco boiler is a specialised water boiler designed for easy, safe use by the elderly or those with reduced mobility. Safer than a standard kettle, the Burco has features to reduce the risk of burns and accidents. SVP responded immediately, providing the device and ensuring Jade understood how to use it properly and safely.

For a time, it seemed the system had worked as intended. SVP had stepped in swiftly to help a vulnerable person. Then, Jade struck. She sent an official complaint to SVP, alleging 'the contents of a boiled kettle of hot water fell onto my lap and scalded me from my groin down'. She then escalated the matter, threatening the possibility of criminal charges against the volunteer who had supplied the boiler, and suggested a figure for compensation: €6,000.

Whether SVP caved in to her demands remains unknown.

The pandemic may have isolated the world, but for Samantha, it became another stage, proving, yet again, just how far a well-constructed lie, delivered in the right place and at the right time, could go. With hospitals overrun and clinics shuttered, she found it easier than ever to avoid scrutiny. She insisted her Huntington's diagnosis was real but, thanks to COVID restrictions, argued that she couldn't attend in-person appointments or scans. This allowed her to sidestep the usual checks that might have exposed her lies. It was at this point that an emboldened Samantha set her by now well-practised mind on the scam that would eventually be her undoing. Having learned from her experience with the Waterford Social Welfare Office, she now decided she was ready to con the Irish welfare system from her new base in Kerry.

To access Irish disability payments, Samantha needed 'proof' of her Huntington's diagnosis and she went to extraordinary lengths to produce it. She constructed tales for visiting officials, exaggerating or fabricating symptoms, describing involuntary arm movements, tremors in her legs, and the desperate need for mobility aids. On 2 September 2021, still firmly in the role of Jade, she became a patient at a local GP's practice, beginning a relentless, calculated con. Over many months, she wove a complex web of lies around the unsuspecting doctor.

She wasn't just seeing her GP. She regularly attended physiotherapy, dietician sessions and consultations with an occupational therapist and speech and language therapists, who all became unwitting players in her grand deception, striving to help a patient who was, in reality, a master manipulator. Using various iterations of her identities with each practitioner, such as Jade Cooke, Jade Williams, Carrie Williams and Carrie Jade Williams, she claimed her tremors made stairs a nightmare and that she struggled to shower safely, despite having grab rails. Her GP notes recorded her hope that neurology and specialist footwear might ease her symptoms. 'I have an appointment for specialist footwear in the hope this could help a little,' she wrote in correspondence with her GP. 'Ultimately, I didn't want to burden anyone, so I just sort of muddled through.'

Behind her carefully crafted complaints, Samantha cleverly avoided attending neurologist appointments or any scans that might have revealed her fraud. Yet the medical professionals, convinced by her consistent narrative, supported her cause. In

November 2021, as her act reached its zenith, an occupational therapist conducted a remote appointment. Convinced by her performance and stories, the therapist produced a formal report stating:

> At this stage both arms are affected by involuntary movement and her left arm is weaker, she experiences tremors in her legs which is affecting her mobility. Jade requires to use a mobility device. Jade's current home is highly unsuitable for her needs as it is in an inaccessible environment. Jade needs an accessible home urgently. An accessible bungalow type house is essential. A ground floor house is preferred; however, HSE has approved funding for a stairlift for Jade.

In an effort to fully convince her GP of her supposed illness and diagnosis, Samantha utilised the difficulties of obtaining medical documents during the COVID-19 lockdowns. With meticulous care, she used a black marker on reports from her medical appointments with specialists – which she attended under a variety of false names – that worked against her narrative. For example, where a neurologist consultant might write, 'reports to have been diagnosed with Huntington's gene', Samantha would black out 'reports to have been', leaving only 'diagnosed with Huntington's disease' visible, shaping the documents precisely to her advantage and presenting them to her GP as evidence. She would misquote disability laws to allow her to provide photocopies of photo ID, such as her provisional driving licence: 'As someone living with terminal HUNTINGTON'S DISEASE, that includes PARKINSON's type symptoms and EARLY ONSET ALZHEIMER's DISEASE, I am legally allowed under the COVID restrictions to have my certificate photocopied due to accessibility barriers under the Disability Discrimination Act.' This licence was doctored to give the false name Carrie Jade Williams. Her clever invocation of disability laws, which protect individuals requiring reasonable adjustments in accessing services, further hid her deception behind an impenetrable façade. By exploiting legal provisions designed to ease the burdens on disabled people, Samantha was able to navigate medical and governmental systems with near-complete immunity from suspicion.

Eventually, worn down by persistent badgering, Jade's GP produced a medical report stating, 'Jade was diagnosed with Huntington's disease in 2019.' Signed and official, this document became Samantha's golden ticket, legitimacy on paper that opened the door to social welfare funding and an elaborate fiction deeply embedded within the medical system.

For Samantha, the chaos of the pandemic wasn't a barrier, it was a crack in the system she could wedge open, slipping past checks and balances that, in quieter times, might have caught her in the act. By mastering the art of remote persuasion, she extended her con further than ever before, laying the groundwork for schemes that would shock even those who thought they knew her best.

During the same turbulent period that Jade Williams was embroiled in a bitter and costly dispute with her landlord Pauline in Cahersiveen and was hoodwinking the Irish health system, another, more personal, battle was unfolding across the sea in the UK, which revealed the cold depths of Samantha's resolve.

Family members back home were witness to a fracture that ran deeper than grief. According to a cousin, when Samantha's name was mentioned to her father, Leslie, in his final days, he insisted that he did not want to see her. The shame her behaviour had cast over the family was unbearable even in his final hours. And when he passed away, Samantha, still playing the role of the vulnerable and charming Jade in Ireland, simultaneously and deliberately engaged in legal action against her mother and brother over the division of her late father's estate. Letters and demands poured in, harsh and unrelenting. Samantha accused her family of cover-ups, alleging they had hidden a supposed Huntington's diagnosis in childhood from her, accusing them of neglect and worse. These accusations were not only baseless but cruel, weaponised in a ruthless pursuit of 'every penny' she could claim. Eventually, Samantha would reveal that she'd received a lump sum from her late father's estate.

This action uncovers something crucial about Samantha. Despite her endless shape-shifting and complex fabrications in Ireland, she had not lost sight of who she really was beneath the disguises. Jade Williams/Cooke was a mask for the outside world, but Samantha Cookes, the woman writing the legal letters, was present, aware and calculating. She knew her backstory intimately, she just chose whom to share it with, and when. Her dual existence – Jade the injured and vulnerable in Cahersiveen, Samantha the litigator demanding justice in England – showcases an unnerving clarity and control. Far from losing herself in the lies, she wielded her multiple identities adeptly, orchestrating parallel lives as skilfully as a conductor leads an orchestra.

Central to Samantha's deceit in Ireland was a claim that would mobilise empathy. She said she had Huntington's disease, but why chose this specific condition? For Samantha, it wasn't just about the illness, it could also have been about a desperate bid to be special, to stand out in a world where she felt insignificant. Psychologists studying pathological lying report that these individuals often wrestle with low self-esteem. Their lies aren't mere fabrications, they are carefully crafted masks designed to elevate their wounded sense of self and manipulate how others see them. Samantha's story was no exception. By claiming a rare, devastating disease, she painted herself as uniquely vulnerable, someone deserving of sympathy, attention and, above all, help.

Yet her lies served another, more calculated purpose. Beyond playing the victim, Samantha knew the power of the system she exploited. She sought welfare payments and free housing, not out of need, but out of cold opportunity. Targeting Kerry County Council, she turned her fabricated illness into a golden ticket, leveraging the Irish State's generosity towards the vulnerable to secure financial gain and, if possible, a free roof over her head.

This was no innocent white lie. It was a weapon forged in a mind driven by a cocktail of insecurity and greed. Samantha invited in pity and resources, all while meticulously ensuring her story had the perfect mix of tragedy and urgency. The result? A serial scammer who was as much a master storyteller as she was a criminal, her deception forged in the very human need to be seen, to be special, even if it meant living a lie. And the lie was about to become even bolder.

* * *

With the world at her feet during the COVID-19 pandemic, Samantha Cookes shed the last vestiges of Jade as she blossomed into Carrie Jade Williams full time, a persona carefully sculpted. This was not merely a reinvention after being exposed, as seen before – this was an evolution, a calculated metamorphosis that transcended survival and her schemes. With the constant need to evolve and fabricate newer and greater identities, Jade was no longer enough. And so Carrie Jade was birthed into the wider world. A fully rounded character for her to step into. It had taken some time to build a legitimate backstory, infusing the terminally ill Jade persona with the character of a genuine author. Now Carrie Jade was no longer just a fabricated identity, she was a storyteller given form, a martyr clad in the guise of a woman grappling with Huntington's disease, wielding words as weapons and shields alike.

For years, Samantha had created fictional scams with an artist's finesse, crafting lives teetering on the edge of reality. This time, she harnessed the raw emotional power of her supposed affliction not just to deceive but to dominate. As Carrie Jade Williams, she embraced the mantle of author, channelling her knack for storytelling to a chilling new level. Her writings, rich with empathy and heartbreak, painted a portrait of suffering that was all the more potent because it was built on lies that were perfectly rehearsed.

Fully becoming and embodying Carrie Jade Williams was Samantha's crowning achievement, a symphony of deception, vulnerability and calculated cruelty, played out on the world's stage with relentless grace and horrifying intent.

And the world eagerly lapped it up.

A young Samantha Cookes in 2006 in Gloucester when dating her first boyfriend.

Above: Samantha in Gloucester, 2007.

Right: Partying with friends.

Samantha Cookes walking free from Teeside Crown Court after her conviction for surrogacy fraud, October 2011. (Courtesy of North News and Pictures)

Samantha posing as Lucy Fitzwilliams (*left*) in Dublin and Lucy Fitzpatrick (*above*) in Mayo, 2016.

Samantha posing as Carrie Jade Williams in Cahersiveen, County Kerry, 2021. (Courtesy of Ronan Kelly, RTÉ)

Samantha as Carrie Jade Williams, trying on wedding dresses for her bogus wedding, in Kenmare, County Kerry, 2022.

Samantha posing as terminally ill author Carrie Jade Williams, photographed at Listowel Writers Week, County Kerry, 2022. (© Ger Holland)

Samantha as Carrie Jade Williams, at the St John's Theatre Artist Residency, in Listowel in 2022.

Samantha, posing as Sadie Harris, as she fled from Celbridge, 2024.

15

CARRIE JADE WILLIAMS

In the suffocating quiet of the 2020 COVID-19 lockdown, Carrie Jade Williams emerged as a beacon of resilience and creativity in the writing world, building a reputation and, in turn, legitimacy for herself. Hosting writers' sessions through Zoom, she brought together a vibrant community of storytellers from every corner of the globe. Her positivity shone brightly despite the shadow of her supposed terminal illness, and she carried an aura of kindness and authority that captivated all who joined. Every session ended with her signature sign-off – 'love and light' – a mantra that became synonymous with her online presence and inspirational spirit.

Carrie Jade became a fascinating character who drew in all around her. She befriended a well-respected British writer who runs a popular monthly newsletter for emerging writers via her Substack account. After Carrie Jade reached out to the writer praising her work, they exchanged a few complimentary emails. Learning of Carrie Jade's terminal illness, the writer was so bowled over by the dying woman's positivity and kindness in the face of adversity that she wrote a newsletter post containing an interview with Carrie Jade. Shared to the writer's large following, this further legitimised Carrie Jade Williams in writing circles.

The interview was spellbinding. In it, Carrie Jade revealed her Huntington's diagnosis:

> My neurologist explained that there was no cure, very few treatments and I might not live past 35. We don't see pictures of our brains. I saw mine and I was like a Matisse painting. There are black marks on it which look like someone had cut bits out. It was a horrific day. The biggest thing for me was that I was about to buy a house and I had to pull out because the bank refused to allow people with a terminal diagnosis to have a mortgage. I lost my deposit, which was all my savings. Then I was told I would never be allowed to drive again. I was a very keen rock climber ... I was told I would never do that again ... the same with rowing ... The only saving grace was that I was self-employed so I knew that financially I would dig myself out of this, but it was awful. I had lived this life where you save up to buy a house, you find a sensible man, you marry him and you live a normal life and everything will be ok. I lived a life not rocking the boat.
>
> But actually, we are not promised long lives. Anything can happen at any moment, so it was very arrogant of me to be living like that – and it's pretty boring. So when I got my diagnosis, it was like, well, if the worst-case scenario is another three years – what are those three years going to look like? I started thinking: 'How do I want to spend my days? What do I want to do on a daily basis?'

Reeling in her audience, Carrie Jade then shared details of her 'bucket list', the things she wanted to achieve before she died prematurely from her devastating diagnosis. 'Some stuff was crazy – like climbing Everest and joining Elon Musk's space programme – and other stuff was small, like I wanted to make artisanal bread and pasta from scratch and serve it to friends.' She shared that she also wanted to write a book, hence falling into becoming an author. 'I'd never written anything before but I've got lots of godchildren and I wanted to write something for them, so that they'd have it after I'd gone.'

Carrie shared an inspiring message of hope, not one to be beaten down by the weight of her crippling condition:

> Many people see my diagnosis as a terrible thing but if I'm completely honest, I love the freedom. I love that I just embrace the day. I'm going to spend the next however many years I'm graced with on this planet doing things that really matter, rather than plodding along until I'm 55 and waiting to start living then. I feel like I live life in all the colours now, whereas, before, I was living a very drab beige life and planned on it becoming colourful when I retired – how ridiculous! I didn't know that I could simply reach out and hold onto life, that I didn't have to wait. I laugh more now. I used to be quite a serious person and I didn't really laugh, whereas now, I love to laugh. I find life quite funny. You have to laugh and take yourself less seriously – because the likelihood of me falling over and dropping things is quite high! Recently I forgot the word for 'human', so I phoned a few people and asked for the word for what I am. Mum said 'noisy', a friend said 'awesome', and my

goddaughter said 'human'. Whenever I get too frustrated with my situation, it helps to remember that everybody has a struggle – it just presents itself in different ways. I will probably, at some point, go on a feeding tube because I don't want to get to the point where I'm fearful of choking. I do not agree with euthanasia, so if it gets to the point where I am living alone, or my support needs are too high, I'll go to a nursing home. I've done a living will that details very clearly on paper what I want. But you never know what tomorrow will bring. I don't sit there and plan what I'm going to be wearing in the nursing home. Next year, I'm hoping I can travel a bit. I'm hoping I can stay on my feet as long as possible.

I've now been told my life expectancy is probably going to be closer to seven years because there's always new information coming through. I live in hope every day that there will be a cure because watching other people suffer on the Neuro ward is awful – but I don't regret having it. If I look at Huntington's as purely a diagnosis of what will happen to me, it's a pretty awful disease, but I always factor in all the living I will do BEFORE that happens. I am grateful for what this illness continues to teach me, the amazing people I have met because of it, and the opportunities I have created in its wake.

True to form, Carrie Jade pushed her lies another step further. For no reason other than to elevate herself further in the eyes of others, she claimed to work part-time offering free STI tests to sex workers in her community:

> I believe that community, and thinking about people, and just being there are all so important. We have to get in the trenches with people and be willing to get a bit dirty. Then, when they come out on the other side, they know that they have true friendship and many people are craving that. Sometimes we're really scared to just be next to somebody who's going through a hard time and be like: 'I don't have the answers, I can't change this, but I can love you and we can walk through this together.' So that's how I live my life and I have met the most awesome people.

No one seemed to question the likelihood of such a service being regularly required in rural Kerry.

Carrie Jade's growing reputation earned her more prestigious writer residencies at esteemed institutions, such as the St John's Theatre & Arts Centre in Listowel. The writing community embraced her warmly, recognising the undeniable talent underlying her carefully crafted persona. Her work was not just good, it was masterful storytelling, honed by years of intricate deceit turned into art. One of her short stories was a finalist in the London Independent Story Prize, a testament to her storytelling prowess.

Then came her crowning achievement – winning the prestigious and highly competitive *Financial Times* Bodley Head Essay Prize in autumn 2020 with her essay 'When I Edit With Assistive Tech'. This was a stirring and powerful narrative told from the point of view of a woman living with a terminal illness and forced to rely on voice-command technology when losing the use of her hands. One judge praised it as 'a tour-de-force in miniature, a startlingly gripping piece of writing, the product of the gravely challenged circumstances of the author'. Carrie Jade Williams reacted with grace and determination, saying, 'This has been overwhelming and I am now excited to try and find a home for my novel. Writing has become my sanctuary in a world that's very slow to be fully accessible for those living with neurological illnesses.'

The win of the Bodley Head Essay Prize opened a dazzling new chapter for Samantha Cookes, now fully embodying Carrie Jade Williams. With the esteemed seal of approval from such a prestigious institution, her story of battling a terminal illness was no longer simply heard, it was validated, published and celebrated. On 28 November 2020, Penguin Random House published a copy of her award-winning essay in book form, providing the authoritative platform that transformed the fiction of Carrie Jade Williams into undeniable literary legitimacy. The £1,000 prize, alongside a prominent feature in the *Financial Times*, propelled Carrie Jade into the spotlight. Yet beneath this glowing success lay an unsettling truth. Following years of deception, families scammed across Ireland, and webs of lies sustaining her, Samantha's confidence had hardened into bold audacity.

The accolades triggered a wave of opportunity. Multiple online meetings with literary agents followed, each encounter reinforcing the growing hunger for Carrie Jade Williams' voice and story. Ultimately, she signed with Greene and Heaton, one of London's leading literary agencies, a move that firmly planted her feet on the path to widespread acclaim and influence. Suddenly, Samantha's alter ego was everywhere, the darling of the literary scene, a symbol of courage and creativity whom everyone wanted on their side. Carrie Jade wasn't just a character anymore, she was a force wielding the power of her storytelling to command attention, sympathy and success on the world stage.

Flourishing in her new role, she began to court publicity, appearing as a guest on local and national radio speaking of her illness and championing a world of greater accessibility for those like her with life-limiting disabilities. Her appearances included an interview on Newstalk's *Lunchtime Live* and multiple appearances on Radio Kerry. She wrote a long letter to the editor of the *Irish Examiner* in response to an article featuring a contribution from a young woman suffering a neurological condition who was pro-euthanasia. This letter was published in June 2021:

> Accessibility before euthanasia choice
>
> Firstly, I want to express my sincere love for the woman telling her story – 'Why, oh why can't I die in peace?' As a 32-year-old woman living with a terminal, degenerative, neurological illness I can empathise with her experience.
>
> I live with a neurological disease frequently described as one of the most horrific neurological illnesses. Imagine a mixture of Alzheimer's, Parkinson's and ALS in one disease. Yet my life has value.
>
> I will not consent to euthanasia and hope that before euthanasia is legalised in Ireland we will ensure there is full accessibility for all disabled people. We will ensure that accessibility barriers are removed.
>
> By ensuring disabled individuals are included and supported we can ensure that euthanasia is a genuine

> choice and not simply a reaction to a world that is currently not accessible.
>
> I know what it is like to have to fight to be included. There are spaces and government departments still inaccessible to me. There are still presumptions made about me as a disabled person that I do not agree with. One of the most concerning being that the concept of allyship with the disability community being a pro-euthanasia position. I am not necessarily writing this to try and change anyone's mind on euthanasia, more as a plea, that all the energy going into giving me and others like me the right to die could be split between the right to die and the right to accessibility while I'm living, because I can't help but feel that euthanasia is seen as the easier solution than ensuring assistive technology becomes socially normalised.
>
> Carrie Jade Williams
> Cahersiveen
> Kerry

Emboldened by her recent acclaim and subsequent media attention, Samantha made an even bolder move. She reached out to RTÉ, Ireland's national public service broadcaster, known for its trusted news, radio and television programming. With a carefully crafted email, she pitched a story to the producers of *Doc on One*, RTÉ's flagship documentary radio series renowned for telling powerful real-life stories in compelling audio form. The email landed on the desks of Ronan Kelly and Liam O'Brien, two veteran producers of *Doc on One*, who read it with growing disbelief. Never before had a pitch so perfectly captured the drama, pathos and urgency they sought:

> Subject: Documentary Pitch
>
> To Whom It May Concern
>
> I am a young 32-year-old Irish woman living with a terminal degenerative neurological illness that was misdiagnosed due to the fact I was adopted. I have Huntington's disease, which is ALS meets Alzheimer's meets Parkinson's, a pretty tough disease. Irish neurological wards are increasingly becoming full of young Irish women like me who are terminally ill due to the secrets and lies around adoption. I have accepted that I will die because I was misdiagnosed. I have accepted that I will more than likely die without meeting my birth mother. What I cannot accept is that this is going to continue impacting women until something is done, until people hear my story and realise change is urgently needed and not only for adoptees. We have a chance to save a life if just one woman thinks to question their GP after hearing my story, that's a positive.

For Ronan and Liam, the email was irresistible. It promised an intimate, heartrending investigation into illness, identity and systemic failure, a story perfectly suited to *Doc on One*'s mission. What they didn't yet know was the true depths behind the voice reaching out to them, attempting to set the stage for a national audience to be drawn into one of Ireland's most intricate and audacious cons.

Ronan Kelly made the trip from Dublin to Cahersiveen to

meet Carrie Jade Williams. The rolling green hills and misty coastline painted a serene backdrop as he arrived, expecting a story; what he didn't expect was the sheer force of personality he encountered. Carrie Jade was extraordinary – radiant despite the heavy shadows of her claimed illness, articulate with an irrepressible wit, drawing Ronan into a world of tangled emotions and raw authenticity. As she shared her story, she spoke with the candour and passion of someone driven not just by circumstance, but a fierce urgency to be heard.

Claiming to have been born in Ireland but adopted by an English woman and raised in the idyllic Cotswolds, Carrie Jade described a childhood shaped amidst wealth (the family owned a diamond abrasives cutting factory), but also by her mother's fierce free spirit and activism. She recounted how her mother had brought her to marches and protests, instilling in her a sense of justice and rebellion. 'Always knew I was adopted. It was never some big secret,' she told Ronan. 'There was never a day where I found out. I thought everybody was adopted!'

She described the confusion of childhood, learning that other children were raised differently. 'It was a shock to me when I learned some people weren't adopted because my mum would always say, "Oh, I chose you. You were my gift." And I thought, well, I must not be that great if some people just kept their babies.' She laughed softly, the vulnerability cracking through the strength.

Her story unfolded like a vivid tapestry woven with joy, loss, rebellion and a profound search for identity and truth. Ronan found Carrie deeply intriguing; he believed that voice carried the kind of complexity and gravitas that could grip listeners across Ireland. The story was destined to be a compelling, deeply human exploration of adoption, illness and the meaning of family. She sat across from him, her voice steady but laced with raw emotion as she unfolded the layers of her story. 'I didn't know I had Huntington's because the gene runs down from my birth parents, people I never knew,' she explained. Ronan's head swam as she wove together the threads of her past, a degree in engineering, then water testing, and finally health and safety work during the pandemic.

'Huntington's disease,' she said, 'when you get diagnosed, it's a list of all the things you're suddenly not allowed to do anymore. You're not allowed to drive, to make many decisions. I was a mad rower, I'm not allowed to row anymore. Not allowed to rock climb.' Her voice cracked slightly. 'For me, it felt like my life suddenly got very, very small.'

Carrie described having a neurological condition as 'like moving into a town where nobody wants to be, and everyone's desperate to leave'. 'I have accepted there's no cure,' she said bluntly. 'It's a really shit disease. If I could get rid of it in the morning, I absolutely would. Because it's heartbreaking, heartbreaking to live with.' But she also shared how Huntington's gave her courage. 'People tell me I'm brave or inspirational. I hate that sometimes, because I just want accessibility barriers to vanish. It's 2021, we should do better. I'm polite, but I won't back down. If something can be fixed for less than €40, like closed captions or better tech for booking trains, I force the issue.'

She explained how Ireland's laws made it hard for someone like her to apply for social welfare without relinquishing mental capacity. So she developed her own technology, programming voice-controlled software to navigate her computer because hand tremors made using a mouse and keyboard nearly impossible. 'I had to figure it out,' she said. 'The first program I coded moved my mouse by voice control. Then I created text-to-speech tools. It was about survival.' Despite the hurdles, she found joy in storytelling, crafting essays and bucket lists for her godchildren. Through voice recognition and sheer determination, she became a writer, joining an online community inspired by her resilience.

Carrie Jade then leaned in, her eyes sparkling with the mix of hope and harsh reality as she explained deep brain stimulation to Ronan. 'In the US, they look at neurology and brain health completely differently than we do here or in most of the world,' she said. 'It's treated as separate from psychiatry and even neurology, to an extent. In Los Angeles, there are real opportunities now, especially with deep brain stimulation.'

She described it with fervour: 'Deep brain stimulation is like a little pacemaker for your brain. It's a tiny device they implant through a 15-millimetre hole drilled in your skull. Electrodes deliver electrical pulses that interrupt abnormal brain signals causing seizures or movement disorders like Parkinson's. The idea is it "hits pause" on Huntington's disease, doesn't undo the damage, but slows or stops the progression.'

Carrie explained how she was preparing to travel to LA for the surgery, undergoing MRIs and intensive studies to target where the electrodes would be placed. 'They think they'll put one in the back of my brain, the other in the middle left side, my front brain is too damaged for anything there. The surgery's done under conscious sedation, you're awake but relaxed. I've had practice runs, like having a tooth removed this way. To keep calm, during surgery I'll watch *The Real Housewives of Beverly Hills* on a screen, they'll keep me talking about nonsense to distract me from the drilling noises.'

Her humour cut through the grim setting, but beneath it lay the steely nerve to endure the unknown. She invited Ronan to come along and record her story for the *Doc on One* documentary: an unprecedented journey into the heart of a brave, complex woman fighting a cruel disease with science and spirit intertwined.

This unfiltered narrative left Ronan captivated, a portrait of a woman shrinking from and fighting against the cruel restraints of Huntington's disease, wielding technology and grit to keep her voice alive. It promised listeners not just a story of illness, but of resilience, innovation and a rare glimpse into cutting-edge medicine bristling against the odds. It was a story ripe for *Doc on One*.

As Ronan drove back to Dublin, the rolling hills of Kerry fading in his rearview mirror, his mind swirled with the stories and revelations he had absorbed from Carrie Jade Williams. She was unlike anyone he had ever met, a dazzling mix of wit and raw vulnerability, wrapped in layers of complexity. Her tales of growing up adopted in the Cotswolds, her fight with Huntington's disease, and her fierce advocacy for accessibility were compelling and heartbreaking in equal measure. The stark reality of her upcoming deep brain stimulation surgery and her determination to find humour even in the darkest moments, painted the portrait of a woman who was defiant in the face of overwhelming odds. Each anecdote, each sharp insight, felt like a thread pulling him deeper into her world, yet leaving him tangled in questions.

Ronan felt the weight of the story's potential, not just for listeners craving truth and humanity, but for himself, now caught in the gravitational pull of a woman whose layers were as intricate as the diagnosis she carried. Carrie Jade was a captivating character, a paradox wrapped in mystery, and as the motorway blurred by, Ronan knew that this meeting would stay with him long after the microphones were turned off.

However, after that electrifying meeting, Carrie Jade seemed to vanish. Ronan drove to her place again, recorder in hand, eager to dive deeper into her story, only to get a last-minute message cancelling their appointment. Days turned into weeks, messages about the critical LA surgery remaining unanswered. His research following their meeting failed to uncover any evidence of the experimental treatment she spoke of. Ronan and his colleague Liam began to exchange uneasy glances. Was Carrie truly grappling with her health, or was something more elusive going on?

Suspicion tickled at the edges of their thoughts, yet compassion held sway. After all, she was claiming to be terminally ill, so they gave her the benefit of the doubt. Time slipped away, and without new contact or updates, the story quietly slipped off their radar, marked down to either the tragedy of a spiralling mind or the cruel weight of illness.

Ignoring Ronan, whom she had hooked in, knowing full well she would not be able to deliver on her promise of a ringside seat to groundbreaking experimental treatment in LA, Carrie Jade set her sights on a new community to infiltrate.

* * *

Nestled amid the natural beauty of County Kerry, the town of Kenmare is a quiet sanctuary where ancient history and rugged landscapes meet a warm and close-knit community. This quaint town, affectionately known in Irish as An Neidín, or 'Little Nest', is a place where time seems to slow, inviting strolls between moss-covered stone walls and along a vibrant patchwork of colourful shopfronts. Amid the rolling hills, salt-kissed air and peaceful river banks, Kenmare's understated charm permeates everyday life, from the bustling town square where locals gather in cosy pubs filled with trad music, and inviting cafés where neighbours exchange stories over flat whites and fresh pastries.

It was into this serene, slow-beating heart of Kenmare that Carrie Jade Williams arrived, claiming the identity of a health and safety officer and award-winning author, stepping lightly into the rhythms of the town with calculated ease. In the lead-up to her move she had been giving different versions of her alias name to different groups she was connected to; in Kenmare, she was finally Carrie Jade Williams to everyone.

In Kenmare, Samantha Cookes prepared to perform her grandest act, changing lives and shaking the very fabric of this serene town. When Carrie Jade Williams set her sights on this community, she arrived not as an intruder but as someone who gave the impression she was returning to a place that had always been waiting for her. She was disarmingly ordinary, with her sensible shoes, a cardigan the colour of weak tea and an easy smile, but there was a focus in her listening, in the way she watched people's faces when they spoke, as though cataloguing them for later use.

In those first weeks, she was everywhere yet never obvious, turning up at book clubs, volunteering for charity drives, helping at the church hall. She spoke of her illness, gently, never fishing for sympathy, simply laying it down like a fact of life. But that detail, her terminal diagnosis, created a hush around her. People wanted to protect her, make her final years meaningful. That was how she gained ground.

16

VALIDATION

Over her time in Cahersiveen, and now in Kenmare, Samantha Cookes perfected the art of illusion. As Jade and then Carrie Jade, she continued her scams and wielded her pen like a scalpel, piercing institutions, drafting complaints and crafting narratives that made systems bend under her hand. For years, her written words had been her greatest con: sharp, plausible and compassionate enough to deflect suspicion. But one winter afternoon, as rain threaded down her windowpane, she decided to reach beyond her usual marks and perform what perhaps she believed would be a gesture of kindness, or else an experiment in power.

The international news had been dominated for months by the downfall of Elizabeth Holmes, the formerly celebrated founder of Theranos. Once hailed as Silicon Valley's next great visionary, Holmes had promised to revolutionise the process of blood testing. When it all collapsed, with investors defrauded, patients misled and reputations ruined, the trial became a cultural reckoning. Presiding over the case in a San Jose courtroom was Judge Edward Davila, a man who had already warned that the consequences would be 'measured not by loss of funds, but by the loss of trust'.

It was to this figure of judgment that Carrie Jade Williams addressed her letter. Typed on her laptop, printed off and posted from a quiet Irish post office, the message carried all the hallmarks of sincerity. She introduced herself as a thirty-four-year-old woman diagnosed with an incurable neurological disorder. The letter pleaded for mercy, appealing to the humanity of the court with a tone that teetered between reverence and self-righteousness. When Holmes' defence team submitted character references, Carrie Jade's letter was the only one read aloud in court from a stranger, so out of the ordinary, in fact, that excerpts later found their way into *The Wall Street Journal*:

> I am writing from Ireland in the hopes that you will consider the other side to the mistakes made by Elizabeth Holmes. I am a 34-year-old woman with a degenerative neurological illness [...] As someone with a neurological illness with no hope of a cure, I need people like Elizabeth to continue to innovate. If you send Elizabeth to jail, you are essentially sending every young person with a terminal illness like me with her [...] please remember the world is watching.

When Samantha learned that her fabrication, her voice, had crossed the ocean and echoed in an American courtroom she would never see, she must have felt the old thrill return. For a moment, she was untouchable, as though her lies had taken flight and found a higher purpose.

Perhaps that was what drew Samantha to Holmes in the first place – the recognition of something shared. Two women, each in her own way guilty of selling faith and fiction dressed as hope. As she watched the trial unfold from across the Atlantic Ocean, Samantha may have seen not a disgraced entrepreneur, but a mirror, one that reflected her own belief that the story, if told beautifully enough, could become its own truth.

* * *

Carrie Jade Williams was doing remarkably well in her self-crafted role as an emerging writer and advocate. Behind the scenes, she had received significant support from the Arts Council of Ireland – a €15,000 bursary in 2021 for an English-language literature project, followed by a €21,250 award in 2022 for another writing endeavour. These grants were for literary projects submitted under one of her earlier aliases, Jade Cooke. When asked about this, the Arts Council later stated that its application process was based strictly on the 'artistic merit' of the proposals, and previous criminal convictions, like Samantha's fraud convictions, were not considered in funding decisions. These grants allowed Samantha to present herself publicly as a serious and talented artist, further bolstering her credibility and deepening community trust.

During this time, Carrie Jade Williams' writing career seemed to be unstoppable. Her public appearances and social media presence were building a profile of resilience and creative success, all of which helped Chloe and others believe in her authenticity. She appeared as a guest speaker at the renowned Listowel Writers' Week, for which she received a fee of €200 alongside a festival lanyard granting her access to all events across the festival. She was a special guest on the hugely popular *The Guilty Feminist*, a podcast hosted by Deborah Frances-White. With millions of listeners worldwide, it features discussions on feminism, mixing humour with candid conversations about the contradictions, insecurities and hypocrisies faced by twenty-first-century feminists. Carrie Jade did a stellar turn on the programme and unexpectedly struck gold.

During the episode, she shared her Huntington's diagnosis with the world using a potent mix of vulnerability and determination: 'I'm doing great things like, you know, I am terminally ill. It is tragic in some ways, but how many people would love to throw all the rubbish out of their lives and just live for the moment, like, loads of people crave that and I'm doing it.' She spoke passionately about advocating for assistive technology to improve not only her own life but also those of countless others living with neurological conditions. She painted a compelling vision of how technology could revolutionise communication and independence for those whose bodies gradually fail them:

> I'm very tech focused because I think we have technology and why not use it for good? ... I always say to people, do you enjoy typing? And most people are like, no, I really don't like typing. I find it really difficult and I'll say, why don't you switch to talk-to-text technology? It saves time. I mean, I've written a novel from my shower because I, you know, I just shout it out and it records my notes while I'm walking around the house.
>
> So my whole house is assistive tech. Because I live with memory loss. I use assistive tech because my whole life that's how I'm able to function. That's how I carry on doing things.
>
> I use an electronic braille reader that I designed myself.

Carrie Jade waxed lyrical about her tech inventions that enhanced her life. Then came the crucial moment. The host, blown away by her tales, interjected the conversation with enthusiasm, 'Carrie, because a lot of people listen to the show and a lot of feminists listen to this show. If somebody has an ethical tech company ... because you don't want to make money out of the things that you've made ...?' She was giving a subtle nudge to any tech company listeners to consider backing Carrie Jade's groundbreaking work.

Jumping at the idea of backing from a tech company and any potential source of revenue out there listening, Carrie Jade replied, 'So I've got four patents out and I'm willing to gift it all over because I'm dying, so there's only so much you need to buy, you know?'

With this seemingly offhand comment, she indicated a desire to connect with investors to support a business idea focused on 'talk to text' assistive innovation. That casual remark did not go unnoticed. Shortly after the broadcast of the podcast episode, in October 2021, a member of the Alzheimer's Society UK, who had been listening in, reached out. They had identified Carrie Jade's project as a perfect fit for their Accelerator Programme, a prestigious initiative designed to nurture early-stage companies developing pioneering solutions for people with dementia and neurological diseases. The programme offers funding, expert mentorship and vital networking opportunities to help transform ideas into impactful products. They encouraged Carrie Jade to apply.

This connection offered Samantha something she had never fully achieved before – genuine access and legitimacy within a respected, cause-driven organisation. The layers of credibility she built, from winning the *Financial Times* Bodley Head Essay Prize to the endorsement of a widely respected feminist podcast, to now tying her narrative to a trusted UK health institution, created an almost impenetrable fabric of validation around the persona of Carrie Jade Williams. Each endorsement lent its own hard-earned authority, deepening the illusion and making it nearly impossible for anyone to question her story.

When Carrie Jade Williams applied to the Alzheimer's Society UK's Accelerator Programme, her proposal – an innovative app designed to support those with neurological conditions to communicate more easily – was accepted. In the relentless march of her deception, she now made a calculated leap forward. She officially registered a company in the UK, headquartered in Belfast, under the name 'Start Voice Control'. Her project description was a masterclass in persuasive innovation:

> This app is designed as an integrated memory prompt and communication support system, empowering those living with memory-based complexities. It uses machine learning to tailor communication support to each individual's needs. Whether on a smartphone, tablet, or stand-alone device, the app prompts words, visual cues, and grammatical patterns to counteract the effects of frontal lobe deterioration, enabling continuous self-expression despite progressive memory challenges.

The supposed 'talk-to-text' app would be incredibly helpful for a person living with Alzheimer's disease, which often affects word retrieval and sentence structure, making expressing thoughts difficult, leading to frustration and isolation. By prompting words, images and familiar grammatical patterns, the app would help a person finish sentences or convey meaning even when their memory faltered, preserving their ability to be understood and protecting dignity and self-confidence. If it had been real, it could have been a truly life-changing piece of technology.

In early 2022, pitching this vision, Carrie Jade secured a coveted twelve-month partnership from the Accelerator Programme offering up to £100,000 in investment, expert guidance and peer support. After being paid an initial £8,750 by the Alzheimer's Society, however, months passed with no news from Carrie Jade. Grand promises evaporated into silence, emails from the society went unanswered or were met with stories of hospital stays and urgent surgeries. The revolutionary app remained as elusive as its inventor.

At the same time, Samantha expanded her reach locally, becoming involved in a project with a local primary school. Harnessing the zeitgeist of the Irish government's impending 2023 nationwide voluntary ban on mobile phones in schools, Samantha promised the principal of the school a cutting-edge solution: technology to block mobile signals within the school, an innovation meant to save teachers from the grind of phone-guarding duties. But, as with her app, the school was met only with delays and unfulfilled promises.

On top of this, the Wellcome Collection, the renowned London museum and library connecting science, medicine and art, stepped into the story during this time. After she applied to them, they granted Carrie Jade funding and featured her in an article highlighting her supposed pioneering work with assistive technology. The Wellcome Collection, known for fostering innovative health projects, paid her fees of £500 and £587.70. This wove a further tangible thread into the fabric of Carrie Jade's legitimacy.

It was around this time that, under the name 'Jade Williams Cooke, t/a Start Voice Control', Samantha applied for and was awarded €2,500 from Kerry County Council as part of the Trading Online Voucher Scheme. This is a government-funded grant to help small businesses build or improve their online trading presence.

In a strategic move of confidence, Carrie Jade leased office space in Kenmare. During negotiations, she portrayed herself as 'an engineer with a background in assistive technology,' emphasising accelerated business growth fuelled by innovation awards and funding. She boldly declared plans to hire a team of three to four employees immediately, promised a November launch for her app, and even touted exclusive international exposure through an impending Netflix documentary, a claim unverified but potent in its allure. 'I prefer to keep the exact totals of my innovation awards private as I do not like to boast,' she told the landlord, layering humility atop ambition.

Through these intertwined ventures, each a mixture of promise, partial truth and deception, Samantha crafted a complex tableau of credibility. The prestigious Alzheimer's Society Accelerator Programme demanded a registered business, a prototype, a detailed business plan and commitment to develop solutions for people affected by dementia. Her company registration and polished project proposal met these criteria on paper, lending her false persona a shield of authenticity. Her association with the Wellcome Collection, a respected institution at the crossroads of humanities and medical innovation, added another gleaming layer of legitimacy. Yet beneath this intricate mirage, months of silence and unfulfilled commitments told a different story. The grand vision of Start Voice Control remained just that – a vision.

The ever-industrious Carrie Jade Williams was, at the same time, tightening a web around her London literary agent at Greene and Heaton. The agent, patient yet growing weary, awaited manuscripts that never came. Weeks turned into months of unanswered emails, punctuated only by Carrie Jade's convoluted excuses laden with medical despair. Huntington's had robbed her of the ability to type, the assistive technology she depended upon was malfunctioning, she was undergoing emergency surgeries. Her messages were laced with the quiet desperation of a woman constrained by incurable decline. She portrayed herself as trapped in silence, her voice carried only by the fragile help of technology that too often failed her.

Yet behind these digital silences, another contradiction simmered. While telling her literary agent she could not even send a typed document, as Samantha she was meticulously filling out welfare paperwork by hand, every signature and form penned with deliberate clarity that belied her professed physical limitations.

The stark dissonance between her whispered claims of helplessness to one world and her accurate, handwritten fraud in another framed her genius as both a master manipulator and an unrepentant chameleon, capable of playing victim and predator simultaneously, navigating her lies with chilling dexterity. The truth lingered in the shadows and Samantha Cookes, a phantom of contradiction, knew exactly which mask to wear, and when.

17

THE PEAK OF HER POWERS

Over the course of 2020 to 2022, under a host of guises and when registered at addresses in both Cahersiveen and Kenmare, Samantha's ongoing medical con extended deep into the health system, where her cunning proved almost surgical. As well as convincing her GP, through trickery, to write a letter confirming her diagnosis of Huntington's disease, she attended numerous appointments with neurologists and specialists to secure the official records of medical appointments she needed. Attending initial consultations where she would outline her medical complaints, she would then miss crucial scans and follow-up appointments that would reveal how her complaints had no grounding in fact.

However, while she maintained different versions of her name with her GP and medical professionals, Samantha was forced to use her real identity for social welfare payments, since funds were deposited directly into her bank account and linked to her Personal Public Service (PPS) number. Drawing from the art projects she once did as a nanny with children, she printed out text versions of the necessary identity in small cutouts and carefully glued them over different names on official forms, such as pasting Samantha onto a consultant's report and the GP's letter originally addressed to Carrie or Jade. She then photocopied these doctored pages, disguising the telltale bumps and textures of the alteration, making the falsified papers appear seamless to unsuspecting eyes.

These multiple identities, fluid in medical contexts yet anchored in reality for finance, were the culmination of her artistry and calculation, a reminder that beneath the layers of deception, Samantha retained full control.

* * *

On 27 January 2021, a letter arrived that would mark a defining moment in Samantha's long and twisted game. From the Irish social welfare services office came confirmation that Samantha had been awarded a disability allowance. The letter detailed her entitlement, a weekly personal rate of €203, supplemented by a €19 increase for living alone, plus a fuel allowance of €28 during the colder months. Samantha later also began receiving €2.50 a week telephone support allowance. Payments were to be ongoing.

In black and white, the State had affirmed Samantha's claim, validating the complex set of lies she had carefully crafted. She had successfully fooled not just individuals, neighbours and local charities, but the very machinery of the State itself. This moment was more than just a financial victory. It was proof that Samantha's deepest con had taken root, that her fabrications had passed the highest forms of scrutiny, and that her presence in the system was secure, for now. Behind the official letter lay months of impersonation, forged documents, remote medical consultations and cold calculation, the culmination of a psychological mastery in deception.

The Irish taxpayers, unknowingly, were now footing the bill for Samantha's carefully choreographed illusion, and, as the weeks turned to months and then years, the shadow of what she might do next stretched ever longer.

During this audacious phase, Samantha's duplicity took on new and shocking dimensions. She enrolled at two Irish universities under false names. She attended Sligo Institute of Technology in 2021, posing as Jade Williams, where she studied for a Bachelor of Science in Occupational Safety and Health. During her time there, she lodged formal disability discrimination and data breach complaints. Although she initially demanded compensation of €26,040, the dispute was settled through mediation for €3,962.94, along with an official apology letter from the college president. She then ceased her study there.

Her academic chicanery also extended, once again, to Dublin City University (DCU). Having enrolled in 2016 as Lucy Fitzwilliams, she returned under the new guise of Carrie Jade Williams in 2021 to study for a Bachelor of Arts in English and History. There, she filed a formal complaint alleging that, due to her claimed Huntington's disease, there were accessibility barriers on their online platforms preventing her from submitting coursework. She intensified the pressure by informing DCU of a commissioned podcast and documentary exposing their discrimination, and boasting of a 'considerable social media presence'. The outcome of this complaint is not known.

Samantha also attempted to register for a BSc in Immersive Software Engineering at the University of Limerick, but her application was denied due to incompleteness.

These exploits underscore the ambitious extent of Samantha Cookes' deception, infiltrating respected educational institutions, manipulating discrimination laws and weaponising disability claims for personal gain, all while weaving false identities and narratives that shielded her true self.

* * *

Samantha Cookes was at the height of her powers during her time as Carrie Jade Williams. In early 2022, when she had moved into her new home in Sheen View, Kenmare, the first impression was universally positive. Tim, the landlord, couldn't believe his luck. 'Finally,' he told her new neighbour Chloe, 'someone reliable. An English lady, polite, professional, a writer, a health and safety officer. Quiet as a mouse, too.'

To Tim, she was the ideal tenant. Rent always on time, emails full of gratitude, everything neat and proper. She'd even left fresh flowers on the windowsill the day she moved in, as though determined to make the house look well-loved. When she spoke about her writing, a book, she said, about resilience and illness, Tim was in awe. 'You'd swear she was famous,' he told Chloe. 'She's been on the radio.'

Chloe remembered their first meeting vividly. Carrie Jade had appeared on her doorstep holding a plate of scones, shy but bright-eyed. Her accent was soft, clipped English with an undercurrent of warmth that made conversation feel effortless. She was younger than Chloe had expected, with a fragility that seemed to make her glow rather than fade. 'She was lovely,' Chloe recalled later. 'Gentle, a bit quirky. The kind of person you just want to look after.'

It was the details that drew her in. Carrie Jade told her about the Huntington's diagnosis, how it stole her words and, most recently, her ability to swallow. 'I can't even eat a sandwich now,' she'd said with a rueful smile, gesturing towards her cup of tea. 'Liquids only.' Chloe had been horrified. Yet Carrie Jade spoke with such grace, such acceptance, that pity turned into admiration. How could someone so ill still be doing so much?

When Chloe later googled her name, up came articles and blog posts, even a profile from the *Financial Times* mentioning a 'Bodley' essay prize she'd apparently won. There were interviews too, including one on a national radio station, Newstalk, where Carrie Jade's lilting voice spoke of courage and terminal illness. Chloe was stunned. Everything she'd heard seemed confirmed in black and white.

The invention of further complex false narratives came hard and fast. Carrie Jade had an easy way of making her life sound extraordinary. Over late coffees that stretched into dusk, she told Chloe about her adoption story, how she'd been born in the old Bessborough Mother and Baby Home in Cork before being sent to an English family. Perhaps Samantha was appropriating details from stories heard during her time studying for the Leaving Certificate exam as a mature student next to the old Bessborough home. 'My mother was barely more than a child herself,' she said softly. 'I've been searching for her my whole life.'

Chloe was rapt. The story had weight, sadness, the kind of depth that made you feel privileged to be trusted with it. Some of her new neighbour's tales seemed almost cinematic, but Chloe brushed off her instinct to question them. People with lives that rich were bound to sound improbable at times. When Carrie Jade dropped the bombshell that Netflix were producing a documentary about her life, Chloe left the conversation dazed but dazzled.

Later came stories of finding her birth mother in Cork, a woman who was both deaf and non-verbal. Then came Fionn. Carrie Jade spoke of him so vividly that Chloe felt she could almost picture him: the ruggedly spiritual fiancé, kind-eyed and earnest, born-again through faith. The two had met at an evangelical church retreat, Carrie Jade said. Their connection had been immediate, divine almost. There was talk of a wedding, invitations were printed and Chloe even received one, tied with a satin ribbon. She was genuinely moved. 'A miracle,' she told her mother over the phone. 'Someone like her deserves happiness.' Carrie Jade even shared a photograph of herself in the perfect white wedding dress, snapped during a fitting at White Ivy Bridal Boutique in Kenmare. The kind-hearted shop owner, Katrina, would later recall that the dress in question, although ordered, was never paid for.

In the end, however, Chloe began to notice how, now and then, a story delivered would tilt slightly off balance. The honeymoon plans, for instance. One morning, between talk of wedding favours and playlists, Carrie Jade casually mentioned that she and Fionn were going to 'Burning Man'. Chloe laughed, thinking she'd misheard. 'The festival? The one in the desert?'

Carrie Jade nodded earnestly. 'Yes, we both want to experience something spiritual before the next chapter begins. It's freeing, apparently. A place where the soul meets itself.'

Chloe tried to reconcile the image of a devout evangelical Christian, terminally ill, preparing for marriage, with the chaotic festival she'd only ever seen in glossy documentaries, alive with sandstorms, neon lights, people draped in feathers and sequins, and huge wooden effigies set ablaze under a desert sky. It didn't fit.

Then there was the mention of visiting the set of hit American television series *The Walking Dead*, which Carrie Jade spoke of that same week, her tone brimming with excitement. 'Fionn knows someone on the crew.' It was only later Chloe remembered she'd been chatting on the phone about that exact show a few nights earlier, standing out in her garden while light glowed faintly behind the curtains next door. Just a coincidence, she told herself then.

Not satisfied with just the rapt audience sitting at her kitchen table, Carrie Jade, ever the industry of output, also began a podcast during this time, though she only released one episode to the public. The podcast, entitled 'Dying Alone', claimed to follow Carrie and her fiancé on their journey as 'an inter-abler couple living life, falling in love and all the odd things people say!' Not surprisingly, her supposed fiancé, Fionn, didn't make an appearance throughout the recording. As of 2026, this episode still remains available online.

Samantha, as Carrie Jade Williams, appeared unstoppable. 'She mentioned once she was involved in 3D printing,' Chloe remembered, 'making sensory toys for children with autism and additional needs. She said she had these big light tubes, flashing colours and sounds, it was incredible. But she told me so much about herself it was almost too much to take in.'

* * *

Unbeknownst to Chloe and everyone else in Kenmare, Carrie Jade Williams had built an entire world beyond the quiet cottage walls, one that was vast, adoring and entirely under her control. Online, she was luminous. Using TikTok, the short-form video platform that had exploded during the long isolation of the Covid lockdowns in 2020 and throughout 2021 and 2022, Carrie shared fragments of her life and illness in fifteen-second bursts that captured millions of hearts.

During the global pandemic people were watching TikTok more than ever, at kitchen tables, in bedrooms, on their phones late into the night, and Carrie understood instinctively how to speak to that loneliness. She would look straight into the camera, her voice trembling slightly, speaking about Huntington's disease, about courage, about finding light in darkness. She read extracts from her essays, smiled gently when she faltered, and laughed softly at her own effort. Sympathy followed in waves.

Writers adored her, and she became a small celebrity in online literary circles. She hosted workshops on Zoom, teaching others to 'write through adversity'. Participants left feeling inspired, chatting about her kindness, her spirituality, her humour. No one questioned her story. The tremor in her voice, the conviction in her words made it impossible to doubt. Online she was untouchable, framed always in soft light.

Then came her 'mission.' She launched a website under the name '1820 Things', selling 3D-printed sensory toys for autistic children and those with additional needs. She claimed in a TikTok video that the name for the website had come from the fact that, according to Carrie Jade, a person with Alzheimer's forgets five things per day, and so 1,820 things per year. There is no known medical truth to this statement. The branding of the website was artfully simple with a white background and soft blues, and advocacy woven through every word. It was created by Samantha on the graphic design website 'Canva', copying and pasting images from other websites and genuine retailers. The toys, light tubes, tactile cubes, spinning discs and weighted blankets were displayed in glossy photographs. Normally, items like these could cost hundreds of euros. Carrie claimed she made them herself on her 3D printer, allowing her to sell them at a fraction of the cost – €40, €60, sometimes less. Her goal, she said, was to make life better for children with special needs before her illness took her. It was all part of 'her legacy'. Orders for hundreds and hundreds of euros worth of equipment started rolling in.

In September 2022 one of those who watched, utterly entranced, was Krissie Edwards from Coventry in England. A single mother of two autistic boys, she had grown used to scraping by. Her days were relentless, managing meltdowns, contacting schools and services, fighting through the tangle of waiting lists for appointments with specialists that never came. Late at night, when her sons finally slept, she would scroll TikTok for a few stolen moments of peace. That's where she found Carrie Jade Williams.

There was something about the way Carrie Jade spoke – gentle, unhurried, almost saintly – that made Krissie stop. She followed her, then watched everything: the workshops, the story about her faith, her frailty. The idea that someone so ill would spend her time helping others felt profound, even sacred.

When Carrie Jade mentioned that she wanted to provide affordable sensory equipment to struggling families, Krissie's heart leapt. She watched footage of Carrie Jade showing a brightly coloured fidget board turning slowly under the light. Carrie Jade said she had a team of over twenty employees helping her to produce sensory rooms for families across the UK and Ireland. The aim was to create calming, interactive spaces that helped children regulate their moods, bubbles and colours that soothed overstimulated minds, gentle vibrations that eased sensory overload, textures that replaced distress with focus.

Krissie knew immediately what that could mean for her boys. She sent a message. Within days, Carrie Jade replied, inviting her to join a Zoom call. When they connected, Carrie Jade appeared on screen in a neat cardigan and soft scarf, her voice slow, slightly trembling, eyes warm behind the camera. She told Krissie she had reviewed her application personally and wanted to help her. The kindness in her tone drew instant tears. Carrie Jade shared mocked-up plans for a sensory room, photos, 3D designs and lists of equipment. When Krissie gasped at the detail, she smiled. 'I want to do something special for you,' she said. 'You remind me why I started this. Let me double your package so the boys have everything they deserve.'

It was the first time in years Krissie had felt pure hope. She transferred the £200 'contribution' – her savings and the boys' Christmas money – and marked the day the sensory kit would arrive on her calendar. Her sons talked about it for weeks, imagining bubble lamps and light-up walls. But nothing came.

The messages slowed, then stopped. The website persisted, but Carrie Jade no longer replied. Krissie's stomach sank with every passing day. What Carrie didn't realise, however, was that she had crossed the wrong mother. Krissie Edwards was about to start asking questions.

* * *

Offline, in Kenmare, others were starting to ask questions too. Locals, including Chloe, had started to notice that Carrie Jade's claimed symptoms of Huntington's were strangely inconsistent. Her voice quivered some days and seemed steady on others. Her hands shook while she poured tea but were still when she typed. She said she couldn't eat solid food, that she'd once nearly choked to death on pasta, that she lived now on smoothies and soups. This all felt tragic and believable, except when she forgot that detail and was seen eating toast on her porch one morning.

Regardless, Carrie Jade's charm was seamless and her network expanded. Over the summer of 2022, a small circle of local women began visiting the cottage regularly, chatting over tea, bringing groceries, sitting beside her laptop as she spoke gently about advocacy, illness and hope. Seeing her surrounded by such kind people reassured Chloe. 'I thought maybe they were part-time carers,' she said, 'helping her with her illness.'

By September 2022, however, things began to feel less benevolent. Carrie Jade offered jobs to locals, positions she said were part of a charitable venture she was managing remotely. Several people had Zoom interviews with her; others came to her home for meetings. Then, suddenly, everything went quiet. Promised start dates came and went. Messages went unanswered. 'That's when alarm bells started,' Chloe recalled. 'I bumped into another woman in town, and she said, "What on earth is going on with Carrie Jade?"'

Around the same time, Chloe stopped feeling comfortable in her own garden. If she went outside to make a call, her neighbour seemed to appear. If she lingered too long, she could feel her gaze. 'I started closing my windows,' she said. 'I didn't want her to hear me.'

When they were around others, she became suddenly distant with Chloe, self-contained, subtly warning Chloe away. It was clever, almost imperceptible. 'She kept people separate,' Chloe said later. 'She didn't want us comparing stories.'

By then, the name Carrie Jade Williams was circulating far beyond Kenmare. Her online presence, videos, interviews and elaborate narratives had attracted attention she hadn't anticipated. A reckoning was beginning to build, invisible but inevitable. As Chloe sat one evening by her darkened window, watching the light glow faintly from next door, she had the strange, sinking feeling that the woman who'd moved in smiling, fragile and full of impossible stories had already begun to disappear.

18

A TIKTOK DOWNFALL

Maz McClelland hadn't meant to become an influencer. She was a mum from Dorset – sharp, funny, a bit of a firecracker – and TikTok had seemed like a strange new world, one meant for teenagers and dancers, not women with children and shopping lists. But during the long stretch of lockdown, her friends had insisted, 'You'd be brilliant on there, Maz. People would love you.'

For months she resisted, rolling her eyes every time someone brought it up. What would anyone want to watch her for? But isolation does odd things to the imagination, and one afternoon she downloaded the app just to look. Within days she was hooked, not by lip-syncs or trends, but by the courtroom livestream dominating the platform: the Johnny Depp and Amber Heard trial. The case was everywhere, an online circus of celebrity, heartbreak and conflict. Maz became transfixed, not by the fame but by the psychology. The body language, the choice of clothes, the small tells in every gesture. She began recording nightly video summaries from her kitchen table, her cup of tea steaming in the corner, analysing what each side's performance revealed.

To her surprise, people listened. Thousands turned up in her comments overnight, calling her insights 'uncannily accurate'. She began venturing predictions, what Amber Heard might wear next, how she might present herself in court. When Maz said, almost laughing, that Heard would likely choose yellow, 'not for cheer,' she explained, 'but for control; yellow projects calm, optimism, authority in the storm', her followers laughed with her. The next morning, Amber walked into the courthouse in a buttery yellow suit.

Maz's follower count exploded. Hundreds of thousands tuned in daily, hungry for her warmth and quick wit. When the trial ended, she felt a void, like someone had turned off the power. For weeks she wasn't sure what to do next. She had built this huge, positive audience, but she didn't want to squander it on gossip. So she began doing what came naturally to her: lifting others up. Promoting small creators, sharing fundraisers, cheering for strangers who needed encouragement. 'Let's use this platform for good,' she said in one video, and her followers echoed her call.

Then, on the evening of 4 October 2022, her notifications lit up. Dozens of people had tagged her in a video from a woman called Carrie Jade Williams. Maz clicked, curious. What played on her screen was extraordinary, a young woman, with a well-spoken English accent, deeply upset. She said she was living with Huntington's disease and had been renting out her home through Airbnb to make ends meet. But now, she explained tearfully, she was being sued by her guests for 'emotional distress' after they had stayed in her home and were triggered by the sight of her disability aids, hoists, rails and specialist chairs. The woman shared a link to an online petition she had created to help her in her plight, encouraging those watching her TikTok video to sign it and share it far and wide. The petition read:

> **Help me show a Judge that disabled people aren't scary**
>
> Hello, I am starting this petition as I am about to be sued by guests who stayed with me – who have stated that they are traumatised due ot [*sic*] being forced to be around a disabled person (me).
>
> I would like ot [*sic*] be able to show a Judge (when this case goes to Court) that 100 people (and I know that is a lot) support the following statement:
>
> **Disabled people are not scary and should not have to pay compensation if someone dislikes their disability.**
>
> I can only share my side of this situation legally, so I am not asking you to support me personally – simply to support the statement that disabled people should not risk being sued for thier [*sic*] disability allegedly 'traumatising' another person.
>
> As a disabled person I cannot hide myself away. I cannot change my disability (I have Huntington's Disease which is genetic) and I cannot hide myself away in case I 'trigger' someone. I have also put up videos online about this situation in much more detail (ThisWorldCanBeAccessible both on YouTube and Tiktok), but I would very much love to have 100 people show their support to highlight that there are others like me who believe that disability is never something to be feared.
>
> Happy to answer any questions.

Maz gasped aloud. The story was outrageous, cruel, unthinkable. As someone who had worked as a carer, she knew how misunderstood disability could be, but to imagine a terminally ill woman being dragged through the courts for trying to live with dignity? It struck her deeply. Within moments, she was filming.

'Right,' she said, her tone both maternal and fierce, 'we're not having this. This woman needs our help. Go to her petition. Sign it. Share it. Let's do something that matters.'

Her followers answered immediately. That night, Carrie Jade Williams' petition began to climb, with hundreds, then thousands of signatures. Maz watched the view count on Carrie Jade's video surge into the millions. It was everywhere. The hashtag of Carrie Jade's TikTok username, #thisworldcanbeaccessible, trended across the platform for all to see. And for a few shining days, the internet moved as one.

TikTok filled with videos of disbelief and outrage, young women crying at the injustice, older men shaking their heads in fury, creators with millions of followers calling Airbnb out by name. Others used content from Carrie Jade's original video, reading comments from her petition in trembling voices. The platform pulsed with moral clarity, with empathy, with anger.

Carrie Jade basked in it, sharing more details, expanding on the story to hooked viewers, claiming that she was being sued for £250,000. Her soft features, illuminated by the glow of her phone screen, watched her follower count tick ever higher. To her audience, she was a symbol of courage against cruelty, a woman fighting not just a lawsuit but a world too callous to understand illness.

Maz, meanwhile, went to bed that first night proud, believing she'd done something good. She had helped change a stranger's life. The next morning, her video had half a million likes. The world seemed to be uniting behind one fragile woman.

No one, not even Maz, could have guessed that the story wasn't true.

* * *

The smell of wet grass and the sound of laughter carried on the wind. It was a Sunday afternoon, and Maz McClelland was in her happy place: the sidelines of a children's football pitch in Dorset, coffee in one hand, cheering as her son charged across the field. The air was sharp, the world simple for once. No TikTok notifications, no DMs, just the comforting rhythm of ordinary life.

Then her phone pinged. At first, she ignored it. Another comment, she thought, or a tag from her latest upload. But the subject line caught her eye: 'Carrie Jade is not who you think she is.'

Maz frowned. The sender was anonymous. No name, no signature, just a blank address and that one chilling sentence and a link to an online news article. For a long moment she hesitated, thumb hovering above the screen. Her pulse quickened. Curiosity won. She tapped the link.

The browser loaded slowly, the weak pitchside signal dragging out the moment until she almost wished she hadn't clicked at all. Finally, a news article appeared. The headline was from 2011, blunt, factual and utterly bewildering: 'Woman convicted of surrogacy scam'. Maz scrolled. Paragraph after paragraph detailed a complex fraud case involving a young couple, money, fraud and a woman named Samantha Cookes. Beneath the text was a small, grainy photograph. The face was younger, thinner, framed by dark hair, but the eyes stopped Maz cold. The same shape. The same begging vulnerability that had captivated millions online.

Her coffee slipped from her grip, splashing into the mud. She barely noticed. For a moment she just stared at the screen, her breath caught in her chest. It couldn't be. It must be a mistake, a coincidence. The internet loved twisting stories, feeding on doubt. She read the name aloud: 'Samantha Cookes.'

Maz felt a prickle of nausea. She glanced back towards the pitch where her son was shouting joyfully with his friends, completely unaware that his mother's world had tilted beneath her feet. The article said that Cookes had run a fraudulent surrogacy scheme, convincing a couple in Yorkshire that she could provide them with a baby, exploiting their vulnerability, their grief. Maz's hands shook as she read the details, the manipulation, the pattern of deception, the carefully constructed lies. She wondered if it was possible that Carrie Jade Williams, the dying writer the internet adored, could actually be Samantha Cookes, the convicted fraudster.

Her mind scrambled for logic. The time line almost fit. Over a decade had passed and faces change as time and age morphs them. But still. If it were true, then she, Maz McClelland, the supposed good Samaritan of TikTok, had sent millions to this woman's page. She had told them to trust her, to sign petitions. Maz felt sick.

The noise of the match faded into a dull hum as the realisation settled. If this was the same woman, then she was running a con on a scale that Maz couldn't have imagined. A woman who had exploited strangers offline might now be doing the same online, behind the soft lighting of a camera lens, and she had made Maz an unwitting conspirator in her scheme. Maz's heart thudded hard against her ribs. Her son was calling for her – he'd scored – but she barely heard. She forced a smile, waved back, applauded mechanically, then looked down at her phone once more.

The anonymous email glared up at her, cold and absolute. She knew what she had to do.

The drive home from the match had passed in a blur, Maz's son was chatting happily beside her about goals and passes while her mind whirled in tight, frantic circles. She nodded in all the right places, smiled when she needed to, but her thoughts were somewhere else, on the woman behind the phone screen, the voicc that had sounded so gentle and true.

At dinner, she chopped, stirred, plated, all by rote. The smell of spaghetti bolognese filled the kitchen, the everyday masking the extraordinary. Her son hummed as he ate. Maz forced down a few bites, her stomach in knots.

When the house was finally quiet, she sat down at the kitchen table with her laptop and a cup of tea gone cold. The room was dim except for the blue light of the screen and the faint hum of the fridge. She exhaled and whispered to herself, 'Right, Maz. Let's find her.' She felt, absurdly, like a detective in a spy film. Except this was real, and her gut told her she was about to uncover something dark. Typing the name Samantha Cookes felt almost illicit.

The first search brought up fragments, an old court report, an online news article, a few stray comments beneath old news posts. Then a school reference from Denmark Road High School for Girls. Maz's heartbeat faster. She clicked, scrolling through archived websites, alumni pages, staff lists, photographs of students, of class trips abroad. Slowly, she pieced together the trail, the kind of invisible thread that most people assume the internet forgets. She worked late into the night, and the night after, trawling page after page. Each tiny confirmation drew her deeper. Online forums. Photo archives. Social media scraps. Somewhere, she told herself, there had to be a clear connection, an image that would leave no room for doubt.

By the third day, she was barely sleeping. Mugs of half-finished coffee littered the worktop. Her notes filled a pad, lines of connection scrawled in blue ink: 'Surrogacy scam', 'Yorkshire', 'Gloucester', 'Same timeline??' Then she found it, the revelation hiding in plain sight.

Maz had been comparing video stills of Carrie Jade speaking on TikTok, analysing them side-by-side with old pictures of Samantha Cookes. Samantha Cookes was young, petite, blonde. Carrie Jade was larger, older with chestnut-brown locks. However, something about the shape of the jaw, the kind eyes, the set of the smile, felt too familiar. It wasn't until her cursor lingered over one particular image, a still frame from one of Carrie Jade's advocacy talks, that it struck her. There were three tiny moles on Carrie Jade's neck, just below her collarbone. Perfectly spaced.

She froze. If she could find an old photo of Samantha's neck, the match would prove everything.

She scoured the press images from the surrogacy case, her pulse quickening with each click. Annoyingly, in all of them Samantha wore a scarf, coiled high, obscuring her neck. Still, Maz refused to stop. She searched local papers, web archives, anywhere she could think of. Then, in a buried gallery on an old community newspaper's site, she found it. A candid shot. Samantha, younger, thinner, caught mid-step with no scarf around her neck.

Maz zoomed in. Three moles. The exact same pattern.

Her breath caught audibly. For a moment she did nothing, just stared, blinking, the static buzz of disbelief filling her head. She whispered, 'It's her.'

She felt a strange thrill, triumph laced with horror. She'd cracked it. The face that had smiled out from TikTok, that had captivated millions, that had asked for empathy, support and understanding in the face of adversity, belonged to a convicted fraudster. And she, Maz, had inadvertently helped her.

The victory instantly turned sour. Heavy nausea roiled her stomach. She closed the laptop, then opened it again, hovering between needing to walk away and needing to do more. But she was unsure of what she should do. Go public? Go to the police? How would she even begin to tell her followers that the woman they'd raised up, that she had raised up, was most likely not dying, but lying?

Maz sat in the half-dark kitchen, the glow of the laptop still flickering, her reflection pale on the screen. She had uncovered the truth, but the truth was unbearable. Because once you see something clearly, you can't unsee it. And Maz now knew what Carrie Jade Williams really was.

She realised what she had to do. Conscience wouldn't let her rest. She took out her phone and hit record. Her reflection blinked back, tired but resolute. The red light glowed. She took a breath.

'There's something I need to tell you,' she began, her voice low and steady, the words landing like stones in a still pond. 'You know Carrie Jade Williams, the woman with Huntington's, the one we all rallied behind? I supported her too. I believed her story. But after something's come to my attention, I started looking into her past. And what I found …'

She paused. The silence felt enormous.

'What I found is that Carrie Jade Williams is not who she says she is. Her real name is Samantha Cookes. In 2011 she was convicted of surrogacy fraud. I have verified it. The photos match. It's her.'

She could feel her pulse in her throat as she spoke, the enormity of it pressing down. 'I don't take this lightly,' she continued. 'I wish it weren't true. But people need to know who they are supporting.'

She stopped recording. Sat still. For a long time, she couldn't bring herself to play it back. The room was so quiet that she could hear the central heating creak. Finally, she pressed post.

Her phone hummed once as the video uploaded, then fell silent. There was no going back.

Maz sat there in the half-dark, staring at the blue glow of the screen until the first notifications began to appear, likes, comments, questions. The ripples of truth moving outwards, unstoppable. And somewhere, far away, another phone would soon light up. One belonging to the woman who called herself Carrie Jade Williams.

A reckoning had begun.

19

EXPOSING THE TRUTH

On the morning of 7 October 2022, in Coventry, single mum Krissie Edwards woke in the blue dawn light, her dreams heavy with tangled worry. She had paid all of her children's Christmas money to Carrie Jade Williams on the promise of a life-changing 3D-printed sensory room for her two sons with autism. Carrie Jade had gone quiet on her and no items had yet arrived as promised. She knew something was wrong, but she couldn't help but second-guess herself. The terminally ill woman online had seemed so gentle, so caring, so kind.

Reaching for her phone, she found TikTok lit up with dozens of notifications; something big was happening. Sleepily, she scrolled, and Maz McClelland's face appeared in video after video. Krissie had followed Maz online for some time and knew she never looked this serious. Curious, she tapped on the video. She watched, wide-eyed, as Maz spoke of fraud, of betrayal, of a woman called Samantha Cookes hiding behind the name Carrie Jade Williams.

The words landed on Krissie's chest like a stone slab, silent but impossible to lift. At first, she shook her head, but then the sinking realisation hit her. Maz's video was confirming her worst fears. She went to Carrie Jade's page, desperate for reassurance that her instincts were wrong, that Maz was wrong. But things had changed. There, under Carrie Jade's latest post, strangers were flooding the comments section:

> 'Hi Rebecca.'
> 'Omg it's Lucy, she's back.'
> 'She was with us in Cork, called herself Rebecca.'

Line after line was filled with fragments of a bigger story, one that didn't belong to the woman Krissie had trusted. Krissie's heart rattled in her chest. Had she really been fooled? Were these just trolls, or was there more? She couldn't let it go. Not now.

Krissie's tenacity kicked in and she began digging online. Birth records, address searches, social media handles, her screen time soared. She looked up Samantha Cookes and traced registration trails, housing, court documents, any breadcrumb she could follow. Stories and aliases unspooled – Rebecca, Lucy, Jade – stretching across counties and years. Empowered, Krissie started making TikTok videos of her own. She showed screenshots, read out old news clippings, walked viewers through what she was piecing together. Each new clue invited more comments, her followers growing as others tried to understand how they'd been collectively scammed.

As the wave of truth built, something strange rippled through Carrie Jade's page. Krissie was one of the first to notice that comments under Carrie Jade's videos, especially those questioning her story or dropping old names, began to vanish. Krissie watched in real time as these comments disappeared. Then, suddenly, Carrie Jade turned off the permission to comment on her site altogether. A day later, her videos started evaporating, one by one; the tributes, the writings on hope, the smiling workshops, all gone in the space of hours. Only blank spaces remained, a digital vanishing act.

And then, nothing. The account went dark, the profile picture disappeared, every trace was scrubbed. Carrie Jade Williams, her voice, her story, her pleas for help, were gone. Wiped out by her own hand.

Krissie lowered her phone, pulse thumping, her sense of outrage and vindication warring with something deeper – the ache of hope lost, trust betrayed. For a moment, all was silent. But one thing was certain. Carrie Jade, or rather Samantha, could run, but her digital footprints would always remain, and the women she had deceived were not so easily erased.

* * *

The fallout from Samantha Cookes' time in Dublin in 2016, when she was living as Lucy Fitzwilliams, had not ended. The trio of best friends – Lorraine, Hillery and Lynn – were still trying to come to terms with what had happened. Lynn described living in constant fear, installing security cameras and living with the dread that Lucy might return to abduct her daughter Ellie.

One day in 2022 Lorraine, technologically inexperienced, downloaded the app TikTok onto her phone to search for information on a woman in Dublin called 'Kerry', about whom she had heard a story. That story, shared by one of her hairdressing clients, was a wild true-crime tale of a crazed woman and the juicy details were available on TikTok. Lorraine was keen to find out more. Unfamiliar with using the platform, when searching the name 'Kerry', by complete chance she stumbled onto a video of someone called Carrie Jade Williams, whose face was unmistakably that of the woman she had known as Lucy Fitzwilliams. Her mouth dropped open. 'She's back,' Lorraine gasped as she called Hillery. 'Lucy's back, on TikTok!'

'What do you mean she's back?' Hillery exclaimed.

'I don't know how, but she's back and she's on TikTok!' replied Lorraine in a panic.

Confused by her friend's outpouring, Hillery decided to download the app. She quickly discovered Krissie Edwards, who was already investigating Carrie Jade Williams/Samantha Cookes online and decided to contact her. 'Krissie, I know you don't know me, but I need to speak to you. I know Samantha Cookes, she scammed us!' Krissie's response was instant and inviting, 'Come join the group.'

Lorraine, Hillery and Lynn all joined the WhatsApp group Krissie had created for Samantha's victims. This moment marked their uniting, creating a powerful network of survivors and sleuths determined to expose Samantha's continuing lies. As they shared their individual stories with each other in the WhatsApp group, their heads swam with the extensive length and breadth of Samantha Cookes' scamming. For Lorraine, Lynn and Hillery, the return of Samantha under yet another name brought the past rushing back.

Lorraine also reached out to Sinead in Mayo, telling her, 'Sinead, she's back, we have to stop her.' Sinead, too, was added to the WhatsApp group.

Krissie and fellow TikToker Maz's videos exposing Samantha Cookes as Carrie Jade Williams and unveiling the intricate web of lies were ripping through TikTok like wildfire. Each upload drew thousands of viewers, then tens of thousands. Comments flooded in, messages from women, men, families who had been touched, hurt, or outright conned by the same woman Krissie was exposing. Among the many voices reaching out to Krissie, one stood out. Layla sent her a private message that read simply but powerfully, 'I need to share my story.' In a matter of hours, she was added to the WhatsApp group Krissie had created. Lorraine, Hillery, Lynn, Sinead, Maz McClelland and others, all victims of Samantha's lies, welcomed her.

This was no longer a solo crusade. It was a movement gathering momentum and fury, a collective of survivors piecing together a picture of deception too vast for any one person to hold alone. Every new voice added a strand to the growing narrative – a mother burned by a broken promise, a family beguiled by false charity, a friend betrayed by a smiling stranger. Layla still remembered the initially sweet, angelic, au pair she hired almost a decade ago, who left behind a note in a discarded journal: *I did not murder my daughter*. 'I struggled to believe at first,' Layla said, 'but it felt like the same Samantha. The same pattern of lies, the same charm, the same scars she left behind.'

Together, these women parsed every detail, shared evidence, strategised next steps. Krissie found herself juggling online research, video production and managing a sensitive, growing community fuelled by hope and justice. The stakes couldn't have been higher. Samantha Cookes wasn't just a flimflam con-artist, she was a relentless predator who had told lies for decades, drawing sympathy and aid while breaking trust and leaving a trail of heartbreak behind her. Now, in the glow of phone screens and video calls, the battle for truth and justice flared into life.

* * *

For Samantha Cookes, the glow of the screen became cold and unforgiving as she logged on to her online world in the carefully constructed mask of Carrie Jade Williams. What she saw sent a chill racing down her spine. Comments came at her like knives. 'Hi Rebecca,' one sneered. 'It's Lucy,' taunted another. The online community she had once commanded was turning against her, a tidal wave of scepticism and fury crashing over everything she had built.

The truth had been laid bare by Maz's video. Carrie Jade Williams was no champion suffering from Huntington's disease but a fraudster hiding behind a thousand lies. Her surrogacy scam was dragged back into the harsh light of day, viral and merciless. The fragile fortress of her invented world crumbled, bricks falling with every accusation.

In a last, frantic gambit, Samantha turned to the one weapon she had left – her words, which had previously served her so well. On her 1820 Things website she posted a measured statement, calculated to stem the flood:

> My name is Carrie Jade Williams and I am writing this on the advice of my legal team. I am an entirely separate individual to my sister whose mental health past has been dragged into my life as an attempt to discredit my advocacy work.
>
> It is illegal and defamation to attempt to suggest that my sister's past is mine, when I am an entirely different individual. Legal steps have already been undertaken to stop this illegal defamation. I am an entirely separate individual and appalled that internet trolls have attempted to discredit my advocacy by bringing my sister's past and suggesting I am she. This mixing of people's lives is defamation.

> I am my own, individual person.
>
> I was not aware of the full history of my sister's mental health difficulties, though we support and love her. She has moved her life onwards and not had any legal trouble in nearly a decade. I will not be providing any further comment on my sister, due to the threats received.
>
> I stand in support of all those with mental health difficulties. My sister has had a long history of mental health difficulties and is suffering due to internet trolls attacking both of us. Internet platforms need to urgently take steps to ensure their platforms are not used to defame individuals and their families. I am not my sister and although we look similar (like many families) I am older and heavier. We live in separate locations and lead separate lives. It is defamatory to suggest that we are the same people when we are in fact separate individuals. Anyone suggesting we are the same individual will face the full force of the law.
>
> To any of those of you looking to cancel orders (which I take no profit from) please email hello@1820Things.com and we will arrange for a refund through Stripe.
>
> We ask for peace and quiet during this devastating time for me to mind my sister and take the legal steps to protect my reputation, as per the law.

She hit publish. The words were out there, cold, indelible armour amid the maelstrom of accusation. But this story could be no salvation. Samantha Cookes had no sister. The night was closing in, and Carrie Jade Williams – the creation, the myth, the lie – was bleeding out before a merciless world. However, the fight for her carefully created illusion was far from over. Samantha clambered to grasp control of the chaos, surrender never an option. Filled with the fierce fire of desperation, she leapt into action.

For the previous two years, usually under the guise of Jade Cookes, she had been campaigning relentlessly for accessible housing from Kerry County Council. According to the council's Housing Allocation Scheme, applicants with disabilities may receive priority status if their current accommodation fails to meet their medical needs. The process requires a detailed application, including medical documentation, and applicants are placed in order of priority on a waiting list assessed on eligibility and housing need. Samantha had weaponised this system, relentlessly driving her case with urgency and tragic narrative, leveraging the council's legal duties to persons with disabilities. Using every contact she could, from local officials to national politicians, her prolific letters and emails included urgent appeals to Minister for Special Education and Inclusion Josepha Madigan, Housing Minister Darragh O'Brien, Taoiseach Micheál Martin and Education Minister Norma Foley. In one stark plea, she wrote, 'I am writing as I am seeking euthanasia abroad on the grounds of inaccessible housing for disabled people.' She pressed them to intervene, demanding Kerry County Council expedite her 'medically necessary housing'.

Now, with her life as Carrie Jade Williams unravelling, Samantha sensed the pressure to secure this alternative housing. She poured herself into accelerating her campaign, petitioning, calling, emailing everyone she could think of, desperate to stave off the collapse of everything she had fought so hard for. She needed a new roof over her head, a fresh start, somewhere to concoct the next version of herself. With the world closing in fast, she was no longer just fighting for housing, she was fighting for survival. The clock was ticking.

20

THE END OF CARRIE JADE WILLIAMS

Chloe, living next door to Carrie Jade Williams, felt her phone buzzing incessantly late one evening in the middle of October 2022. Curious to see what the commotion was, she discovered multiple messages from a woman in her circle who had grown suspicious of Carrie Jade Williams. The urgent messages came with a link to a Reddit group that had outed Carrie Jade as Samantha Cookes and outlined her history of scams. Chloe's heart sank the moment she saw the grainy court photo; it was undeniably the woman she had thought she knew as Carrie Jade.

'It was like falling down a rabbit hole,' Chloe recalled. The Reddit thread was filled with messages from women claiming to know Samantha under different aliases, such as Rebecca and Lucy. The truth began to unravel with terrifying speed.

Chloe admitted she struggled to grasp the enormity of what was unfolding. 'I was piecing things together slowly,' she said, 'trying to understand what it all meant. I had to create a TikTok account just to connect with other women who had been caught in her web.' A phone call with one of the women from the group shook her deeply. Krissie Edwards warned Chloe to prepare herself, that Samantha was not just a compulsive liar but potentially dangerous. Chloe, with two young children, felt her stomach tighten as she wondered what the woman next door wanted.

Meanwhile, Samantha Cookes knew it was time to vanish again. With the online world alive with exposés tying her back to her real identity, she slipped out of her home, leaving her belongings behind. She checked into a hotel sixty-five kilometres away in Tralee, close enough to her life in Kenmare but far enough to stay under the radar, buying herself time to think. At the same time, she continued to bombard Kerry County Council with emails demanding emergency accommodation, while clinging to her 'Carrie Jade' persona. She even floated the idea of being placed in a nursing home as a last-ditch measure, threatening legal action if her demands were ignored. She claimed she was under palliative care, that she was on morphine and following a medically specialised diet, emphasising just how fragile and urgent her situation was.

When the council couldn't or wouldn't find her suitable accommodation, she asked if they would at least pay for her hotel or a B&B. They offered her a bed in a shared hostel, but she refused. For the first time in a long time, Samantha was not getting her way.

Back in Kenmare, Chloe had noticed there was no sign of Carrie Jade. The lights remained off, no one home. As the WhatsApp group pinged and chimed with text message revelations unfolding a chilling backstory, Chloe grappled with the new revelations about the woman she thought she knew. 'The fear of her coming back to the house was overwhelming,' she said. The group, initially all women, grew as survivors shared their stories, uniting in shared trauma and vigilance. 'The others said it was a pattern – when Samantha was outed, she vanished, abandoned her situation. I clung to that hope.' Yet Chloe felt a palpable paranoia, with her children in the house, and she spent nights awake on the couch, glued to the WhatsApp group, trying to make sense of the chaos.

Days passed with no sign of Carrie Jade. Chloe finally decided to send her a text. Just something simple, innocent. 'Hey Carrie, haven't seen you in a while, hope all okay x.' Instantly she received a response. 'Hi Chloe, I'm in hospital at the moment, be back soon x.' Chloe was dumbstruck by the continuing lies. Her nerves that night, after receiving that message, were shredded. She sat on the couch, watching out the window in fear.

And then, three days later, Samantha returned, stepping out of a taxi. Chloe, watching through the window, felt her body flinch involuntarily. Before she knew it, she was outside, face to face with Samantha Cookes. Chloe forced herself to breathe. Her voice almost caught, but her words came, soft, neutral, carefully measured. 'Hi, Carrie. How are you doing? Back from the hospital?'

Carrie Jade's face held its familiar warmth for a moment, but then, in a split-second shift, her smile thinned. The gentle attentiveness gave way to something colder, sharp, almost brittle. 'I'm just back for the night,' she replied, her tone clipped, no longer the kindly woman so many believed her to be. Her eyes bore into Chloe's, and for the first time Chloe saw not softness, but calculation. 'Is that okay with you?'

Chloe nodded, swallowing the lump in her throat, and turned away before the tremor she felt could betray her fear. Inside, her hands trembled as she closed and locked the door firmly behind her. She then watched from her window as, minutes later, this unknown woman walked back out through the front door of her rental home with a small bag, turned the key, walked down the short driveway and climbed into a taxi waiting to whisk her away. The solitary vehicle cut through the quiet hum of Kenmare's sleeping houses. Inside, Samantha Cookes knew she must leave Carrie Jade Williams behind, shed her skin and don a new identity. And she did.

Chloe's call to Tim the next morning, Carrie Jade's landlord as well as hers, was urgent and tinged with fear and disbelief. As she filled him in on the unfolding truth about Carrie Jade, his shock grew. After the call, Chloe sent him the link to the online melee exposing Carrie Jade Williams as Samantha Cookes, the serial fraudster. Tim was stunned. 'We all thought she was a suffering, dying woman,' he said later. 'My wife's a nurse and knew how brutal Huntington's disease could be. I didn't want to add to her stress, so I never chased her about rent.' Carrie had recently stopped paying her rent, citing hospital stays. Now, Tim realised that wasn't true. 'She had us all fooled. It's like that movie *Catch Me If You Can*.'

With no communication from a now vanished Carrie Jade and knowing Chloe, a young single mother, lived next door, Tim was worried about the situation. He decided to inspect the house himself one night. When he opened the door, the sight struck him speechless. His beautiful home was devastated, food rotted on the floor, walls gouged, furniture damaged, some missing, and piles of clutter everywhere. The stench was overwhelming. Among the wreckage, he found burner phones, modified fake provisional driver's licences and photocopies of passports. The magnitude of the betrayal made him physically ill. He was facing thousands of euros in losses.

But the worst was yet to come. Just a week later, Tim received shocking news. Carrie Jade Williams had lodged a complaint against him with the Residential Tenancies Board, just as she had done to her landlord in Cahersiveen. She claimed unlawful eviction, despite having fled the house in the dead of night, leaving unpaid rent and living under a false identity. The board informed Tim they would proceed to review her claim under the alias Carrie Jade Williams.

Tim was trapped in a limbo; he could neither re-rent the property nor clear his name without legal cost, all while dealing with the distress of feeling duped. On the day of the mediation hearing, unsurprisingly, Carrie Jade didn't show up. Tim sat alone on the Zoom call with the Residential Tenancies Board invigilator waiting in vain. 'A farce,' he called it. The experience left him disillusioned, just like Pauline in Cahersiveen, and he quit the rental business altogether, feeling abandoned by the system that offered him no real protection against someone like Samantha Cookes, a manipulator who turned tenancy laws into another tool for deception and gain.

Soon the whole of Kenmare would be left with a similar sense of disillusionment over the woman they had known as Carrie Jade Williams.

* * *

The story of Samantha Cookes' trail of devastation exploded into the mainstream on 9 December 2022, when Katherine Denkinson of *VICE* published an in-depth exposé titled '"Made My Blood Run Cold": Unmasking a TikTok Creator Who Doesn't Really Exist'. The meticulously researched article revealed that Carrie Jade Williams, known online for being an advocate for the terminally ill, as well as an award-winning writer, was in fact Samantha Cookes, a serial fraudster with a long history of scams. Denkinson's investigation revealed Samantha's real identity, her multiple aliases and how she had manipulated the internet and real-world communities alike for over a decade.

The *VICE* article was the spark that pushed the story from viral online chatter into the heart of mainstream media. Outlets like the *Irish Independent* quickly followed suit, with Ellen Coyne and Mark Tighe reporting on the unbelievable tale of how this woman had crafted a web of lies that entwined victims in Ireland and the UK. The story's gravity and shocking twists captured public attention worldwide.

The *Financial Times* swiftly withdrew their prestigious Bodley Head Essay Prize from Williams and deleted her article from their website. Penguin Random House followed suit. The Alzheimer's Society UK ceased all association with her and her company, Start Voice Control, terminating their project. Her literary agent at Greene and Heaton terminated the contract. The Wellcome Collection removed any mention of Carrie Jade Williams from their website. The world that had been so carefully crafted by Samantha Cookes collapsed like a house of cards.

In Kenmare, Carrie's unsuspecting neighbours and friends were faced with a shock they could never have anticipated. To them, Carrie had been a kind, quietly suffering woman with a huge heart, someone many deeply admired and trusted. The revelation that she was really Samantha Cookes, a con artist, was almost unthinkable. As the media delved deeper, the small community found itself at the epicentre of a huge scandal where personal betrayals met public exposure in a perfect storm. The quiet town of Kenmare would never be the same.

One December evening in 2022, the phone of Ronan Kelly, the RTÉ producer who had once met Carrie Jade Williams in Cahersiveen, buzzed with a message from his boss, Liam O'Brien. The text contained a link labelled, 'Is this your Carrie?' Hesitant but curious, Ronan clicked the link and was plunged into a revelation that shook him to his core. The article detailed the shocking truth that Carrie Jade was not who she claimed to be but was actually a serial con artist known for crafting elaborate scams. His mind raced as he read about the women whose lives Samantha Cookes had shattered through lies and manipulation. The sweet, vulnerable woman he had met was a fraud, but her con was about far more than money – she preyed on trust, hope and the kindness of others, leaving emotional devastation in her wake.

Feeling hoodwinked himself, he recognised that this was a story of extraordinary importance and deeply personal betrayal. Ronan and Liam resolved to help amplify the voices of Samantha's victims, and from this resolve was born the acclaimed hit RTÉ podcast *The Real Carrie Jade*, which was an immersive deep dive into unravelling the tangled narrative, exposing the deceit and seeking justice for those affected. The series not only chronicled the astonishing cons and hidden truths but gave a platform to those who had suffered silently for years, uncovering a modern tale of manipulation, resilience and reckoning that gripped the nation and beyond.

The podcast tore up the charts, topping true crime lists in both the UK and Ireland. Its meticulous unravelling of Samantha's lies, backed by expert interviews and survivor testimonies, gripped listeners like a vice. Each episode peeled back another layer of the story, compelling the audience to hold their breath alongside the victims. It was a chart-topping success.

A podcast series in the UK, *Carrie Jade Does Not Exist*, also covered the story, hosted by journalist Katherine Denkinson and British comedian, broadcaster and writer Sue Perkins, most widely known for being the former host of hit television series *The Great British Bake Off*. *Carrie Jade Does Not Exist* stormed the popular true crime podcast charts in the UK and pulled even more fascinated listeners into the complicated world of Samantha Cookes.

The media caught fire. Alleycats Films, a BAFTA-award-winning production company known for shining light on some of the darkest human stories, took up the cause. This author, who works as a director with Alleycats Films, partnered with RTÉ and BBC Northern Ireland to produce a two-part documentary series exposing Samantha's trail of wreckage on both sides of the Irish Sea. The documentary promised unflinching truth, a portrait of a predator who preyed on trust and hope with equal cruelty.

Yet despite the swell of public attention, the omnipresent question gnawing at every forum, every headline, every whispered conversation in smoky pubs and quiet homes was: Where is Samantha Cookes? The woman had vanished with a cold calculation that chilled even the most seasoned investigators. No trace, no pattern, just the echoes of her name, a ghost haunting both nations.

* * *

The women of the WhatsApp group, once isolated by their individual losses, had morphed into a fierce sisterhood, bound not by choice but by shared betrayal. Each message on their phones brought them closer, adding urgency and resolve into their collective story. Now, more than ever, the women in the group burned with a singular purpose: to illuminate the darkness Samantha Cookes had vanished into.

Samantha, the masterful chameleon, had slipped through every net cast for her. The trail went cold, and the silence around her disappearance rang louder than any accusation. But silence was their enemy, so they made it their battleground. With relentless determination, they crafted a campaign to distribute her photo, tell their stories and rally the public. 'If we raise enough noise,' Hillery told the group during a tense video call, 'somewhere out there, someone will recognise her. We will find her.' The women told their stories to multiple news outlets, including the *Irish Independent* and *The Irish Sun*, drawing more and more attention to the case.

In this fractured world of media frenzy and shattered trust, the women stood resolute, unwavering in their quest not only for Samantha's capture but for closure, justice and the restoration of stolen dignity. Every interview, every broadcast, every shared story was a step towards pushing Samantha Cookes out of the shadows and into the light where she could no longer keep hiding.

Samantha had underestimated her targets' strength, intelligence and resourcefulness. Each woman brought to the group a fierce resolve not just to expose Samantha but to protect others from falling prey to her. As Hillery said, 'She thought we were weak. But we've become unstoppable.'

21

JANE AND SADIE HARRIS

The videos had come first, pacy edits of Samantha's face on TikTok, cross-faded with eerie synth music and captions like #sickfluencer and #SCAMMER. In January 2023 the internet was alive with her name. Fascinated by the tangled web of her story, digital sleuths traced any remnants of the woman who had been Carrie Jade Williams. Victims, including Layla DeJagger and Krissie Edwards, began sharing stories of their interactions with the person they now knew to be Samantha Cookes. True-crime fans posted on Reddit threads in their droves speculating that she'd fled to Spain or Morocco, or a perhaps a little rural village in Wales where no one would notice her. No one guessed the truth – despite being outed in the mainstream Irish media as a fraud, Samantha Cookes was still in the Emerald Isle, this time in New Ross, County Wexford, living under her latest name, Jane Harris.

Coming up for air in February 2023, New Ross suited Samantha Cookes. It was small enough to slip into unnoticed, large enough that strangers didn't know who you were. The River Barrow curved through the town like a secret, and Samantha liked secrets, especially her own.

She spotted the 'To Let' sign on a small shopfront walking through town one wet afternoon. A charming shopfront that could be almost anything – a café, a printer's, a Montessori school, a dream. Within days, she'd charmed her way into a meeting with the owner, Jim Ryan, a man in his eighties whose good nature had outlived his caution. She introduced herself briskly, with that bright smile she'd perfected over years of pretending: 'Jane Harris. I'm an entrepreneur, 3D printing, educational workshops, that sort of thing.'

Jim nodded, warmed by her energy. She explained at pace and with smooth enthusiasm, how she would bring school children in to learn about design and innovation, how she'd even run a small Montessori part-time. New Ross, she said, needed imagination. Jim agreed. He immediately let the property to her, so charmed was he by her joie de vivre.

She paid him €700 in cash, apologising profusely that her bank limit prevented her withdrawing the full €1,000 for the first month's rent. 'I'll have the rest to you tomorrow,' she promised. But tomorrow never came.

Weeks passed. Locals said she'd opened a Montessori of sorts. 'Odd setup,' one commented, 'just a kiddie pool and a few boxes of coloured plastic fish toys.' Upon hearing whispers locally, Jim began to worry. Was this woman all she had built herself up to be? When he finally asked for the next month's rent, the tone shifted. Suddenly, Jane Harris was the aggrieved party.

The emails began, first polite, then insistent, then venomous. Jane wrote of a leak in the ceiling, of ruined stock, of thousands lost. Her tone was clipped, managerial, the voice of someone weary from putting things right. 'I've had to stop trading altogether,' she insisted. 'My printers, all of them, destroyed.'

At first, Jim had felt nothing but concern, already trying to calculate what costs for repairs might entail. Shortly afterwards, Jane Harris transformed herself from victim to creditor, now claiming that he owed her money, €25,000 for damages. The figure left him speechless.

When he visited the premises the next morning to see the damage for himself, he couldn't believe his eyes. The floor bore no sign of a leak. A cheap, blue paddling pool sat in the centre of the room, half-collapsed, its plastic walls wrinkled like deflated skin. Around it, heaps of black bin bags and wrung-out takeaway cartons slumped against the skirting boards. And in the far corner, by the shuttered back window, an inflatable mattress lay half-inflated, draped with a dirty blanket. Jim's heart sank as he realised she'd been living there.

There was no 3D printer. No workstation. Not even an extension lead. And what's more, no sign of Jane Harris. He stood in silence for a long time, the faint hum of traffic outside mixing with the slow tick of the clock behind the counter. He felt foolish, an old man duped by confidence and charm. He didn't realise then that he would in fact never see Jane Harris in person again. She had vanished from New Ross as quickly as she had arrived. However, she was not finished with Jim, not yet.

That evening another email arrived, polite, clipped and signed 'Jane Harris'. The next came hours later. Then another. They grew darker, demanding restitution, asking for his home address 'for correspondence'. Within a week they were threats, dressed up as legal formalities. Words like 'negligence', 'settlement' and 'court papers' appeared in bold. She added more allegations, the building not being fit for purpose, of having severe mould issues.

Sleep no longer came easily for Jim. The phone would light up with each new message, her name sitting like a curse on the screen. Linda, his daughter, found him at the kitchen table one night, staring at an email that opened with 'Final notice before legal action'. His hands trembled slightly as he read aloud to her.

'I think she's serious, Linda. I think I owe her something.'

Linda was appalled. Her father had never dealt with this kind of deceit. As Jim told her the story of this English woman and her grand tales of 3D printing, Linda knew something didn't add up. She told him, firmly, to stop responding and to let a solicitor handle it. 'She doesn't get to bully you into paying her, Dad. That's what she wants.'

He agreed, though his confidence was frayed. It would take weeks, and the quiet reassurance of his children, to steady him again.

Weeks passed with increased communications from Jane Harris. On 21 April 2023 she wrote:

> It is disappointing that we have not heard anything from you or your solicitor (which you stated you had instructed). Never before have I had to consider legal action and find it very unprofessional that you are refusing to negotiate.
>
> I am sending this in the hope you will negotiate this situation as Court will be extremely costly for you given how strong our case is. I do not want to financially cause you difficulties but I do need this situation resolved fairly and swiftly.
>
> We lost a lot of time and money due to your failures to be transparent and that needs rectifying. As you will

see from this email we are offering you one final chance to return our deposit and first month's rent, otherwise we will have to seek damages of over €20,000 through the Courts.

Unfortunately if this situation cannot be negotiated between ourselves we will be forced to initiate Court Action to recover damages.

As stated in our previous email we are out of pocket €22600 due to your failure to supply the information regarding the building failing to meet standard.

As stated below to avoid court all we are requesting is that you return our deposit and first month's rent. Should this proceed to court as stated below we will be forced to seek the full amount – and given the amount of evidence we have we have a strong case. We want this sorted swiftly and are willing to accept a far lower amount if this is dealt with quickly.

If you could confirm if you are willing to accept our offer by Monday – otherwise we will proceed to court. This situation has been extremely disappointing for us and we hope you will finally respond to this email rather than attempting to distract from the situation.

As a landlord it is your responsibility to ensure the statements made about your property are legally sound. I hope you will learn from this situation and ensure any future tenants are furnished with the leaking and flooding issue with this building.

Regards

Just after lunch on 24 April 2023, Jim received yet another email threatening court action:

> It is disappointing that after making a very fair offer to settle this situation you have decided to ignore our requests to avoid court and reach a resolution.
>
> If we have not had an offer to settle from you by 5pm we will be starting legal action tomorrow. Given the strength of our case and the fact we have 4 professional reports supporting that the unit was not as advertised we hope that the Courts will move quickly.
>
> As a reminder we have agreed to accept €1350 to avoid this going to Court.
>
> Should this proceed to court we will be seeking the full amount of €22,000 plus legal costs as standard.
>
> If you could please inform us by 5pm of you intend to settle before court action is started.
>
> Regards

Jane didn't used her name to sign off the email. Perhaps even she couldn't attach herself to the act of defrauding a kind, old man. When the emails stopped abruptly, without cause, after that day, the silence was almost as unnerving as her words had been.

Jim Ryan has kept a copy of the email correspondence printed out and saved. The printouts are fading now, but the memory isn't. He still marvels at how intelligent she seemed, how bright her eyes had shone when she said, 'This town deserves something new.' Only later did he realise everything about Jane had been new as well, right down to her name.

* * *

By May 2023, those looking for her still didn't know where Carrie Jade Williams, or rather Samantha Cookes, had vanished to. With a media storm continuing to swirl around her from Ireland to the UK, many continued to believe she had fled the island. TikToker Maz, who was the first to break the story on the social media app, got numerous tip-offs from people who thought they had spotted Samantha. One woman wrote in a DM:

> While out visiting family in Co Waterford on May 5th, I saw a woman who strongly resembled her on a bike at the Suir Valley Train Station in Kilmeaden and a while later at the Coach House in Kilmacthomas. She was with a male, also on a bike. It was approximately between 3–5pm. It might be nothing but I thought I'd pass on the info. I couldn't get her out of my head in case it was her. She needs to be stopped hurting all these innocent people.

Nothing ever came from any of these alleged sightings. Samantha wasn't in Waterford with a man on a bike. In fact, she was hiding in plain sight, right under everyone's noses in Celbridge, County Kildare. She had shed her latest guise of Jane Harris like a snake shedding old skin and become Sadie Harris. This time she reverted to something more familiar – the role of a Mary Poppins-esque nanny.

Nestled on the River Liffey, some twenty-three kilometres west of Dublin, Celbridge is a commuter town that blends ancient charm with the bustle of modern life. The town has just over 20,000 inhabitants, dense enough for life to pulse vividly but small enough that neighbours still greet one another by name. It's the kind of town where trust is currency and privacy is hard to come by.

Into this community stepped Sadie Harris, a name that held an odd echo for those tuned into popular culture. Sadie Harris was also a character on hit American television medical drama *Grey's Anatomy*. The character is a fiercely competent, vibrant surgical resident known for resilience under pressure. Whether Samantha Cookes knew this or simply liked the sound of the name remains unknown, but the choice seemed fitting: a woman stepping into a role requiring adaptability and strength.

In September 2023, Sadie arrived at the home of Maria and Fred Ward (not their real names) like a whirlwind of warmth and efficiency. Maria was preparing to return to work after maternity leave and needed someone she could trust implicitly to care for her two young children. Both Maria and Fred were busy professionals, juggling full-time careers and the intense demands of parenthood. They knew how important it was to find the right person – not just a caretaker, but someone who would be part of their family's daily life.

The couple had a spare room prepared, complete with a private bathroom, ready for the new nanny. When Sadie responded to their advertisement placed on www.mindme.ie, she sealed the deal with her background story. Over a Zoom online interview she claimed to have spent over seven years working as a nanny in Los Angeles, caring for the children of high-profile clients. Discretion had been paramount, she said, and she was bound by non-disclosure agreements that forbade her from revealing any identities. These legal contracts, common in elite childcare circles, ensured that the privacy of celebrity families was protected. Sadie's silence, ostensibly, was a badge of her professionalism. She spoke eloquently about the Junior Infants school curriculum, about the use of 'jolly phonics' to help children to begin to read and write. She really seemed to know her stuff.

Maria couldn't believe their luck. To find someone not only experienced but also immediately available in a town like Celbridge felt like a gift. A meeting with Sadie in person sealed the deal. Her easy smile, unfailing kindness and seemingly genuine warmth quickly earned their trust.

The two children, aged five and three, adored her from the start. Every morning, Sadie walked the oldest to the nearby local school, a charming stone building not far from the house, then brought him home in the afternoon, becoming an integral part of his daily routine.

Sadie also wasted no time finding her way into Celbridge's evangelical community, based at The Bridge Church, a warm and friendly congregation led by Pastor Matt Ryals, an American who had made Ireland his home. Matt remembered their first meeting clearly and, unlike many others who had been charmed by her, felt from the start that something was off about Sadie. Her stories were strange, tall tales, and her speech bore an odd cadence, peppered with the phrase 'Oh, that's so L.A.', something Matt knew no one who had lived there would actually say. That artificiality set his suspicions alight.

Nevertheless, Sadie fed an intricate web of falsehoods to the mostly female congregation members. She claimed her mother owned a diamond business in Israel, making her a wealthy heiress, and that she ran a women's refuge in Dublin to help prostitutes escape the streets. She spoke of an office in Dublin's city centre where she conducted this outreach work. To Matt, all of this seemed far-fetched and bizarre, but one particularly vulnerable woman, Simone (not her real name), was drawn to Sadie's charm.

In her forties, Simone was navigating a lonely stretch in life, longing for a connection and love that had so far eluded her. Sadie became her steadfast companion, and Simone would pick her up from Maria and Fred's home for joint gym sessions, during which they would have heartfelt conversations. Maria and Fred, who were not part of the church, were unaware of Simone's close bond with Sadie.

Sadie claimed to have attended a mega evangelical church in Los Angeles, a booming, conservative movement filled with strict teachings. She portrayed herself as devout, often remarking that women shouldn't wear trousers, broadcasting a holier-than-thou persona that seemed to give her power and a sense of superiority. She embraced the spotlight, speaking her mind boldly, an audacious move for someone hiding from the world. No one could have guessed she was a woman on the run.

Simone confided secrets to Sadie that she had never shared with anyone else, feeling safe and supported for the first time in years. Through these conversations she exposed her vulnerability to Sadie, who exploited it with ruthless precision. Where Simone longed for connection and validation, Sadie wielded that need like a weapon to maintain power and control. She dazzled Simone with stories of independence and strength, claiming she didn't need a man, but then slyly inserted the illusion of a perfect partner to keep her envious. It was a classic manipulation of hope and jealousy – Sadie could have a man, even if she pretended she didn't want one, while Simone was left feeling worthless, her own desires unfulfilled.

This manipulation echoed one of the hallmarks of covert narcissism, where feigned vulnerability and strategic emotional control cloak a deeper agenda. Sadie's care was a hollow pretence, wrapped in charm yet devoid of true empathy, making Simone feel safe enough to share her deepest fears, only to have them quietly used against her. In this toxic dynamic, Simone's self-worth steadily eroded, leaving her isolated in a friendship that was anything but nurturing. Sadie, in contrast, would have experienced a rush of power from this silent, insidious dismantling of another's confidence, maintaining dominance while masquerading as a devoted friend.

During this period of hiding in plain sight, Samantha led a deceptively busy life. She cared for Maria and Fred's children with great attention, organising arts and crafts projects that filled the home with colour and laughter. When the school had a bake sale to raise money, Sadie had a batch of brownies made and ready to go. Every morning and afternoon, she dutifully dropped the eldest to and from school, inserting herself deeper into the fabric of the family's daily routine.

However, Maria did begin to notice strange things about her new nanny. Sadie would never answer her mobile phone. It would ring and ring sometimes in the house and Sadie would simply ignore the call. On the rare occasion Maria needed to phone Sadie from work, Sadie would never answer but would soon call back from a withheld number. She shared complex stories of her life over dinner with great detail and embellishment. She claimed she had been adopted as a child by a wealthy Jewish woman. Her birth mother had been Irish, and hence Sadie had come to Ireland to seek her out. She had to do it in person in Ireland as her mother was deaf so could not take phone calls. She claimed to have been born in Bessborough Mother and Baby Home, the same location where the real Samantha Cookes had sat her Leaving Cert some years prior. Maria thought her stories outlandish, but they were delivered with such conviction and detail that she didn't think she could question them.

An active member of The Bridge Church, Sadie never missed services or weekly prayer meetings, fully embracing her devout image in front of the congregation. Yet Sundays were only part of the picture. On her days off, Maria recalled Sadie frequently taking trips into Dublin city. There, unknown to her employers, she engaged with the controversial Trans-Exclusionary Radical Feminists (TERF) movement, which opposes the inclusion of transgender women within women's spaces and rights campaigns, arguing from a gender-critical feminist perspective that womanhood is strictly biological. The movement is deeply polarising, sparking fierce debate about gender identity, rights and feminism worldwide.

Sadie kept her different worlds rigidly separate. Her TERF activism was never mentioned at the open-minded Bridge Church gatherings, where she displayed a warm Christian persona. To Maria and Fred, meanwhile, she projected a different image, that of a liberal feminist trying to fit into their progressive bubble, sympathetic to equality and women's rights. The couple remained oblivious to the more shadowy corners of Sadie's life, believing her to be the trustworthy, kind nanny they had welcomed into their home.

Each facet of Sadie's personality was crafted for maximum effect, whether devout Christian, radical feminist or liberal caretaker, always tailored to best manipulate those around her and evade detection. With her constant shape-shifting, she became a living lie, threading her way deeper into the lives she immersed herself in. But reality was about to catch up with her.

* * *

One calm February morning in 2024, Sadie did what she always did, walking Maria and Fred's eldest child to school, her smile warm, her manner gentle. The little boy laughed around her as they reached the school gates, his tiny hands holding hers, his trust complete. Another mother, having just dropped her own children off, caught sight of Sadie and the little boy. The kindness in Sadie's eyes, the easy grace with which she handled the child, it was impossible not to notice. There was a genuine affection there that made Sadie seem like a guardian angel in a world of hurried parents and chaotic mornings.

Later, on her journey home, the other mother tuned in to a podcast she had been meaning to catch. *The Real Carrie Jade* filled her ears, a riveting tale of a woman who wasn't who she claimed to be. A con artist, a master of disguise, a woman on the run. The story of Carrie Jade Williams, the nanny who had fooled family after family in Ireland, was wild, tangled with lies and heartbreak.

Once back home, her curiosity piqued, the mother's fingers searched for Carrie Jade Williams on her phone. Her breath hitched as the Google image results loaded. The face staring back was impossibly familiar. It was Sadie.

Her heart slammed against her ribs. *No, this can't be*, she thought, but as she continued to swipe, what she saw confirmed every fearful doubt. That gentle, kind nanny with the sparkling eyes and calm voice was the very woman the podcast had exposed. The woman behind the lies and broken lives.

'Oh my God,' she whispered, hands trembling. 'That poor family ... they have no idea.'

In that moment, the quiet, sunny streets of Celbridge seemed to hold a dark secret: a cruel con artist walking in plain sight unnoticed among the innocent.

The mother's car raced through the quiet streets of Celbridge, the podcast's harrowing story echoing in her mind like a siren. Her pulse pounded in her ears as memories of the gentle, smiling nanny at the school gates collided violently with the chilling truth she had just uncovered. She pulled into the school's narrow driveway, then propelled herself through the doors and into the reception with a fierce urgency. 'I need to speak to the principal immediately,' she said, breathless.

Within minutes, the principal appeared, her calm demeanour quickly disturbed by a realisation that the situation was grave. The mother laid out her evidence – the podcast, the images, the shocking realisation that Sadie Harris was none other than the elusive Carrie Jade Williams, a con artist and fugitive. The principal's face paled, lines of worry creasing her forehead. 'This ... this is very serious,' she murmured, voice tight.

The principal knew such news had to be handled with the utmost care. Were the family aware of who their nanny was? Was there some kind of explanation? Maybe they were somehow related to this woman? The principal's mind was swirling, trying to make sense of what she had just been told. A private meeting with Maria and Fred was essential, a phone call would not do. As it so happened, parent–teacher meetings were taking place that very day, and Maria and Fred were due to arrive that evening. Only a few hours away. It was decided it would be best to inform them then, discreetly, in person. This was sensitive, delicate, a situation that demanded compassion and caution.

* * *

The tiny chairs always made Maria smile. Every parent–teacher meeting began the same way, knees folded awkwardly beneath tables designed for five-year-olds, polite nods, and that faint smell of glue sticks and poster paint hanging in the air. Fred sat beside her, straight-backed and proud, glancing at the neat stacks of exercise books the teacher had laid out.

Their son's report was glowing. 'He's doing very well,' the teacher said warmly, pushing her glasses up her nose. 'Kind, curious, with lots of friends. He's a thoughtful boy, always the first to make sure everyone's included.'

Maria felt her chest fill with quiet relief, that soft parental satisfaction of knowing something in their careful scaffolding of life was working. Fred grinned, already planning a celebratory beer on the couch when he got home. Everything about the afternoon felt comfortingly routine. Sadie at home with the two children, dinner already prepped, rain easing off outside.

They stood to leave, thanking the teacher, when she added, almost as an afterthought, 'Oh, before you go, the principal would like a quick word with you. She's just down the hall.' Maria and Fred exchanged a puzzled glance but didn't think much of it. Principals liked to make an appearance; perhaps it was about a school fundraiser or a new extracurricular. Fred joked lightly, 'Maybe she's getting an award,' as they followed the familiar corridor lined with children's paintings, a blur of smiling suns, paper-cut rainbows, names printed in wobbly marker pen.

The hum of chatting parents faded as they neared the principal's office. The door stood slightly ajar, light spilling across the tiled floor. On the wall, the noticeboard was crammed with certificates of attendance and photos from the Christmas concert. Everything so ordinary, everything so safe.

Maria knocked once and stepped inside, still smiling. The principal looked up from behind the desk, her expression composed but weighted with something that didn't belong to an evening like this. She gestured to the two chairs in front of her.

'Maria, Fred, thank you for coming. Please, have a seat,' she said softly.

And in that pause, before a single explanation was given, Maria felt it. That small, sinking shift in the room. The sense that the ground beneath their well-ordered life had just, imperceptibly, begun to move.

'There's something you need to see,' the principal said, sliding her laptop towards them. The screen glowed with the headline of an article: 'Samantha Cookes, a serial scammer and fraudster'. More tabs opened, revealing news reports, podcasts and police statements. Stories of betrayal, hundreds of pounds stolen. And then there was the image. Carrie Jade Williams. It was the worst kind of news – their trusted nanny, Sadie Harris, was not who she claimed to be.

Maria's composure shattered. Hot tears spilled down her cheeks as the weight of the revelation hit her. Fred sat frozen, numb, panic lurking beneath a mask of calm. The question looped endlessly, 'Who is the person who has been looking after our children?' The feelings that washed over them defied words – pure, unfiltered terror; profound betrayal; confusion that made the world tilt and a panic that clawed at every breath.

They left the principal's office in a daze, their reality fractured. As they drove home under the dark sky of early nightfall, Maria wept quietly in the passenger seat, inconsolable.

Fred's mind raced, a cool head amidst the storm. 'Maria,' he said quietly, 'we need to play this right. We have no idea what she wants or how dangerous she really is. She's with the kids right now. We don't want to spook her. Who knows how she will react if confronted?'

The principal's words still hung between them, unreal, weightless, too large to fit inside the car. Sadie isn't who she says she is. Her real name is Samantha Cookes. We believe she's the woman from the news.

Maria's fingers twisted the ring on her hand until her skin felt raw.

'What if she's gone?' Maria's voice cracked. 'What if ...?'

Fred didn't answer. His jaw was set, eyes locked on the road ahead. He'd gone pale, his hands gripping the steering wheel so tightly his knuckles gleamed white.

The car fishtailed slightly as they turned off the main road onto their street. Maria's eyes darted to their house, lights on, curtains drawn, everything outwardly normal. Too normal. It made her stomach twist.

Fred, steady and resolute, said, 'We wait this out tonight. In the morning, first thing, we call the Gardaí. They're the only ones who should confront her, it's the safest way.'

Maria wanted to recoil from the nightmare, but she knew Fred was right. She didn't want to confront a potentially hostile Samantha Cookes alone in their home right then. She whispered, voice trembling, 'I can't believe this is real life.'

She fumbled with her seatbelt before the car had even stopped. Every step towards the front door stretched like a lifetime. She felt torn in two, the instinct to run away battling with the greater instinct to run in.

'This can't be real,' she muttered. 'She can't be, she's been with us for months.'

Somewhere inside, their children were playing, laughing, maybe watching television with the woman Maria had trusted completely. Only now did she feel the full terror of what that trust might have cost.

* * *

The family dinner that evening was a study in strained normality, a fragile theatre of calm desperately maintained over a bubbling undercurrent of dread. Maria forced herself to sit upright, her fingers trembling slightly as she served the food, determined to mask the storm raging inside her. The sight of her children's bright eyes filled with trust in this woman who was not who she seemed made Maria's stomach churn. Every time Sadie's gentle voice bubbled up in laughter with the children, or she saw her reach out to clasp their hands in a tender grip, her throat tightened as bile threatened to rise.

Fred, ever the stoic, tried to keep the mood light-hearted, engaging the children in playful banter, but the air between the couple was taut, heavy with unspoken fear. To the children, the world remained reassuringly untouched, their conversation about schoolyard games and the simple pleasures of their day. 'And then we made a rainbow with the paints!' one gushed, eyes wide. Their voices were warm as they confided in the nanny they adored. Meanwhile, their parents mechanically picked at their food, each bite feeling like a performance piece played out for Sadie's benefit.

Sadie, perceptive as ever, sensed the shift in Maria's demeanour immediately. She tried to draw her into conversation, but Maria's answers were clipped and sparse, an excuse of tiredness used to mask the tempest of emotions raging beneath. She fought hard to maintain the veneer of normality, the last thing holding her family's world together, but the façade was cracking.

Later, with the children long asleep, the silence in the house deepened. Maria and Fred lay awake, minds racing, hearts pounding. The woman who slept mere rooms away was a stranger, a liar, a fraudster and a fugitive. The weight of that truth pressed down upon them both, a silent spectre casting shadows over their every thought. In the quiet dark, only one certainty remained – their lives were forever changed. Maria was sure she would never trust another stranger again for as long as she lived. Not after this.

In the dark stillness of the night, the sound was unmistakable. Maria's breath caught as footsteps sounded in the hallway. Every muscle tensed and she froze, the weight of terror pressing down like a lead cloak. It was the middle of the night, but Sadie was not asleep. The faint rustle of movement drifted towards the kitchen. Panic flared.

'Fred, she's up. She's up,' Maria whispered urgently, shaking him lightly. He stirred, eyes fluttering open from a light sleep. Together, they crept silently through the shadows towards the kitchen, dread knitting their thoughts. Could she have one of the children? The nightmare spun through every possibility.

As they reached the kitchen door, it swung open. Their eyes locked on the figure of Sadie climbing out the window, a bag slung across her back. The outward calm they had barely maintained shattered in an instant. Fred sprang forward to grab her, shouting, 'We know who you are! You're Samantha Cookes! A fraud!' Maria fumbled for her phone, snapping photos, capturing proof of the fugitive in their home.

A tussle erupted and Fred yanked the bag from her grasp, fearing she was stealing from them. Samantha twisted to flee, nimble and desperate. Then, under the cover of night, she was gone, vanished once more, escaping before the Gardaí could be summoned. It was another failed attempt to catch a woman who was always one step ahead. Sadie had sensed the change, the tightening noose, back at dinner. She knew the jig was up and planned accordingly.

Maria rushed to their children's rooms, desperate to know they were safe in their beds where they belonged. She wrapped them in tight hugs. The invader was gone, but how long could freedom last for this woman they barely knew, the stranger who had blown their sense of safety to pieces?

Fred made his way down the narrow hallway towards Sadie's bedroom, the weight of what had happened pressing down on his shoulders. With every step, questions raced through his mind. What did this woman want? Why had she never asked to borrow money or for anything material? Were they just a safe place to hide? Her motives remained a mystery. The door creaked softly as he pushed it open, the room bathed in shadows.

What he found there deepened the confusion. Hidden in a corner lay a burqa, an unexpected and perplexing item considering Sadie had never claimed to be Muslim. It seemed like the identity she was hiding was even more complex than they could have imagined. A careful search also uncovered an arsenal of eighteen pointed implements called kubotans, designed for self-defence. Why would their supposed sweet nanny need such a thing? The chilling thought that these weapons had been in their home, where their young children slept, played and wandered freely, twisted Fred's stomach into knots. He felt sick as the full weight of the danger they had unknowingly harboured enveloped him. Sadie had been a master manipulator, living alongside them, savvy, prepared and possibly more dangerous than anyone could have guessed. The burqa and implements were clues to a covert world she had carefully concealed.

The Gardaí were called later that morning and arrived to take statements from Fred and Maria. They searched Samantha Cookes' bedroom and seized electronic devices left behind. That evening Fred changed the locks on the front and back doors as the children cried for their disappeared nanny. The family was left reeling, their sense of safety in their own home broken, their trust in humanity gone, facing work in the morning and no childcare available to them for the foreseeable future.

22

A SENSE OF PURPOSE

Pastor Matt Ryals was sitting in the half-light of early evening when his phone vibrated on the table. A message blinked up from a parishioner containing no words, just a link. He hesitated, then tapped.

A podcast began mid-sentence, a clipped, urgent voice detailing the rise and fall of a woman named Carrie Jade Williams, her string of aliases, the money trails, the betrayals spun like fine silk. Matt's heart slowed as he listened, the voice layering detail upon detail.

A new message arrived. Another link. This time, a news article with a photograph. It was Sadie. Except the caption didn't say Sadie. It said Samantha Cookes, also known as Carrie Jade Williams.

Matt stared at the screen until the image blurred. The room pulsed faintly with the sound of cartoons on the television, his children laughing somewhere out of sight. The world felt indecently normal. He tried to breathe, but his chest was tight with the implications of this revelation. Then, a name punched through the haze: Simone. Simone, who had trusted her, who had leaned on her. Did she already know?

Matt closed his eyes. All his quiet instincts, all the small hesitations he'd buried under the easy decency of faith, were suddenly laid bare. He had always sensed there was something off with the newest addition to his congregation. There had always been something beneath Sadie's calm. Something just slightly … rehearsed. Now, seeing the truth, everything suddenly made sense.

The following morning, Simone sat across from Matt in the church office, the faint scent of polish and candle wax in the air. She could tell from his face before he spoke that whatever he was about to say would change something she didn't want changed. When the words came, she could barely take them in. Samantha Cookes. Carrie Jade Williams. Fraud. Lies whispered into every conversation they ever had.

Her throat burned. 'No,' she said, shaking her head. 'You must be mistaken. Sadie would never …' But Matt only looked at her, sorrow etching his features.

The room faded as Simone tried to make sense of it. Every coffee shared, every prayer spoken in confidence, every tear shed in that woman's presence, each memory was now hollowed out. What had any of it meant? Was it all performance? For money? For attention? For some dark, private satisfaction? She pressed her palms to her eyes, but the tears came anyway. 'I trusted her,' she whispered. 'I let her into my home, around my child.' The words cracked in the stillness.

Her faith, once her anchor, suddenly tilted. How could someone who spoke of grace and light commit such deception and smile so sweetly while doing it? The betrayal wasn't just personal, it was spiritual. Simone felt stripped bare before the enormity of it.

Matt reached across the desk, but she pulled back, shaking, her grief folding into a quiet, consuming disbelief. Somewhere deep down she wondered if she would ever be able to look at kindness the same way again.

* * *

The story Celbridge held close to its chest couldn't be contained for long. By ten o'clock the following morning it was everywhere, on radio bulletins, as online headlines. The *Irish Independent* had named her. Samantha Cookes, alias Carrie Jade Williams, alias Sadie Harris. A serial scammer, operating once again under the guise of a perfect nanny.

For Celbridge, the revelation landed like a blow. It was one thing to scroll past a story like that when it belonged to another town, another set of faces. Quite another when you recognised the places in the photograph, when the cottage with the blue door splashed across the news was one you'd passed on the way to Mass.

Matt Ryals watched the coverage unfold with a strange hollowness. By noon, journalists began calling, first from Dublin, then from London. They wanted background, anecdotes, reactions. The BBC and RTÉ had already announced a joint documentary; they asked if he would take part in it. Fred and Maria, still numb, had refused. So did Simone. They didn't want people with microphones and cameras invading their sorrow. They wanted distance, quiet, the chance to reclaim something from the shock.

However, Matt said yes. Not for attention, but for warning. If his voice could help someone see through Samantha's charm before it was too late, then maybe some good could come of all this.

In the meantime, somewhere far from Celbridge, Samantha Cookes was still out there, watching, waiting, already assembling the pieces of her next illusion.

* * *

When the news of Samantha's appearance in Celbridge broke, Lorraine's phone in Dublin began to light up before she had finished her morning tea. Ping after ping, one notification after another, the WhatsApp group alive again. Messages flooded in. Shock first. Then anger. Then a kind of weary disbelief that tipped towards despair.

Lorraine read through the thread slowly, her stomach tightening as each new comment chimed in. 'She's done it again.' 'In another family's house.' 'With children.' It wasn't only the fresh betrayal that hit her, it was the thought of the children. Someone else's children now. The words blurred on the screen, but she could almost hear the tremor in everyone's texting rhythm as the fury that Samantha had done it again overwhelmed them. She stared out the kitchen window at the slow Dublin drizzle, remembering the day she'd first met Samantha – the charm, the competence, the calm. The shame of bringing someone like that into her friends' lives hadn't left her; it lived somewhere quiet and constant inside her.

By midday the tone had shifted. The pain was still there, raw and real, but beneath it pulsed something new: resolve. The group pinged on, long voice-notes, fragments of memory, plans quickly forming. They spoke of the upcoming documentary, how they would show up, speak out, lend their faces, their voices. No more anonymity. No more silence. The country needed to see Samantha Cookes for who she truly was, and they would make sure it did. They couldn't undo what had been done, but they could make sure no one else welcomed her into their home thinking she was Mary Poppins.

Lorraine closed her phone and sat for a long time in the quiet kitchen. Outside, the rain ran down the glass like thin threads. For the first time in months, she felt the faintest edge of purpose.

* * *

Though weeks had passed since that terrifying day, Maria still woke some mornings with Samantha's voice echoing faintly in her head, soft, practised and soothing. She and Fred were barely keeping the household afloat now, juggling two jobs and patchwork childcare. Each evening, after tucking the children into bed, Maria sat staring at the empty space where Sadie's things used to be, wondering how she could have been so deceived.

Then one morning, as she sorted through the post left on the hallway table, a white envelope caught her eye. No return address. The handwriting neat, deliberate. She tore it open, expecting perhaps a 'thinking of you' card or a note from school. Instead, she found a single sheet of lined paper, written in looping blue ink:

> I am writing as my solicitor has advised I give you the opportunity to correct your failings as an employer. I

am open to negotiating this situation and hope you will respond within 14 days with a resolution to avoid this being progressed through the Civil Court options available.

During my time employed by you, I experienced deeply unfair conditions and unpaid wages. I am therefore requesting payment of €7,183.70 to rectify these matters immediately.

Please correspond regarding settlement to the email address below.

Regards,
S H.

Her pulse hammering, Maria read the letter twice, then a third time, waiting for the words to change, for the sense to shift into something understandable. But it stayed absurdly, terrifyingly real.

'S H'. Sadie Harris. She was still pretending.

Fred found his wife standing in the kitchen, the paper trembling in her hands. 'It's her,' Maria whispered. 'She's still out there. Still playing games.' They stared at the letter together, until Fred stated what she already knew. There was no return address, no solicitor's name, no way of getting in touch. It was just an audacious taunt thrown from the shadows.

The national papers had plastered Samantha Cookes' face across every newsstand in Ireland. Still, somehow, she had found a way to reach them, to turn herself from villain back into victim, to make even her crimes sound administrative. Maria folded the letter and sat down hard at the table. The kettle boiled in the background, unseen, hissing like static. For the first time since the story broke, she felt hunted instead of simply bewildered.

✻ ✻ ✻

Samantha Cookes had vanished from Celbridge the night she realised she'd been rumbled, leaving behind a quiet estate and traces of another life she'd worn like a costume. Celbridge was no longer safe for her. By the time her name hit the national airwaves, she was already two counties away, moving through the edges of anonymity that still existed if one knew where to look.

This time she had nothing. No suitcase, no savings, not even a change of clothes. Her photograph was all over the news, her story repeated and dissected. A woman without a past and with far too many names. But Samantha had been here before.

She sat in a small café near a bus stop in the midlands, nursing a cup of coffee she hadn't paid for, thinking. She wasn't finished. People said she was reckless, destructive, but Samantha probably preferred a different word: adaptive. Yes, she had lost her place in Celbridge, but that was only one version of herself. There would be others. There always were.

By evening, she had wiped her phone and created a fresh email account. As the streets darkened outside, inside her mind another story was already forming. She would find a new family in a small town where people still left their doors unlocked. Somewhere her charm could take root again. It never took her long to rebuild.

For a while, Samantha kept her head down. The media storm passed on to other scandals, other faces. She had learned when to vanish into the background and when to reappear under a different light. In April 2024, she enrolled in Education and

Training Board programmes designed for adult learners looking to upskill or change careers. They were the kind of classes that drew a mix of people, including parents returning to work, recent graduates between jobs and workers retraining after the pandemic. Accessible, friendly, anonymous enough for someone like her.

To her new classmates, she introduced herself as Jade Cooke, a name she had used before. She said she lived in Cahersiveen, a place she had lived before. Sarah (not her real name) met Jade on one of these ETB courses, a ten-week programme combining online tutorials with an in-person skills presentation in Thurles. The group met twice weekly on camera, a grid of polite smiles and kitchen backdrops. Jade was always there, cheerful, attentive, sometimes over-prepared.

In messages, she shared fragments of her life, wheeling out her usual tropes. The medical problems – a claim that the COVID-19 vaccine had given her epilepsy, that she was suing AstraZeneca. She told stories of being adopted, of recently reconnecting with her birth mother and a deeply troubled sister. The details were elaborate, emotionally charged, yet strangely performative, as if she tilted each disclosure towards pity, then curiosity. Sarah found some of the turns in those conversations odd. But she dismissed it as simply someone oversharing.

It wasn't until a week after an in-person session in Thurles that everything clicked into place. Scrolling the news late one night, Sarah stopped cold. There it was, the name Samantha Cookes, a photograph beside it. The face was unmistakable: Jade, smiling faintly at the camera. Her stomach dropped. The same woman who had hoodwinked a family in Celbridge, who had vanished into scandal, was now using yet another alias.

Jade's texts about course assignments kept coming for a few days after that, polite and upbeat, but Sarah couldn't bring herself to reply. Perhaps Samantha sensed the change, because one evening the messages simply stopped. Her square on the class video grid online went blank, the name 'Jade Cooke' deleted.

23

TRALEE

Detective Garda Ray Liston's office sat at the far end of a long corridor in Anglesea Street Garda Station in Cork. The building itself was unremarkable, with its grey walls, a flickering fluorescent light and the hum of a heater that worked only when it felt like it. Yet from this plain little room, a trail of deception was about to be unravelled. Many of the details of Ray's careful work would only emerge later through court records and media coverage.

Ray was a man with a knack for pattern work, for following inconsistencies in reports that others dismissed as clerical errors. The kind of mind that saw shapes in the chaos. In 2024, he was on secondment to the Department of Social Protection, where he was tasked with investigating welfare fraud.

It seems that the Cookes file landed on his desk on a Tuesday morning in a tide of digital paperwork. He nearly missed it, buried as it was between two larger files dealing with VAT theft. But the details were odd.

The name: Samantha Cookes.

The declared condition: Huntington's disease.

The claim: disability welfare, backdated for two years.

When Ray began to read, the inconsistencies soon appeared. The medical forms had gaps. There were bank transfers, but the addresses changed every few months. A quick google of the name would reveal news reports, headlines screaming about a 'Mary Poppins Conwoman'. Photographs. A woman caught half-smiling outside a courthouse, then again outside a neat suburban home. Whatever her story was, it had burned through more than one community. And now, it seemed, she had found her way to the State's accounts.

Many cases would have crossed Ray's desk where the perpetrator was never traced, but this one pulled at him. The scheme was too intricate, too confident. A patient predator disguised as an ordinary woman. He picked up the phone and called in a request for verification from the Department of Social Protection of medical records, addresses and a banking investigation.

Meanwhile, unbelievably, his target sat in a rented room in a housing estate 95 kilometres as the crow flies from the station Ray in which was operating. Her laptop was open, the hum of its fan drowning out the muffled noise of the traffic on the road below. She was absorbed in another reinvention – new email, new name, new story. She had started where she always did, at the beginning, with details small enough to be believable, birthdates altered by weeks, qualifications borrowed from the profiles of others. Samantha thought she had slipped the net once again, her name lost in the crowded fog of online bureaucracy. She didn't know that a young detective had begun tracing her through the very systems she lived off.

Ray printed a map of Ireland and began to mark sightings, a red pin for every place she'd touched: Tullamore, Dublin, Mayo,

Cork, Galway, Waterford, Cahersiveen, Kenmare, Wexford, Celbridge. One by one, the red marks formed a crooked path, a trail of broken trust. Finished, he stood back and studied it, the rhythm of it, the pattern. It was never random. There was logic to her movement. She always chose trust-rich environments.

The fraud committed was rarely just about money. It was theatre. It was control. And from now on, he told himself, his pursuit would reflect this control.

Outside, the Cork night deepened, the wind rising off the wild Atlantic. Inside the office, a lone lamp burned above Ray's desk as he began to write her name onto the first line of a new case file – Investigation: Samantha Cookes.

Now, at last, Samantha Cookes was being watched.

When the Cookes file slid into his queue, Ray Liston would have seen enough cases to know that even the neatest narratives rarely survived close inspection. He began with the GP, the doctor whose signature had legitimised Samantha Cookes' disability claim by confirming the diagnosis of Huntington's disease, one of the rarest and cruellest genetic conditions. The GP answered the phone on a damp morning, their voice courteous but cautious. When Ray explained the purpose of his call, there was a long silence, the kind that settles thickly over a room before confession.

'Well,' the GP said at last, 'she told me she'd been diagnosed while under a consultant in Dublin. Her symptoms seemed ... plausible. Tremor, unsteady gait, slurred speech. But no, I never saw the specialist's letter myself. I believed her.'

No evidence. No neurologist's report. The house of cards swayed.

Ray drove to the clinic that afternoon, the road narrow and shining with rain. He collected a copy of the file, which was thin, too thin for a chronic neurological diagnosis, and scanned through the notes in his car. It was, as he would come to know, classic Samantha Cookes, with well-constructed detail presented with enough authority that people stopped asking questions.

Later, poring over the files in closer detail, he realised they contained no conclusive proof that Samantha Cookes had Huntington's disease. There was no official diagnosis signed off by a specialist consultant as you would expect. But with the GP's sign off, the Department of Social Protection had been steadily paying hundreds of euros every month in disability benefits to a ghost moving under false names.

Leaning back in his chair, arms folded, Ray stared at the map that hung on his wall. It showed all the post office withdrawals of the disability payment. Recent collections clustered around one branch on Edward Street, Tralee. It was something. The first solid trace of Samantha's whereabouts in months. She wasn't online or renting property under her real name, and she had no known friends or family who would shield her in Ireland, yet records showed someone was walking into that Tralee post office every week to collect the payments. It had to be her.

The following day, Ray drove to the town, parked discreetly on the street, and watched the glow of the post office sign humming in the early morning rain. Through the windscreen he'd watch. He'd wait. A week, two if he had to. He knew her pattern now. She couldn't resist routine, and from what he'd read of her history, she always came back to collect what she thought she was owed.

As the rain ticked down on the car roof, Ray settled deeper into his seat. Somewhere out there in the wet anonymity, Samantha Cookes was still moving, still scheming and, he was certain, still within reach. The hunt had entered its quietest, most dangerous phase.

* * *

Week one passed in patient silence. No sign of her. But the payment was released weekly, so Ray knew he would have other chances. However, the following week there was again no sign of Samantha. Ray returned to his office frustrated but uneasy. He knew she was out there; someone was collecting the payments.

On week three, he changed tactics. He parked at a different angle, closer to the post office this time, with her photograph tucked just inside a notebook on the passenger seat of his car. He watched, scanning each passerby against that sharp, steady face he'd memorised.

Then he saw her. Her hair was shorter and she wore sunglasses despite the dull light. A neat trench coat was belted at her waist and a canvas bag hung from one shoulder. She moved with calm purpose, the kind of calculated casualness he had read about in every report. Even at a glance, Ray knew. The weight of recognition hit him. He leaned forward slightly, fingers tightening on the steering wheel.

Samantha entered the post office. Ray waited thirty seconds, then another thirty, before stepping out of the car. The air was cool, the town moving quietly around him. Crossing the street felt like stepping through water, the sound dulled by adrenaline.

Inside, the post office smelled of paper and polish. The line was short. At the counter, Samantha was asking for her payment with the same calm sweetness she had once used to comfort children and charm parishioners. Ray stood just behind her, watching the transaction unfold.

When the teller handed over the cash and she reached to slip it into her bag, Ray spoke. His voice came out level, deliberate.

'Ms Cookes.'

She froze. Not dramatically, just enough that the moment stretched thin. Her shoulder blades squared. Then, slowly, she turned. For a breath, neither spoke in the heavy silence. Then Ray, showing his badge, said quietly, 'I think you and I need to have a chat.'

Her expression didn't break. Not a flicker of panic, not even surprise, only the faintest smile that never reached her eyes. As he escorted her towards the door, she looked around the post office at the curious faces and the teller, frozen mid-motion. 'You've been waiting for me,' she murmured.

Ray guided her out of the building. 'For a while.'

It was 12 July 2024. Outside, the air smelled of wet tarmac and salt. Somewhere a church bell started to ring, distant but clear. The past was finally about to catch up with Samantha Cookes.

24

THE LIES REVEALED

The news broke just after six. Lorraine was cooking dinner when her phone started to buzz, one message, then another, then the familiar flurry from the WhatsApp group that had bound the group of women together over months of shared disbelief and pain.

'SHE'S BEEN ARRESTED.'

'Tralee.'

'It's on RTÉ news!'

She froze where she stood, wooden spoon midair, the sound of the radio filling the kitchen. The broadcaster's steady tone cut through the soft crackle of the pan. 'An arrest has been made in Tralee today in connection with a major welfare fraud investigation. The woman, understood to be using multiple aliases, including Samantha Cookes, will appear before court later this week.'

Lorraine sank into the chair beside the table, weak with an emotion she could barely name. It wasn't joy exactly, but the easing of a constant tension. After all the false leads, all the appearances and disappearances, someone had finally caught her.

Within minutes, the WhatsApp group erupted, messages pouring in. Hillery typing in all caps. Krissie sending voice-notes through tears. Lynn, Layla, Sinead, Maz, one after another, their disbelief turned to a shared, cautious triumph.

The following evening, after Samantha had appeared before a Special Hearing of Tralee District Court to be denied bail, *RTÉ News* replayed the shaky footage of her arrival at the Tralee courthouse steps, the press packed tight. A glimpse of Samantha's face as she was led from the car – almost serene, the same faint, unreadable smile she'd worn in all those old photographs.

Chloe messaged the group, 'She doesn't even look sorry.'

Lorraine stared at the television screen for a long time, her heart hammering. For years they had lived in the shadow of that woman's deceit, second-guessing, doubting their instincts, trying to rebuild trust in themselves and others.

Now, maybe, it was over.

But even as the women typed out messages of relief, the mood underneath remained fragile. 'Let's see if she's actually charged,' Maz wrote. 'We've been here before, feeling like things are finally catching up on her only for her to get away with it again.'

Lorraine understood. Justice never moved quickly and Samantha was an expert in finding ways to twist circumstances in her favour. But this time it felt different. The State was involved. The evidence was conclusive. Lorraine typed slowly: 'She can't talk her way out of this one.'

After years of silence, years of explaining and waiting for someone in authority to take action, they finally had proof. And somewhere in Tralee, under the harsh light of an interview room, the woman who had wrecked so many lives was learning how it felt to be the one cornered at last.

* * *

A few short days later the *Irish Mirror* reported:

> Samantha Cookes charged with defrauding the Department of Social Protection of almost €60,000. She was arrested outside Edward St post office in Tralee on Friday when she was due to collect a weekly disability allowance worth €232.
>
> The 36-year-old is suspected to have collected 238 payments totalling €59,094 over a four-year period, Tralee District Court heard on Saturday.
>
> Gardaí allege that she initially submitted a claim for Supplementary Welfare Allowance in February 2020 on the basis that she had Huntington's disease.

Krissie, always the first off the mark, sent the article straight to the WhatsApp group. The women knew that her upcoming trial would be their chance to face Samantha Cookes. 'I want to go to court and look her in the eye,' Hillery texted the group. So a plan was formed that those who were able to attend would do so.

Samantha, initially, did not enter a guilty plea. She maintained her innocence and the case was moved from the District Court to the Circuit Court, meaning a trial by jury would be required. After eight months of delays and setbacks the trial was scheduled for 18 February 2025. However, in typical Samantha Cookes style, she once again surprised everybody by unexpectedly entering a guilty plea on 11 February, thereby avoiding a trial. A deal was agreed that she would plead guilty to a figure of €60,334 claimed fraudulently between the dates of 28 February 2020 and 12 June 2024.

Robbed of the chance of seeing Samantha's case played out in front of a jury, her victims knew that sentencing day in court was their last chance to see her in cuffs in person. Although they knew they would probably never get justice for the psychological pain she had put them through, the sentencing would at least be a justice of sorts.

With Samantha Cookes in custody in Limerick Prison, the morning of sentencing broke damp and pale over Dublin, that cool slate-grey light that never quite becomes daylight. Lynn zipped her coat to her chin, nerves tightening her chest. Beside her, Hillery gripped a coffee that had long gone cold. It had been nine long years since they'd last seen Samantha in the flesh. Nine years of waiting, explaining, reliving. And now, finally, their chance to witness justice being done, however narrow its scope, had arrived.

The two women met the Alleycats film crew, including this author, with cameras stowed in padded cases, in a near-empty car park near the M7, the air heavy with anticipation. The documentary crew would be accompanying them to record this journey of closure. The drive to Tralee was long and silent in stretches, the road winding through misty lowlands, the windows streaked with drizzle. Each woman carried her own heavy thoughts, memories of phone calls, messages, moments of betrayal replayed until they were worn thin.

The spire of Tralee's courthouse rose from the town like something ancient and watchful, its stone façade damp with rain. The square buzzed with low chatter, Garda cars lined the kerb, and camera tripods brushed against umbrellas. Chloe, Samantha Cookes' former neighbour in Kenmare, was waiting outside, hands gripping a folded umbrella. She had spoken with the other women on WhatsApp almost every day for the past three years, bound by fury and grief through the blue-lit glass of their phones, but meeting in person made them all suddenly emotional.

'You made it,' Chloe said, her voice trembling. Lynn nodded, unable to speak. They hugged tightly, the kind of embrace made taut with shared history.

Inside Tralee Circuit Court, the air felt colder and almost sterile. The ceilings arched high, pale walls echoing with every shuffle and whisper. Rows of dark wooden benches gleamed under harsh strip lighting. Garda officers stood at measured intervals, neutral faces betraying nothing. At the front, the judge's bench rose above the room like a stage. The Irish harp carved in dark relief stood behind it, a symbol of State authority casting long shadows. Journalists filled one corner, murmuring as they readied their notepads. In the hush between sounds, the second hand of the courtroom clock was the only thing that moved.

Lynn and Hillery sat down with Chloe in the second row, the smell of varnish and old paper sharp in the air. Lynn's hand found Hillery's, Chloe reached across, linking them all.

Then, all of a sudden, from the side door, escorted by two uniformed officers, Samantha Cookes appeared. Her hair clung to her temples, the grease catching in the light. She wore a pale-pink cardigan and black leggings, the same outfit she had worn in the pictures splashed across the newspapers after her arrest. Her wrists glinted in handcuffs.

For a second, the room seemed to narrow around her. The years stripped away, the nanny in Celbridge, the award-winning author in Kenmare, the lodger in Cahersiveen, the occupational therapist in Dublin. All those names, all those stories, collapsed into this single, extraordinary moment. Lynn felt her throat contract. Hillery's grip tightened hard enough to hurt.

Samantha looked up. Her eyes swept the courtroom, glassy but alert. Then she saw them. A flicker of recognition flared across her face, then shock, raw and unguarded, but only for an instant. Like a candle snuffed out, her expression quickly morphed back into something blank, indifferent. She tilted her chin, looking past them as though they were strangers she'd never met.

She walked with a limp, subtle but deliberate. Sitting, she bowed her head, lips twitching, body rocking slightly. It seemed as if she was performing the symptoms of Huntington's again, the same act that had fooled doctors, neighbours and her online audience. The women exchanged glances that carried years of disbelief and outrage.

'She's still pretending,' Chloe whispered.

A hush fell.

The court registrar's voice called out, 'Court rise.'

Everyone stood, the scrape of benches filling the air as the judge, Ronan Munro, entered, robes swinging, the authority of the State now heavy in the room.

Samantha sat motionless, eyes lowered, the faintest tremor convulsing her fingers. A clerk rustled papers, the sound snapping through the air. Then came the voice of Tom Rice for the prosecution, steady, deliberate and unhurried as he began to read into the record: 'Samantha Cookes duped a respected GP into filling out a form saying she had been already diagnosed with Huntington's disease, a condition she claimed was terminal and life-limiting ...'

Each word landed like a weight. Lynn swallowed hard,

stealing a glance at Samantha two rows ahead, seated between her solicitor and the attending Gardaí. Her hair hung limp and stringy, her shoulders curved inward, a pale imitation of the woman who once commanded rooms.

Rice continued, outlining the offences: two charges of deception, sixteen counts of theft. The figure, €60,334, hung in the air. 'She drew seventy-four payments, totalling €17,747 in supplementary payments,' Rice read. 'When the Department of Social Protection sought to verify her diagnosis, Ms Cookes, as Garda Liston put it, fought fire with fire.'

Appearing in the witness stand, Ray Liston's voice was crisp as he outlined his findings of deliberate deception of medical experts and the welfare system. Chloe felt a calm wash over her as she listened to him speak; he knew his stuff. This was the first time she'd seen him, this detective who had tracked Samantha down through quiet persistence, something none of them had managed on their own despite years of trying. His testimony gave flesh to a story they all knew but could never quite prove themselves.

Prosecuting barrister Tom Rice pressed on. 'By her hand, a respected GP was deceived, led to believe she was wasting away. She claimed she could no longer grip a pen, that her balance and coordination were collapsing.'

A pause.

'But hospital records showed otherwise. She missed every appointment. No scans. No tests. No genetic confirmation.'

The judge took notes, silent except for the faint scrape of his pen. The rain tapping the windowpanes filled the spaces between sentences.

Garda Liston agreed with each point, unflinching. 'The façade fell apart with the first verification request. Once the department crosschecked with all of the neurology clinicians in Cork, nothing existed. The lie unravelled.'

Rice moved to the next layer of deception. The pleading letter to the Department of Welfare, handwritten, the appeals for compassion during Covid lockdowns, false claims of epilepsy. 'She wrote that she could no longer hold a pen,' Rice said quietly, 'and yet she did, long enough to write lies that defrauded the State.'

Hillery was horrified by the callousness of it, how Samantha had used illness and vulnerability as theatre.

Then came the list of amounts again, read clearly, the polished rhythm of a court accustomed to repetition. How her bank balance swelled through the pandemic with €17,747 in welfare payments and another €40,264 in disability allowance, a further €2,323.35 in additional payments from the Irish Welfare System. And then, 'Her account also showed payments of €36,250 from the Arts Council.'

Gasps rippled through the courtroom. The judge stilled the room with a brief look over his glasses. Hillery, Lynn and Chloe stared ahead, stunned. Lynn thought of all the months she'd wondered how Samantha always had money for new beginnings, new disguises. Now they knew.

The defence rose. Barrister Richard Liston (no relation to Garda Liston) dignified, composed, but faintly weary said, 'Ms Cookes wishes the court to know she accepts full responsibility. She apologises to the Department of Social Protection, to the GP involved, and recognises the hurt caused.'

Behind him, Samantha nodded slightly, her eyes still fixed on the floor. Then the defence spoke of her psychological state and the words 'mental health' surfaced. At this, the three women felt a wave of disbelief. The retracting of blame, the softening of edges.

'A snowball of deception became an avalanche,' Liston concluded. 'It overwhelmed her capacity to return to the truth.'

The judge's pen stopped mid-stroke. He looked up, his gaze lingering.

Unperturbed, Richard Liston continued, 'My client, Ms Cookes, experienced profound trauma in her formative years. At the age of nineteen, she suffered the tragic loss of her infant daughter, Martha ...' The words seemed to hang in the room, heavy and deliberate. Samantha shifted slightly in her seat, her hair curtaining her face. 'A cot death,' Liston continued softly, 'which has marked her life since. It is our submission that her behaviour, while deplorable, must be understood within that frame of grief.'

Lynn's hands gripped the edge of the bench. She felt her nails bite into the varnished wood. Her heartbeat surged in her ears, a roar of disbelief.

No!

The word rose inside her, pressing hard against her ribs.

No!

The air around her blurred, the edges of the courtroom flashing in and out of focus. She heard Hillery hiss her name, but it was too late.

Lynn stood. 'No,' she said, her voice cracking through the quiet. At first no one moved. The clerk turned sharply as heads twisted along the benches.

'She's lying,' Lynn said louder. Her voice trembled but didn't break. 'That's not how baby Martha died.'

Whispers swept the courtroom, the sort of noise that doesn't belong in these spaces, where dignity and decorum rule. Judge Munro's voice cut through the growing noise. 'Order in the court.'

Lynn, still on her feet, tears bright in her eyes, repeated, 'She's lying again! She said it was a cot death, but it wasn't! The baby didn't die from cot death.'

Liston froze, his mouth slightly open, papers limp in his hands. Samantha looked straight ahead, her expression glassy and unreadable, a faint twitch at the corner of her eye.

'That baby suffocated,' Lynn continued, her voice steadying as if the anger in her had found its rhythm. 'They asked a judge in Birmingham to look at the case again in 2013 because Social Services were suspicious, but she fled. She never went back.'

A silence so complete followed that it seemed as if the whole courtroom was holding its breath.

The defence barrister turned, the colour draining from his face. He looked at Samantha, then the judge. 'Judge,' he began hesitantly, 'perhaps ... a short recess.'

Judge Munro gave a single grave nod. 'Ten minutes.'

As the clerk called order and people shuffled from their benches, Lynn stood shaking. Hillery's hand caught her arm, guiding her back down to the bench.

When the court reconvened, the atmosphere had changed. Richard Liston's face was pale. His voice, when he spoke, was quiet, stripped of its earlier confidence. 'Judge,' he said, swallowing, 'I have discussed the matter with my client during the break. It appears Ms Cookes accepts that Lynn McDonald's statement is correct.'

A stunned murmur rolled through the room. Judge Munro leaned forward. 'To clarify, Ms Cookes confirms the death of the child was not due to a cot death, as previously stated?'

'Yes, judge.'

The sound that followed was not quite outrage, not quite shock, but something in between, the collective noise of people watching a façade collapse.

Lynn sat frozen. She felt the blood rush from her head, her body both light and heavy at once.

The judge closed his file and looked squarely at the defence. 'This court will require the coroner's documentation from the United Kingdom. Until such records are produced and verified, I am adjourning sentencing.'

The clerk marked it down. The words struck like a hammer. Court adjourned.

The women filed out slowly into the corridor. The marble floor gleamed under harsh fluorescent light. Reporters hustled with eagerness for quotes. The world outside had changed, as though the truth had pushed through years of lies, dizzying in its suddenness.

Lynn steadied herself against the wall, her breath ragged. 'I just couldn't let her use that beautiful baby's name again to get out of trouble. I just couldn't let her get away with lying, not again. She'll never stop,' she whispered.

Hillery nodded, voice low. 'No, but neither will we.'

Outside, rain hammered down over Tralee, washing down the courthouse steps as the world shifted just a little closer towards a reckoning.

25

TAKING BACK THE STORY

The morning of 5 March 2025 broke cold over Tralee. The courthouse steps were once again slick with rain, shining under the lights of the cameramen who had been gathering since before dawn. Reporters huddled under umbrellas, murmuring as they rehearsed their live intros. Across Ireland, the story was already being told, headlines flashing words like 'deliberate fraud', 'carefully orchestrated scheme', 'serial deception'. Inside courtroom two, the heat was close. The press benches were full, notebook pages rustling.

Judge Ronan Munro adjusted his glasses, his voice steady as he spoke the words that would echo across the country by evening: 'Ms Cookes, this court finds your offences were deliberate, premeditated and sustained over a protracted period. Your actions involved the calculated manipulation of a respected medical practitioner, as well as State officials. They were not driven by need, but by deceit.'

The clerk then summarised the eighteen counts of theft and deception she had been charged with under the Criminal Justice (Theft and Fraud Offences) Act, 2001. Samantha stood motionless, her hands clasped before her, chin angled down. She wore no makeup and her expression was cold and distant.

Judge Munro continued, 'This was, in every sense, a carefully orchestrated fraud. It exploited the machinery of compassion within the State. You preyed on goodwill and institutional trust. The damage cannot be measured solely in financial loss but in breach of public confidence.'

From the gallery, court reporters leaned forward as Judge Munro delivered his ruling.

'For these offences,' the judge said, 'I sentence you to four years' imprisonment, with the final twelve months suspended, on condition of good behaviour upon release.'

The sound was final, a door closing, a long echo finally landing.

Three years in custody.

Across the courtroom, a quiet shiver moved through those who had spent years waiting for this day. It wasn't triumph, not exactly; it was the weight of something released.

Samantha said nothing as the Gardaí approached. She nodded once to her solicitor, then allowed herself to be led away.

Outside, the rain began again, fine and persistent. Journalists huddled in the courthouse doors, dictating quotes into phones. Their voices carried down the steps: 'Convicted fraudster Samantha Cookes has been jailed for three years ...'; '... over sixty thousand euro stolen ...'; '... fraudulently claiming to suffer from Huntington's disease ...'; '... the judge described her crimes as deliberate and sustained ...'

By afternoon, the story was everywhere. Paschal Sheehy for RTÉ news led the broadcast with footage from Tralee. Images of Samantha Cookes flashed on screen, that same pink top, the handcuffs glinting in the rain. *The Irish Times* called it a calculated campaign of deception during the Covid years. *TheJournal.ie* emphasised the plea, the apology read out by her solicitor.

In Dublin, phones buzzed as the women who had once filled that WhatsApp group with a constant anxiety reacted to the news. Some cried. Some laughed softly through disbelief. Lorraine texted the group first: 'Three years. Finally.'

Within seconds, the replies flooded in.

Lynn: 'She didn't beat it this time.'

Hillery: 'Three years isn't enough. But it's something.'

Chloe: 'She'll still find a way to twist it. But today, the truth won.'

In Tralee, the Garda van pulled away from the courthouse, turning towards Limerick Prison. Samantha sat wordless in the back, the belt tight across her chest. Rain streaked the window, the courthouse receding behind her. She may have been wondering how she could turn herself once again into protagonist rather than perpetrator. This time, however, the people she had betrayed would make sure that was not possible.

* * *

In Dublin, the evening news replayed the footage for the third time. The anchor's voice was calm and clear: 'Serial fraudster Samantha Cookes has today been sentenced to three years in prison after pleading guilty to theft and deception amounting to more than sixty thousand euro.'

Lynn turned off the television. For the first time in nearly a decade, the silence that followed felt peaceful. Somewhere far away, in a concrete cell with a view of high walls and wire, she imagined, Samantha Cookes sat alone, not plotting, not preparing. Just waiting, suspended for once between the life she had lived and the one she would try to reinvent.

Lynn had long thought about this moment: Samantha behind bars, stripped of the performance, of the lies that held so many in her orbit. But she felt no satisfaction, only a hollow, heavy ache in her chest. Because life, she was coming to understand, had a twisted sense of irony.

Her hands trembled slightly as she reached for her teacup, like a leaf shivering in the wind. The doctors said it was early onset Parkinson's. Manageable, treatable, but no cure; the words rolled off their tongues with practised ease. It was almost laughable, grotesque even, that she was now suffering the reality of one of the illnesses Samantha had been pretending to endure.

Even more cruel, her beautiful daughter Daisy was gone, passing away peacefully in Lynn's arms on 28 January 2024. With Daisy's laughter an echo in the house, Lynn now faced an uncertain future with the full knowledge of what a Parkinson's diagnosis meant for her. It galled Lynn that Samantha had the audacity to call herself a survivor.

She pressed her palm against the cold glass of her kitchen window, the tremor more pronounced now. The world outside was quiet, innocent, mocking in its stillness. She thought of justice, and how unevenly it was handed out. Samantha would serve her sentence and walk free someday. But Lynn? She faced a lifetime's sentence, one that would take from her everything steady, everything still.

* * *

When the cameras arrived, Samantha Cookes' victims were cautious, nervous about opening the door to their homes, their lives and the rawest parts of their stories. For years, they had carried an overwhelming mix of betrayal and shame. 'Would the public blame us? Would they say we were foolish for letting this woman near our children?' Layla wondered anxiously.

But the mission was clear, to expose Samantha Cookes' face and name so no one else would fall prey to her. The Alleycats team offered more than just a camera – they offered a platform for these women to reclaim control. 'We wanted to take back the narrative,' said Hillery. 'It's scary but necessary. People need to see the truth, not the lies she spun.'

The resulting two-part documentary series, *Bad Nanny*, peeled back the layers of deception, revealing the devastating toll Samantha had taken on vulnerable families for more than a decade. While promoting the documentary, Hillery and Lorraine, their faces etched with a steely resolve, stepped under the glaring studio lights of ITV's *This Morning*, broadcasting live from London. Cat Deeley's easy warmth and Ben Shephard's probing questions framed them, not as victims, but as warriors demanding justice. Their voices cracked with emotion but never faltered, gripping viewers who saw not just stories of loss but the fierce will to fight back.

On Monday, 12 May 2025, at 9.35 p.m., the victims sat down in front of their screens with the rest of the nation on the night of the documentary's television debut. Viewers watched as 'Lucy' insinuated her way into homes, earning trust before betraying it with shocking cruelty. They saw Samantha evolve through every iteration of herself during her rampage. It was a surreal moment for those whose lives she had impacted. Samantha Cookes was behind bars and now her face was plastered across television screens in Ireland and the UK, a figure of infamy rather than mystery. They had done it. After years of feeling powerless, they were finally in control.

Unlike Samantha's twisted tales, their stories were unflinchingly honest, raw and real. The impact was immediate and powerful. The documentary soared to number one on the RTÉ Player for two consecutive weeks and trended widely across the BBC iPlayer. Social media erupted, TikTok, X and Instagram lit up with debates, personal reflections and widespread support for the victims. Gráinne McAleer, head of documentaries and features at RTÉ, remarked, '*Bad Nanny* is a story of the power of ordinary people working together. From TikTok sleuths to the brave families behind the scenes, it's a cautionary tale for anyone trusting another with their loved ones.'

Reviews praised the victims' courage, which transformed what had been a story of exploitation into one of resilience and justice. The women had pulled it off, not simply revealing the perpetrator but reclaiming their dignity and sense of safety.

* * *

The jailing of Samantha Cookes did not mark the end of these women's stories, but it was, in many ways, a new beginning for them. What had started as a fragmented group of betrayed families, devastated by the uncompromising deceit of one woman, slowly forged itself into a community rooted in resilience and hope. At the heart of this fragile but growing network were women like Krissie Edwards, Hillery Geelan, Lynn McDonald, Katie Taylor and other mothers, fathers and caregivers, many of whom were navigating their own battles caring for children with additional needs or chronic illnesses.

'I actually want to thank Samantha Cookes for the amazing people she introduced me to,' said Hillery quietly one afternoon. 'These are the people who show up when I have a bad day, who offer a shoulder to cry on or a laugh when it's hard to find one. We don't even really talk about Samantha anymore. She's just not important to us now. She's behind bars, and we can go on living our own lives. That's our victory.'

Their shared trauma had blossomed, paradoxically, into a source of strength. What was once a narrative of victimhood became a collective tale of support, friendship and unyielding solidarity. Through online chats, WhatsApp conversations and in-person meetings, they built a network that transcended the scars Samantha left behind.

They are a testament not just to survival, but to transformation. They took something dark and made it light, using their stories not simply to expose a predator but to lift each other up. And yet, amid their triumph, some empathy still lingered for the woman who had upended their lives.

'She was likeable,' Layla DeJagger remembered softly from her home in Offaly. 'Smart, funny, warm. The children loved her, even missed her when she left. It's hard to reconcile that with the truth of what she did.'

Máire Logue, artistic director at St John's Theatre, Listowel, who had known Samantha under her alias Carrie Jade during her residency as a writer, saw a glimmer of the talent that could have flourished. 'She really was a good writer, a great storyteller,' she reflected. 'I hope she holds on to that, the part of her that could create, that could contribute positively. Maybe one day, after she's served her time, she'll find a way to live differently, to use her gifts for something better.'

For the victims, that hope is bittersweet. They wish her no harm, only that she might one day find peace and redemption. Their focus, now, is on themselves, on rebuilding, healing and moving forward. In the quiet moments between their shared laughter and tears, they carry with them an unspoken truth: Samantha Cookes may have been the one weaving tales of fantasy and falsehood, but the true story is theirs, a story of community, endurance and the resolute power of ordinary people united in extraordinary circumstances.

'We may have started as victims,' Lynn said with a steady voice, 'but we are so much more now. Samantha Cookes didn't destroy us, we won't let her.'

26

NO ORDINARY CON ARTIST

In attempting to understand what lay behind Samantha Cookes' complex labyrinth of deception, it is worth considering the fluctuating narrative she spun about the death of her four-month-old baby, Martha in 2008. The official inquest into this death, after a nine-month investigation, recorded the cause as accidental suffocation. Then, in court three years later, during Samantha's 2011 surrogacy fraud trial in Yorkshire, a different explanation emerged. There, Samantha stated that Martha had died of sudden infant death syndrome (SIDS), commonly referred to as 'cot death'. SIDS and accidental suffocation are very different.

In 2013, after Samantha was diagnosed with pseudologia fantastica, or pathological lying, Shropshire Council grew concerned about the original coroner's inquest and requested a judicial review into the inquest. Samantha had left the UK before the review took place and did not attend, so the ruling of accidental death through no fault of Samantha Cookes still stands.

However, Samantha changed the story again in October 2013 when she told a woman in Edenderry that Martha had died in a car crash caused by a drunk driver. She told Collette, the wedding planner she scammed in Dublin in 2016, a similar story, this time adding that her three-year-old daughter had died alongside her husband in a car accident with a drunk driver. Then, on an audio tape recorded by Ronan Kelly for an RTÉ *Doc on One* in 2021, Samantha alleged that Martha died as a baby due to complications from a vaccine, a narrative she repeated to Chloe in Kenmare. Finally, in the 2025 courtroom in Tralee, Samantha reverted back to the cot death story.

These inconsistent versions of the one story reveal a woman entwined in a desperate attempt to justify her losses and manipulate the sympathies of others for her benefit. The introduction of car accidents, vaccine complications and other stories illustrates a complex and contradictory narrative. The repeated and varied fabrications about Martha's demise were part of a broader pattern of deception, extending far beyond this single tragedy, but all designed to elicit sympathy from the listener, a sympathy Samantha could then manipulate to her own benefit, whether financial or otherwise.

Samantha Cookes' scribbled notes from her time as Carrie Jade Williams also reveal a deeply symbolic and psychologically telling pattern. She frequently used the names of her three children as protagonists in fictional stories, with Martha often cast as a heroic figure battling for justice against an uncaring system. This literary choice is consistent with psychological patterns observed in individuals identified as pathological liars. Incorporating real names, especially those of close family members such as children, into grandiose fictional narratives can reflect a complex psychological process. For someone with pseudologia fantastica, these stories may serve multiple purposes: a way to reclaim control over traumatic or unresolved experiences; an unconscious effort to rewrite painful realities into more empowering versions; or a means to garner sympathy and admiration through the crafted persona. The heroisation of Martha and her two living children in Samantha's writings suggests an attempt to process loss and victimhood, while simultaneously constructing a noble narrative that elevates her children and, by extension, Samantha herself.

In some of her unpublished writings Samantha wrote: 'Please protect my family, Lord. I don't understand your purpose in letting us be separated.' Her incessant and meticulous budgeting revealed scribbled records of money squirrelled away for her two remaining children in the UK. Whether they ever actually received this money is unknown, but it demonstrates that despite her often selfish and malicious behaviour, there was some care there, some thought for others, some effort to seek a connection to her children left to grow up with no access to their mother.

But perhaps the most telling insight of all was scribbled in a handwritten note left inside a discarded journal: 'I miss being myself.'

* * *

Since her arrest in July 2024 and subsequent conviction in early 2025, Samantha Cookes has been serving her sentence of three years in Limerick Women's Prison. Her life in prison, according to reports and insiders close to the case, has been a stark contrast to the peripatetic freedom she once enjoyed. Though offered opportunities for education and self-improvement, including courses in sociology, business, personal development and calligraphy, she reportedly remains a difficult and dissatisfied inmate. Sources have noted that Samantha frequently complains about the prison conditions, such as the food, and she does not appear to have adapted easily to incarceration. Her demeanour is described as unhappy, consistent with someone struggling to accept their loss of control and freedom.

Despite this, she is known to maintain a structured routine, working two days a week in the prison laundry and engaging in educational classes. However, there has been no public indication that she has taken any significant steps towards addressing her underlying behavioural issues or seeking rehabilitation beyond the formal offerings.

The outcomes for recovery in those diagnosed with pseudologia fantastica makes for sobering reading. It is not formally recognised as a distinct mental disorder but is closely associated with personality disorders such as psychopathy. Recovery or permanent change in such cases is reported to be very rare. It requires multidisciplinary management that includes cognitive behavioural therapy and pharmacology, which may help manage associated symptoms like anxiety or depression but offers limited success in curing the underlying compulsive deceit.

Judge Ronan Munro, during sentencing, had expressed the hope that suspending the final year of her sentence would incentivise Samantha to get treatment after release, though observers remain uncertain of whether Cookes will pursue that path.

* * *

Samantha Cookes was no ordinary con artist. She was a master at reading the silent fractures running through society, the spaces where hope had withered, where services faltered and where invisible wounds festered. For countless vulnerable people, struggling with illness, financial hardship or isolation, the safety nets had holes too big to catch them. And into those gaps, Samantha slipped like a shadow.

She sought out the desperate – parents clutching at the frayed edges of medical support for their sick children, abandoned by fractured health services, those battling rare diseases with little help from a system too thinly stretched to care. With every whispered lie about a terminal illness, every sob story of loss and tragedy, she built a fortress of sympathy and trust to manipulate those around her. Pretending to suffer from Huntington's disease, she exploited social welfare systems to collect disability payments, a grim parody of the very real hardships faced by people like Lynn McDonald.

Yet, despite the layers of deception, the cracks in justice were equally wide. On two occasions she was caught and convicted but let off with sentences so light they barely left a mark on her freedom. The courts heard her stories, including the tragic death of her infant daughter Martha, stories she twisted masterfully in testimony to mitigate her duplicitous behaviour, yet no meaningful punishment followed for her outright lies under oath. Each gesture of leniency became an unintentional permission slip to continue her charade.

The institutions tasked with protecting the public failed spectacularly. Arts Council funding decisions lacked the rigorous scrutiny needed to unmask a fraudster. The Residential Tenancies Board, the Workplace Relations Commission, the HSE and

Garda systems were blindsided. False claims about decades-long qualifications went unchallenged, revealing the startling ease with which she could slip past essential safeguards.

The crippling cost of childcare in Ireland, amongst some of the highest in Europe, left working parents struggling to get by and desperate for help. HSE waiting lists and a lack of adequate resources and support for families with children with special additional needs created the perfect environment for a cunning con artist to enter and exploit.

Samantha's lies were not just personal betrayals of the victims but systemic exposures of how fragile and porous safety nets can be. Her story is a chilling reminder of how, when social systems fail to protect the vulnerable and oversight is weak, lies can grow unchecked. Her legacy is not just the crimes she committed, but the unmasking of the urgent need for Irish society to mend its fractures and strengthen its safeguards.

ACKNOWLEDGEMENTS

Writing this book has been a long and extraordinary journey, shaped by the generosity, courage and kindness of so many people.

First and foremost, my deepest gratitude goes to the victims and to all who knew Samantha Cookes. Thank you for trusting me with your experiences, for opening up about your stories and for welcoming me so wholeheartedly. Meeting you all, especially the wonderful WhatsApp group gang, left a lasting mark on me. Your warmth, support and honesty carried me through the telling of this complex and sensitive story.

To those who were hesitant but chose to speak anyway, thank you. Your bravery made this work possible.

Many people contributed to the process of telling this story. At RTÉ, I'm so grateful to Gráinne McAleer and Seán Mac Giolla Phádraig for their steadfast backing in the making of the documentary series *Bad Nanny*. A particular thank you to Kathy Fox for always being a listening ear and an encouraging, supportive champion.

To Raphaëlle O'Loan and Eddie Doyle at BBC Northern Ireland, a sincere thank you for your support and creative collaboration throughout.

A heartfelt thank you to Liam O'Brien and Ronan Kelly from

RTÉ's *The Real Carrie Jade* podcast for your generous collaboration and valuable insights.

Massive thanks to everyone at Alleycats Films, in particular Ed Stobart. I doubt I'd be doing this kind of work at all without your early belief and support. I'm also immensely grateful to the documentary dream team Gráinne Creighton, Joseph Ingersoll and Niall Creaven. Big thanks to Sarah Kieran for your steady guidance and clear-headed wisdom when it was most needed.

Conor Graham, Wendy Logue and the brilliant team at Merrion Press, thank you for making this process such a pleasure and for believing I could write a book! Susan McKeever, your sharp insights and thoughtful feedback made a world of difference.

Finally, the biggest thanks of all go to my family and friends – you know who you are. *Go raibh míle maith agaibh* for your patience, love and unwavering support.